INSIDE
ORGANIZATIONAL
COMMUNICATION

LONGMAN SERIES
IN PUBLIC
COMMUNICATION
Series Editor: **Ray Eldon Hiebert**

SECOND EDITION

INSIDE ORGANIZATIONAL COMMUNICATION

International Association of Business Communicators

Edited by
CAROL REUSS *and* DONN SILVIS

Longman
New York & London

Inside Organizational Communication

Longman Inc., 95 Church St., White Plains, N.Y. 10601
Associated companies, branches, and representatives
throughout the world.

Developmental Editor: Gordon T. R. Anderson
Editorial and Design Supervisor: Jennifer C. Barber
Production/Manufacturing: Ferne Y. Kawahara
Composition: Graphicraft Typesetters
Printing and Binding: The Alpine Press

Library of Congress Cataloging in Publication Data
Main entry under title:

Inside organizational communication.
    (Longman series in public communication)
    Bibliography: p.
    Includes index.
    1. Communication in organizations—United States.
I. International Association of Business Communicators.
II. Series.
HD30.36.U5156   1985   658.4'5   84-7896
ISBN 0-582-28540-2
ISBN 0-582-28538-0 (pbk.)

Manufactured in the United States of America
9 8 7 6 5 4 3 2   93 92 91 90 89 88 87 86

Contents

Foreword

No organization can exist without a communication program.

Michael Welch
President
Credit Union Executive Society

Organizational communication has been around forever and, somewhat formally, for more than four hundred years. But its critical importance to the well-being and growth of organizations has become evident only in this century.

That long history is less than proud, too often having been composed primarily of insufferable, paternalistic house organs. Today, many, many organizations publish bold and creative magazines, newsletters, newspapers and magapapers filled with real information about business conditions, public issues and other news far removed from that once standard paean to baby photos, birthday announcements and bowling scores.

Today's publications often are supplemented by other media—bulletin boards; telephone hotlines and news shows; video magazines; films and slide presentations; meetings of all types and sizes; paycheck stuffers; handbooks and manuals; brochures; feedback and speak-up programs; annual reports, and much, much more. Most media are tailored to meet the communication needs of specific audiences.

It has been in the past decade or so that practitioners—communicators—have been recognized as problem solvers and decision makers, and this new role continues to grow as communicators take a more active part in all aspects of organizational management.

"The day is over when communication dealt mainly with emergencies and scheduled routine," says James Beré, chairman and chief executive officer of Borg-Warner Corporation. "From now on, we will demand the same strategic plans from communicators that we expect from production and marketing and research—plans based on where the company wants to be in the years ahead, what it needs to get there and what the communication function can do to help."

Irving Shapiro, former chief executive officer of E. I. duPont de Nemours and Company, says: "Effective business communicators will need to know more about their business, about the marketplace and about the world around them than ever before. You must know the territory if you want to be helpful and effective."

Along with a greater emphasis on communication has come a change in management style from the school of "tell 'em as little as possible but be firm about it" to an approach of genuine respect for the ever-changing, multifaceted audience—an audience that seeks information, not commands.

To meet these changing communication needs, today's professional communicator has had to become more sophisticated and knowledgeable not only about journalism and communication but about the social sciences, business and economics, and organizational dynamics as well.

Opportunities for communication professionals continue to grow. The 1983 Profile survey conducted by the International Association of Business Communicators found that 37 percent of the practitioners were in new positions; in 1981 nearly 35 percent were in new positions and in 1979, 34 percent were in new positions.

And the nature of these positions is changing: salaries average $29,000 and range well into six figures; titles of director or manager are held by nearly half of the communicators with concomitant increases in responsibility for and participation in management decisions.

More and more, communicators are finding satisfaction within this profession rather than trying to use it as a stepping-stone to a more lucrative spot. But the field can provide a leg up the organizational ladder. Paul Lyet, former chairman and chief executive officer of Sperry Corporation, started as a communicator as did Claude Taylor, president and chief executive officer of Air Canada. Mardie McKimm has moved steadily up the ladder since she joined Kraftco in 1972. Today she is senior vice president, public affairs, and is on the board of several other companies.

The authors of this book are well-respected leaders in this paradoxically young profession with a long history.

Through this book, the International Association of Business Communicators, with the assistance of many contributors, seeks to return something to the profession and its practitioners. The chapters have been updated—two have been added—to reflect changes in the profession since the first edition, published in 1981. Yet much of what was orginally written still holds true.

We hope you will find *Inside Organizational Communication* useful, informative, and interesting, whether you are preparing to enter the communication field or already working as a professional communicator.

John N. Bailey, ABC, CAE
Former President
International Association of Business Communicators

Acknowledgments

The International Association of Business Communicators—10,850 members strong—would like to express its appreciation to all the dedicated professionals who assisted with and contributed to this second edition of *Inside Organizational Communication*.

Most of the credit, of course, must go to the twenty-five authors and contributors whose talents and contributions of time and effort made this book possible. Special thanks go to the book's authors—Carol Reuss, Ph.D., of the School of Journalism at the University of North Carolina, Chapel Hill, and Donn E. Silvis, ABC, director of corporate communications at AVCO Financial Services, Newport Beach, California—who edited the manuscript and supervised myriad details required to produce a book.

Rita Black, ABC, CIBA-GEIGY, IABC director, educational and student relations, coordinated the book project and lent invaluable support.

In addition, Marilyn Baker, of Marilyn Baker & Associates in Austin, Texas, coordinated production of *Inside Organizational Communication* on behalf of the IABC board of directors, and Clara Degen, IABC vice president for research and educational relations, served as liaison with the board, the editors, the authors, and the contributors as well as handling administrative details.

IABC also wishes to thank the many association members who responded when called for information and sample materials to illustrate points made by the authors. Specifically, IABC would like to acknowledge the following people and organizations for their cooperation and kind permission to use illustrative material in this book:

Part I Organizational Communication

The illustration on page 27 is from the *Donnelley Directory Record*, 78/4, p. 10. Reprinted with permission of Reuben H. Donnelley.

Benefits story excerpt on pages 36 and 37 reprinted from *Inside Newsday*, Newsday, Long Island, New York.

Part II Getting Started: Analyzing and Organizing the Work

The illustration on page 47 is reprinted with permission of Digital Equipment Corporation.

Excerpt on pages 53 and 55 reprinted with permission of Xerox Corporation.

The employee survey guide on page 54 is from "Cafeteria Communication: A Survey Menu," Communication & Management, September/ October 1979. Reprinted by permission of Towers, Perrin, Forster & Crosby, Inc.

The figures on pages 79, 83, 86, 87, and 90 are copyright 1983 by Jim Haynes. Reprinted with permission.

The illustrations on pages 102 and 316 are by Curt Hopkins, Curt Hopkins & Associates, Sacramento, California. Reprinted with permission.

Part III   Selecting and Using Various Media and Methods

The upper illustration on page 117 is from Viewpoint, July/August 1983. Reprinted by permission of IBM National Marketing Division.

The lower illustration on page 117 is from Amoco Torch. Reprinted by permission of Standard Oil Company (Indiana).

The illustration on the left on page 119 is reprinted with permission of Resources for Education and Management, Inc., Decatur, Georgia.

The illustration on the right on page 119 is reprinted with permission of Exxon Corporation.

The illustration on the left on page 131 is from ArcoSpark, February 17, 1984. Reprinted with permission of Atlantic Richfield Company.

The illustration on the right on page 131 is from Chase News, December 1983. Reprinted with permission of The Chase Manhattan Bank, N.A.

The illustration on page 135 is from 'Round Robins International, Vol. 4, No. 4, 1983. Reprinted with permission of A. H. Robins Company.

The illustrations on pages 146, 147, 150, 151, 152, 153, 155, 156, 157, 159, 160, 161, and 162 are reprinted with permission of Nebraska Educational Television Network. The illustration on page 146 is from Choice, November 1976, pp. 6 and 7. Image of "The Buffalo Hunt" by Charles Wimar, courtesy of Washington University Gallery of Art, St. Louis. The illustration on the right on page 150 is from Choice, June 1978, p. 7. The illustration on the right on page 151 is from Choice, August 1976, p. 1. The illustration on the right on page 153 is from Choice, October 1977. The illustration on page 155 is from Choice, September 1975, pp. 2 and 3. The illustration on the right on page 156 is from Choice, November 1978, p. 3. The illustrations on page 159 are from Choice, August 1978, p. 1, and May 1976, p. 8. The illustration on the left on page 160 is from Choice, January 1976, p. 1.

The illustrations on pages 148, 149, and 154 are reprinted with permission of TVOntario and art director Dick Derhodge.

The bulletin board on page 168 and the photo on page 185 are courtesy of Southern Company Services, Atlanta, Georgia.

The illustration on page 181 is from the Bulletin Board Resource Kit for 3M bulletin board editors. Reprinted by permission.

The photo on page 183 is courtesy of Triton College, River Grove, Illinois.

The photos on pages 191 and 192 are courtesy of GTE Communication Systems.

Excerpts on pages 209, 210, 213, 214, and 215 are from *Vital Speeches of the Day*, July 1, 1983. Reprinted with permission.

Part IV   Some Special Needs and Techniques

Five suggested goals for an employee orientation program on page 238, suggested elements for an ideal annual report on pages 246 and 247, and excerpt on pages 249 and 250 are reprinted with permission of Towers, Perrin, Forster & Crosby.

The illustration on page 239 is reprinted with permission of the Atlantic Richfield Company.

The illustration on the left on page 245 is reprinted with permission of GTE Corporation.

The illustration in the center on page 245 is reprinted with permission of Standard Oil Company (Indiana).

The illustration on the right on page 245 is reprinted with permission of the Adolph Coors Company.

The illustration on the right on page 248 is from *Monitor*, November/December 1983. Reprinted with permission of Johnson Controls, Inc.

The illustration on the left on page 248 is from *Baylor Progress*, January 1984. Reprinted with permission of Bill Kreighbaum and Baylor University Medical Center, Dallas, Texas.

The illustration on page 251 is reprinted with permission from The Toledo Hospital.

Excerpt on pages 253 and 254 is from *Association Management*, November 1975. Copyright 1975 by the American Society of Association Executives. Reprinted with permission.

The illustration on page 257 is from *Oakton in a Nutshell*. Reprinted with permission of AT&T Communication.

The illustration on the left on page 265 is from "Graduates . . . A Look at Falconbridge." Reprinted with permission of Falconbridge Nickel Mines, Ltd., Falconbridge, Ontario.

The illustration in the center on page 265 is from the "Marathon customer relations manual." Reprinted with permission of Marathon Petroleum.

The illustration on the right on page 265 is from the "Employee Stock Purchase Plan." Reprinted with permission of Informatics General Corporation.

The illustration on page 240 is from *Diamond Shamrock News*. Reprinted with permission of Diamond Shamrock Corporation.

The illustration on page 318 is reprinted with permission of Southwestern Bell Telephone Co.

The illustration on page 324 is reprinted with permission of Weyerhauser Company.

• Part I •

ORGANIZATIONAL COMMUNICATION

◆ 1 ◆

Communication in Contemporary Organizations

Roy G. Foltz, ABC, APR

Fall on your knees if they do not understand you.
Dostoyevsky

Organizations are people, not boxes on a chart. So there's just no way an organization can operate without communication. The organization will die when the communication nerve cells are paralyzed or don't develop. Yet there is probably no other function about which so much discussion has produced so little real understanding. This is a critical issue because the effective use of communication in an organization can mean the ultimate success or failure of that organization.

Organizational communication is *the* vital link in the chain of events that is the process of managing a business. It is the single factor that makes an organization viable, successful, effective, enduring. More than any other element, the communications of an organization project the "personality" of that organization to its internal and external audiences.

Definition

What does *organizational communication* mean? It means different things to different people. In fact, there are probably as many different definitions of the term as there are practitioners in the field. But the definition used here is simply this: organizational communication is the *exchange* of information, ideas and feelings. Or, in a word, *exchange*.

3

Organizational communication isn't and wasn't always defined that way. There are those who think only of communications hardware when they hear the term. Others confine the meaning to the transmission of information, or equate communication and media. But these meanings are only parts of the whole. All must be utilized effectively to promote the *exchange* process and set the tone for communication in an organization.

As I see it, organizational communication has two primary responsibilities: (1) to support organizational objectives, policies and programs, and (2) to meet audience needs. The two responsibilities can be viewed as contradictory or mutually exclusive, but doing both jobs well or closing the gap between the two becomes the real and constant challenge to organizational communication and organizational communicators.

The key to gaining support for organizational objectives, policies and programs is to serve the organization's audiences—to know what information they want and how they prefer to get it. Even though these needs may never be met completely, people who feel they are important to an organization will be much more likely to support it than those who believe that its "management doesn't care about what we think."

The Audience

In recent years, technological advances and the availability of mass media have had an impact on people's perceptions. The social environment has contributed to increased demands for candor. Overall levels of education and income have risen. The work-force profile has changed: more young people, women and members of minority groups are part of it. It is virtually impossible now—and will be even more difficult in the future—to lump employees (or any other audience) into a single group having the same interests and similar information wants and needs.

There is also a growing recognition of the multidimensional nature of audiences. Employees, for example, are also voters, stockholders, consumers, community residents and so forth. Employees have always had more dimensions than most communication would seem to indicate. Certainly there is an awareness that they come from different environments and have different backgrounds and different points of view. Historically, though, employees were viewed as owing gratitude and loyalty to a firm simply because it provided them with jobs and took good care of them. And with respect to communication, the party line was pretty much "just tell 'em what they need to know." It was expected that the organization's philosophy was also the philosophy of employees. This is no longer true. Employees often are every bit as skeptical as the general public on controversial issues facing their organization. And when they are, it can spell t-r-o-u-b-l-e, especially if nothing is done to convert skeptics into advocates.

An example: Employees in a privately owned utility—whose management firmly believes that "nuclear energy is the only way to go ... our employees know this and support this"—don't go along with that position. One employee says, "I'm loyal to a point, but there are too many negatives to be considered when it comes to nuclear energy. I just won't buy the company line that says it's absolutely safe." Another employee adds, "I don't know why the company is closing down these little hydro plants. They run cheap and clean. I really don't know why the company would even *want* to get into something as controversial as nuclear at this point."

If this company wants support from its employees on the nuclear energy question, the company must meet employees' informational needs. It should also reexamine its overall approach to the issue. The company needs to exert considerable effort—be it frequency of message, reasons for its positions, or type of media—to transform disbelievers and doubters into supporters.

The internal audience is not the only one with specific information needs about an organization. There is a rising acknowledgment that the organization must also paint a clear picture of itself and its views to its many diversified "outside" audiences—the general public, customers and potential customers, suppliers, government officials, stockholders, local community residents—and must listen to their views and comments.

Philip Lesly, public relations and public affairs counselor, in 1983, phrased it this way:

> The masterly manager was trained to command the elements that make up the *internal* organization and its functions: finance, production, manpower, distribution, facilities and engineering. The new pattern of *external* forces based on group attitudes is an opposite picture: the elderly, minorities, unions, government, communities, academics, investors, customers, women, media, conservationists, church groups, environmentalists, youth, potential employees, foreign publics.

Coupled with the acknowledgment of the many audiences each organization has is the recognition that the exchange works best when low-ranking as well as high-ranking employees become involved in the communication process. In fact, the lower their rank, the greater their credibility. But employees must understand the organization's mission, objectives and plans, as this quote from an annual report to stockholders suggests:

> Well motivated and skilled employees are essential in meeting our company objectives. Of critical importance to the ability of employees to fully contribute to the future of the enterprise is the degree to which they are kept informed and [are] enabled to understand the increasingly complex issues with which the

business is confronted and how various company functions interrelate in dealing with them.

The implication for organizational communication is clear: find the best way to bring an understanding of these complicated issues to increasingly diverse audiences, both inside and outside the organization.

Support from the Top

Now that we have defined organizational communication and examined audiences, how does the professional communicator cope with it all? How can the pieces of the puzzle be fitted into a down-to-earth, meaningful, practical, affordable program of organizational communication? There's no easy, universal answer. But perhaps the most important requisite is support and involvement from the top.

Organizational communication is the responsibility of line management and, as the top manager, the chief executive officer (CEO) should support and become involved with the objective-setting process for communication. In many organizations, this has been recognized in just the past five to ten years, but there are still many organizations where it isn't recognized at all. In 1978 the International Association of Business Communicators and Towers, Perrin, Forster & Crosby jointly surveyed CEOs for their views on the role of communication and its many functions. The survey showed that more and more chief executives are taking their communication responsibilities to heart. Here are some comments from those CEOs:

> "Any employee communication program that is successful should be administered by the chief executive. The program won't work if the CEO isn't committed to it."

> "The communication department is a tool, but the responsibility for communicating is one we all share."

> "Our job, and mine at the corporate level, is to motivate and support operating managers to communicate. We can help upgrade their communication skills and show that communicating is important, but we have to do it by showing and encouraging, not by edict."

Sometimes the CEO is way ahead of the communication professionals. An example: In a large manufacturing company, the head of the communication department decided that there would have to be severe cutbacks in his budget for organizational communication. Shortly after this decision, the CEO asked about progress on stepped-up communication activity. When told of the planned cutback, the CEO said, "It can't be. Communication is one of my top priorities."

Policies and Objectives

The ideal first step in putting together a communication program is developing an overall policy to set the tone for the program. Mapping it out can be a form of organizational psychoanalysis; much management time and thought are required. Like people, organizations differ widely, so the primary task in developing a policy is to define the organization's unique culture and top management's communication philosophy. Ensuing programs will also differ according to beliefs about why communication is important, what should be communicated, who should do the communicating, and what media should be used. These three points might be included in an internal communication policy:

1. Better communication will encourage employees to make a greater contribution to organizational goals simply because employees will have a clearer understanding of the goals and what they mean to employees' well-being.
2. More effective downward communication will stimulate increased ideas from employees, who will be encouraged to pass ideas upward without fear or concern that their ideas will be considered stupid or beside the point.
3. Better communication will help secure wider support for the organization's stand on important national and local issues. Employees will be better prepared to explain the organization's position in contacts with friends, neighbors and government officials.

After a formal policy has been written, clear and specific objectives should be articulated. The same procedures also apply to communication with other audiences, not just to communication with employees. Here are some examples of specific communication objectives, most of which can be measured:

1. Establish a formal program of regular communication with all employees.
2. Establish one regular channel of downward printed communication to all employees to inform them about all aspects of issues pertinent to the company and industry. Distribute this at least once a week.
3. Issue a publication that will permit more in-depth coverage of internal and external issues. Distribute to all employees and other appropriate audiences on a bimonthly or quarterly basis.
4. Issue a special management publication that will address the special needs of managers.
5. Emphasize subjects that relate to corporate objectives. The subjects will

include competition, government regulation, marketing plans, productivity, pay and benefits.

6. Hold regular meetings between management and employees. Encourage questions from and discussions with employees on problems, and opportunities, and explanations of how employees fit into the big picture.
7. Give employees an annual state-of-the-business review, of corporate as well as local matters.
8. Encourage supervisors to meet regularly with employees to discuss issues, problems and opportunities. (Ideally, specific communication responsibilities should be written into supervisory position descriptions.)
9. Communicate information about the organization to employees no later than it is distributed to outside news media.
10. Install methods and procedures that encourage employees to ask questions, such as telephone hotlines and "speak-up" programs.
11. Conduct surveys every other year to evaluate the effectiveness of the communication program and to determine audience needs and interests.
12. Reexamine these objectives annually to be sure they are in line with organizational objectives.

Audience Needs and Interests

No set of communication objectives can be complete without knowing audience needs and interests. Employee understanding, support and commitment, for example, must be earned. And getting that understanding, support and commitment from employees will come more easily if the employees' needs and interests are addressed regularly.

Survey after survey shows that employees have very specific information needs. Personnel policies (especially regarding pay and benefits), current operations, future plans, products and services usually surface near the top of every list. It's easy to find out what employees are interested in knowing—just ask them. Here are some typical comments:

"We've been hearing of record orders for 14 consecutive quarters, and at the same time we hear of layoffs. How do we reconcile this?"

"Wages and salaries here are a deep, dark secret."

"I'd like to see them publish costs of scrap and repair, or pinpoint the areas causing it—for us."

"We ought to lay all our cards on the table. Why can't management show employees which direction they're taking? We need a better understanding of what the goals and objectives are. How are we going to get there if nobody knows where we're at?"

"Why don't we know further ahead what day around a holiday we will get off—or if we'll get off? It makes it pretty hard to make plans with the family."

IABC and TPF&C conducted a survey of communication effectiveness within 40 organizations in the United States and Canada in 1980, involving more than 45,000 employees. The survey was repeated in 1982, covering 26 organizations and more than 32,000 employees in the two countries. In response to "what subjects are of most, least interest," the responses in the 1982 survey were as follows:

Rank	Subject	Combined "very interested" and "interested" responses
1	Organizational plans for the future	95.3%
2	Productivity improvement	90.3%
3	Personnel policies and practices	89.8%
4	Job-related information	89.2%
5	Job advancement opportunities	87.9%
6	Effect of external events on my job	87.8%
7	How my job fits into the organization	85.4%
8	Operations outside of my department or division	85.1%
9	How we're doing vs. the competition	83.0%
10	Personnel changes and promotions	81.4%
11	Organizational community involvement	81.3%
12	Organizational stand on current issues	79.5%
13	How the organization uses its profits	78.4%
14	Advertising/promotional plans	77.2%
15	Financial results	76.4%
16	Human interest stories about other employees	70.4%
17	Personal news (birthdays, anniversaries, etc.)	57.0%

Employees also have definite ideas on how they would like to receive this information:

"I would welcome more meetings with high-level management telling about specific plans for the present and future."

"That new video equipment is OK, but those interviews with the president have got to go.... Canned questions and canned answers.... And how are you supposed to ask any questions?"

In the same 1982 IABC/TPF&C survey, employees were asked to rank their *preferred* and *current* sources of organizational information. The results were:

Preferred Ranking	Sources of Information	Current Ranking
1	My immediate supervisor	1
2	Small group meetings	4
3	Top executives	11
4	Employee handbook/other brochures	3
5	Local employee publication	8
6	Orientation program	12
7	Organization-wide employee publication	6
8	Annual state-of-the-business report	7
9	Bulletin boards	5
10	Upward communication program	14
11	The union	9
12	Mass meetings	10
13	Audiovisual programs	15
14	Mass media	13
15	The grapevine	2

Employees will also give credit for a good job of communication.

> "The company's safety magazine is just excellent. It's the only magazine my whole family reads."

> "There will always be some problems, but [this survey] is one of the best things about this company. They really want to know what people think, and try to make improvements."

The upward dimension of communication means more than simply giving employees a chance to say what subjects or issues they would like to hear about. It also means openly seeking their opinions and giving them the opportunity to comment on or question anything related to the organization and their own jobs. *People want to know that they're important and that the work they do is valuable.* And they believe that the people who do the work are the ones most likely to know how to improve those operations, as these comments indicate:

> "I don't care so much that they didn't put through my suggestion, but at least they could have told me why. In fact, *why* things are done the way they are is something we never hear."

"Nothing in our communications suggests that the employee might have useful ideas about management policies. It's possible that we might not merely want to hear more, but that we might even have something to say."

Without employee input there is a good chance the message will miss its mark completely. Take this case: The top management of a large multinational company was about to launch an economic education program for employees. The company thought the main problem on employees' minds was the export of jobs overseas. When employees were asked what *they* were concerned about, job export wasn't the problem at all. Someone actually said, "You have to be near where the markets are."

The employees' big concern was to find out when the layoff ax would hit their locations, because they had heard of a major layoff in one of the company's big divisions. They did not know (because no one had told them) that the layoff happened because of a technological breakthrough affecting the manufacturing process in that one division. No other layoffs were in the offing anywhere else in the company. What would have been the result if the company had embarked on a communication program to justify the existence of overseas operations? Achieving *common* goals can best be accomplished by addressing *common* interests and concerns.

The Employee Publication

Although subsequent chapters will describe employee publications, they deserve mention here. After all, the employee publication was once considered to be the sum total of communication in many organizations, and it still is in some, despite all the findings that show employees prefer face-to-face sources of information.

The employee publication was often referred to as the "house organ." Many were often little more than propaganda mills whose main objective (probably not formally stated) was to tell employees only what they needed to know. They concentrated too often on the "three Bs"—births, bowling scores and babble.

The "house's" attitude has changed, and so has the look of the employee publication. The old house organ is playing a different tune, supplying different information. The old predictability is gone, and style and formats of publications are as varied as the organizations they represent.

Least predictable is the content of the publication. In the past decade or so there has been a steadily growing acceptance of the idea that the employee publication—probably still the cornerstone of a well-balanced communication program—should tackle tough issues such as alcoholism and drug addiction, "burned-out" employees, pay and benefits, new product developments, new marketing strategies, possible acquisitions or mergers, effect of government regulations, consumer movements, competition, layoffs.

If the information supplied by the organization is unsatisfactory in quality, amount or timeliness, employees will find out what they want to know from other sources: the grapevine, the union, the local newspaper, radio or television station,—or someone will make up answers. Then the chances are good that incomplete, distorted messages are being sent and acted on.

Other "Downward" Media

Beyond the employee publication are a number of other print media used to communicate downward. There are letters, booklets, bulletin boards, posters, payroll inserts, handbooks. Increasingly, the computer is being used as a downward communication tool; many organizations, for example, now use computerized total compensation statements to give employees personalized reports of their pay and benefits. Beyond the host of printed materials is a variety of audiovisual materials, but for maximum impact, neither should be used alone. Some commonly used audiovisual media are overhead transparencies, slide presentations with live or taped narration, filmstrips, movies, videotape and closed-circuit television.

There continues to be an imbalance between an abundance of excellent hardware and a scarcity of effective software. We have really just begun to utilize the power of television in organizational communication. We can expect further rapid changes in video hardware capabilities in the near future. Satellites and other telecommunication technology make it feasible to reach people both near and far. In the not-too-distant future, two-way picture and sound transmission will permit an exchange of ideas and information with many important audiences.

Informal Media

Informal communicating goes on all the time. The informal channels must exist to provide the avenues of exchange in an organization. In *Communicating at the Top*, George de Mare said: "The first and by far the most common level of communicating is that which goes on below the conscious control of social mechanisms and channels. Perhaps 70 percent of the communication in an organization occurs at this informal, unorganized level." In the past, many organizations were unwilling to recognize or use informal channels. Now, more and more informal communication channels are being used to meet formal organizational communication objectives.

It might not have been defined as an "informal channel," but 25 years ago a half-hour stroll through the plant by a chief executive or senior vice president *was* employee communication in many organizations. Although the difficulty of doing this today is well appreciated, employees keep saying that this kind of face-to-face interaction is the best way to communicate. Here are some employee comments on the subject:

> "I'd like to see top management get out and talk to people. I don't think they give a damn."

> "Chuck has the best organization here. He'll come right down and talk to us about what's going on. There are not too many [other VPs] who will do that."

An employee's desire to come into contact with management is seldom at odds with what management says it *wants* to do. Here is a comment from a CEO:

> "I do believe that communicating cannot be done unless you actually go out and talk to people. I believe that it's important for me to be out there visiting people on the line doing their jobs."

Improving face-to-face communication with executives could well lead to improving the overall organizational climate, because findings in recent studies indicate that employees' perceptions of top management are very closely linked to employees' overall perceptions of the organization and employees' general morale. Employees want to size up top executives, and they want to express their views and feelings directly to top executives.

In any discussion of informal communication media, the importance an organization places on developing, maintaining and nurturing strong and open exchanges between supervisors and subordinates cannot be over-emphasized. Again and again employees say that they prefer to get information about the organization from their supervisors. Communication research shows that this relationship is the element that most strongly affects attitudes about job satisfaction, group cohesiveness and morale. As one top executive summed it up, "First-line supervisors are the window on this organization. An employee who sees good things through that window sees a better organization than someone who sees bad things."

More and more organizations are recognizing the need to develop effective supervisors and are training them in communication skills—speaking, writing and listening—because, as one steelworker observed, "Supervisors with sandpaper personalities just don't belong in today's workplace."

Upward Media

Informal, face-to-face exchanges are valuable, but perhaps the "window on the company" is more of a two-way mirror. The opportunity to communicate upward—to know that one's suggestions and comments are being heard—is the other half of the organizational communication exchange, and whatever can be done to facilitate this exchange, particularly the upward flow, should be done. Informal, face-to-face exchange is by no means the only way to get feedback or an upward flow of communication moving. Other techniques used to spur it are advisory councils, ombudsmen, speak-up programs, attitude or climate surveys and communication audits.

A cautionary note about upward communication: listening implies action. It is not enough to provide the channels and listen attentively. The goodwill derived from such exchanges will quickly turn to disappointment and later to resentment and bitterness if nothing is done to follow up on comments, suggestions, or complaints.

Summary

Organizational communication has come a long way. If nothing else, we are seeing a more businesslike, disciplined approach to communication activity than ever before. Articulating management objectives and getting at audience needs and interests now precede message preparation and media selection. In fact, both message preparation and media selection are easier when communicators know where they're going.

The effectiveness of communication programs will increase as they facilitate the *exchange* of information, ideas and feelings. And the importance of communication in organizations will continue to grow as it becomes apparent that communication activity has a real impact on overall organizational results. In truth, management itself *is* communication.

ROY G. FOLTZ, ABC, APR, is a vice president and director of Towers, Perrin, Forster & Crosby in New York. He is a past chairman of the International Association of Business Communicators and is accredited by IABC and the Public Relations Society of America. He was named a Fellow of IABC in 1984.

◆ 2 ◆

Communicators in Contemporary Organizations

Roger D'Aprix, ABC*

In *Organizational Dynamics*, Jerry Harvey relates an anecdote that has become a classic. He recalls visiting his in-laws in a small Texas town. It was a hot Sunday afternoon and as the family sat languidly on the porch someone suggested that they ought to drive to Abilene for dinner. Seemingly, everyone agreed that it was a fine idea, even though it was a 50-mile drive each way and the family car had no air conditioning.

The meal turned out to be a disappointment, and the drive home seemed almost endless. Once safely home, a tired and hot family member said that she had gone to Abilene reluctantly and that she would have preferred to stay home. In a voice edged with tones of self-sacrifice, she said she made the trip for the others. They sat in irritated and bemused disbelief as first one and then another admitted that he or she had never wanted to get in that hot car in the first place. They had all gone because they thought the others wanted to. No one had the courage to protest.

To some degree, the whole employee communication profession has been on an extended trip to Abilene, with management in the driver's seat.

The trip to Abilene in this case was that most of us, management and professional communicators alike, took the easier and more obvious path of

* This material was originally included in "How to Communicate the Issues," Chapter 4 of *Communicating for Productivity* by Roger D'Aprix. Copyright © 1982 by Roger D'Aprix. By permission of Harper & Row, Publishers, Inc.

15

communicating reactively in media that couldn't possibly keep up with events. Even if the media could have, they would have made little difference, because it wasn't *events* that needed to be communicated; it was, and is, trends and issues that employees need to understand. By and large, the events are simply there. That they have happened is obvious. The question is, what do they mean?

If American institutional organizations are going to deal with the loss of confidence and the mistrust that have been growing in recent years, they must begin to develop new insights into the process of organizational communication.

Survey data accumulated by Opinion Research Corporation (ORC) over the past 25 years show that most institutional managements don't understand the communication process. Those that do haven't taken the trouble to develop a consistent and well-conceived strategy for dealing with the process.

Writing in the *Harvard Business Review*, Michael Cooper and other ORC researchers have documented value changes among employees that have been incubating for two and a half decades. What they see are demands for self-expression and self-fulfillment:

> The changes…are ubiquitous, pervasive, and nontransient; any reversal is unlikely in the forseeable future. The goal for management is to be aware of and prepared for new and surfacing employee needs, before it is forced to take reactive, ignorant, and resistive postures.
>
> What is undeniably required…is that corporations recognize the new realities within which they must function. The crucial issues then become the degree to which management can successfully identify, anticipate, and address these changing values as they surface…. But, make no mistake about it, changing employee values are no myth. They will be the realities that companies must face….

Cooper puts his finger on the key issue for effective communication with the employee constituency. If management is going to address the communication needs of the employee audience, it can understand those needs only by understanding the values that shape them. Then it must identify and talk about the organizational issues that most closely match those needs. And, of course, in the process it must identify, define and articulate those issues that are the product of management's own perspective from the top of the organization. For successful communication to occur, such issues must be presented in terms that are important to the employee audience.

Typically, organizational communication has often worked in almost the opposite way. Following the model of the journalist—the reporter of news—the organizational communicator and his or her management have simply reacted to events as they have happened. The predictable result has been communication anarchy.

To understand why communication anarchy has resulted, look at the journalistic communication process in practically any organization. It is a reactive process triggered by an event either inside or outside the organization. Obviously, the event must be significant enough to make some difference to the people who observe it, enough so that they are inclined to report it to others. If the event doesn't make any difference, it merely becomes one more ripple on the organization pond.

On the other hand, if the event has some significance and it has been witnessed by one or more persons, they will invariably begin the process of recounting it to others, first through the most informal channel of the organization, the grapevine. In any organization, the grapevine normally has credibility. People sometimes resent having to get information from such a source, but the fact is that they usually believe what they hear from it.

Why this is so is instructive. The grapevine, and its mode of operation is a highly personal medium. Messages are delivered face-to-face by other human beings, usually people we know and trust, and with whom we have enough experience to judge how much we should filter the message or how much of it we should discount. Very often, as grapevine sources recount the latest, they become animated, excited, pleased, or angered. They show us a whole range of human emotion and reaction to the message. They speculate about what it means, and they guess about the motives of the people responsible for the event. Regardless of its limitations, getting messages through the grapevine is a satisfactory human experience that most of us take some pleasure in. Figure 2.1 outlines how the process begins to unfold.

Formal channels are brought into play either to confirm or to deny the grapevine message (Fig. 2.2). No matter how much we may pretend

Figure 2.1.

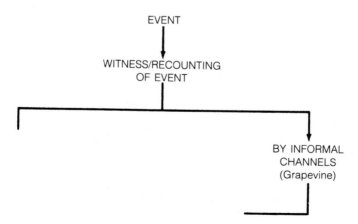

EVENT

WITNESS/RECOUNTING
OF EVENT

BY INFORMAL
CHANNELS
(Grapevine)

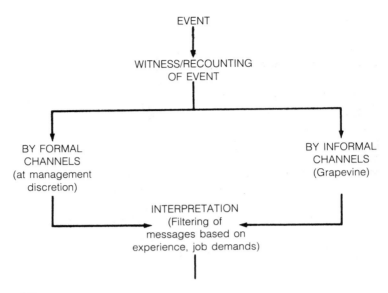

Figure 2.2.

otherwise, the role of the formal channels is practically always confirmation or denial of what everyone already knows. Certainly, the formal channels are more accurate, more detailed and more responsible, but rarely do they give people substantially new information. The reason is that the formal channels presumably operate at management's discretion—"presumably" because the option to communicate or not communicate is more apparent than real.

All too often when a given message is spreading on the grapevine, management convenes meetings to debate whether the event should be acknowledged formally. It is almost as if the event's existence could be denied by ignoring it. Some people who should know better might even argue that nothing should be said because maybe nobody has noticed; a formal statement would dignify the event or confirm it. This was once the justification for keeping the formal channels silent. In the meantime, of course, the grapevine has broadcast the event everywhere with little or no regard for accuracy, personal reputations, or the dignity of those in control.

When those in charge of the formal channels *do* decide to recount a given event through those channels, the audience is left to interpret what they are reading or hearing. The natural way the audience interprets the message is to filter it, generally on the basis of their experience with the other "languages" the organization speaks (namely, action and policy), as well as the job demands that are made on them as employees. It is difficult, for example, for someone in a department that spends lavishly on travel and entertaining customers to believe the message that the company is in a financial squeeze.

In interpreting the message he or she is receiving from both the grapevine and formal channels, the employee frequently tends to believe the grapevine and to be skeptical about the formal channels. Why this is so has much to do with the method of delivery and the tone of the message. The method of delivery used by the grapevine is highly personal, almost intimate; it is one member of the organization talking frankly to another. In the best case, it is honest and reasonably charitable. In the worst case, it is deeply suspicious, cynical and perhaps vicious.

The formal channels, on the other hand, too often dispense carefully laundered messages, with each word measured and sometimes even slightly obscured to disguise an unpleasant reality or put a better face on a particular action. It is not necessarily dishonest communication, but too often it is communication heavily laced with ego. Careers and reputations are on the line in these communications, and everyone knows it.

Lest we be too harsh on those who shape the formal messages, it is important to remember that they are doing only what all of us do all of the time—searching for the best motives to explain our actions, minimizing our responsibility for failures, and presenting our actions in the most favorable light. The grapevine presents a nice balance to this human penchant for self-protection.

Another problem with such a formal presentation of the event is that the language sounds like a parent talking to a child. It is stuffy. It is autocratic and intended to gain respect for the source of the message. But it frequently has the opposite effect.

Once the audience has properly filtered the message and compared the grapevine version with the formal version (Fig. 2.3), the next step is speculation on causes and management motives. Why are *they* doing that? Who is at fault? What will they do about it now? What does it mean to us? When will the other shoe drop? The speculation goes on and on until finally, people are left with one or more perceptions or beliefs about the organization.

The whole reactive or journalistic model is a response to an event. Without the event, the reaction cannot take place. With the event, the communication happens almost of its own will. The momentum, once begun, continues until it is played out in a belief. Except for the shaping of the formal message, no one seems to manage the process particularly or to be accountable for it.

It is impossible to put an end to reactive communication because there are always surprises in life. But it is possible to stop relying on reactive communication as the *primary* mode for organizational communication. In today's organization climate it is essential to do so.

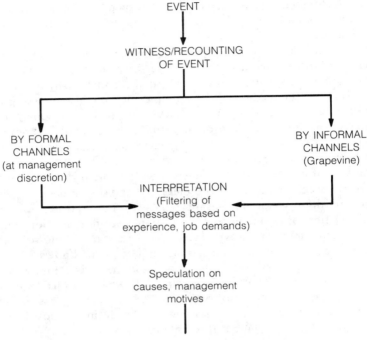

Figure 2.3.

Why this is so is clear from examining some of the limitations of reactive communication. To begin with (Table 2.1), reactive communication focuses on *what* happened, though that's not the major issue. In most organizations it is not difficult to find out what happened: all you have to do is keep your eyes and ears open. What is difficult is to find out *why* something happened. Ironically, this is what we explain least well. In fact, much of the time we simply ignore "the why" in favor of "the what." That's a poor strategy, because people want to know why more than what.

The second limitation of reactive communication is that it leaves the audience to speculate on the event's cause and significance. The danger is that they have so little information from which to speculate intelligently. About all they have is the event itself. From this information they are expected to deduce what caused it and what it means in the scheme of things. It's not surprising that the audience is wrong a good share of the time on both counts. The problem for management is that to talk about the causes and significance of the event is to run the risk of pointing fingers at one of their own or to indulge themselves in adventurous speculation. Most managements don't care for either one of these activities.

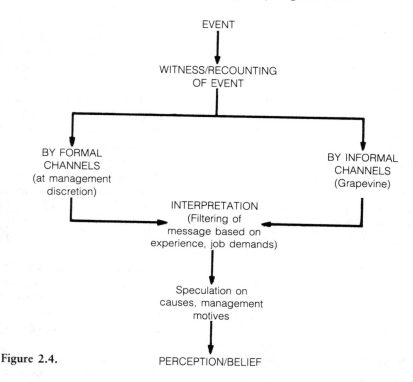

EVENT

WITNESS/RECOUNTING
OF EVENT

BY FORMAL
CHANNELS
(at management
discretion)

BY INFORMAL
CHANNELS
(Grapevine)

INTERPRETATION
(Filtering of
message based on
experience, job demands)

Speculation on
causes, management
motives

PERCEPTION/BELIEF

Figure 2.4.

Table 2.1
Limitations of Reactive Process

- Focuses mainly on what happened
- Leaves audience to speculate on event's cause and significance
- Depends on audience's ability to deduce causes and motivations from event
- Tends to overload audience with raw information, news, rumors and opinions
- Promotes view that organization life is chaotic, unplanned and unmanaged
- Diffuses communication responsibility in the organization

The third limitation is the gravest of all. It is that the reactive process in large measure depends on the audience's ability to figure out causes and management motivations by starting at the event and reasoning back from it. The truth is that the audience has great difficulty doing this because business events generally have complex causes. Rarely are there simple cause–effect relationships. The employee audience usually doesn't have access to all the facts, so the grapevine opts for the simplest explanation and cheerfully spreads it around. "Why did we have to recall the latest model of product Z from the marketplace? It's easy. The vice president in charge of that project was an incompetent who skimped on quality control and reliability studies." That may or may not be true. It may not be the real reason for the recall. But it will do until a better one comes along, probably too late to matter to anybody.

Another reason the audience has difficulty reasoning back from an event is simple distance. Anyone who has ever worked for a large organization is well aware that such organizations are status-laden. From the executive dining room to the isolated and guarded executive suite, the symbols are all over the place. Most employee-senior management encounters occur by chance, and usually make both parties a little uncomfortable. In some companies, employees perceive senior managers merely as names on letterheads or organizational charts.

Given such distance, how on earth can employees hope to guess at management motives with much accuracy? The solution at many places is to omit motive from communication and assume that people will merely accept announcements at face value. This is a naive assumption because audiences will always seek management motives when they aren't given. Even when one is given, audiences will examine it carefully to see if they believe it. The danger in all this is that the audience is usually guessing at the motives of strangers—and powerful strangers at that. It is a dangerous game for management to play either wittingly or unwittingly.

A fourth problem that makes reactive communication the less desirable way to communicate in an organization is its tendency to add to information overload. It's interesting to note that the price of producing and distributing information has decreased dramatically in the past 50 years. But it takes as long to read a page today as it did when the printing press was invented, and with so much more to read, we all pay dearly for the consumption of raw information.

Reactive communication tends to add pieces to the puzzle while doing little to help complete it. The result is that our supply of raw information, news, rumor and opinion is often merely expanded when we read the latest organizational communiqué.

A fifth serious limitation of reactive communication is that it tends to be an organizational stepchild. If you look at the reactive model, it's hard to see who runs the communication process. An instinctive tendency is to give it to senior management because they are, after all, accountable. But given the existence of the grapevine and the likelihood that senior management will be able only to confirm or deny, they're not all that anxious to accept ownership. In fact, many members of senior management would much prefer to ignore everything and let the grapevine have its way. Management in many institutional organizations does the best it can, with an air of cynical resignation and the belief that people will believe the worst anyway.

In some cases, management may wash their hands of the process and hire someone to communicate for them. This never works because the communicator cannot be a proxy for the management. The communicator will ultimately be relegated to the role of manager of employee lip service.

With communication responsibility thus diffused in the reactive process, it is inevitable that the impression created will be that organization life is chaotic, unplanned and unmanaged. Because of the tendency to communicate reactively, organizations seem to be victims of events. They respond, they parry, and they explain, but rarely do they seem to be in control, and this creates a far from comfortable feeling for the people who have cast their lot with a given company or organization. It's not an exaggeration to blame reactive communication for a large part of that feeling.

If reactive communication is ineffective as the primary form of organizational communication, then what is the alternative? First, an important caveat: there is no way to escape the reactive mode completely. There are always surprises. There are always mistakes and accidents to explain. Hence we have to be prepared to react.

But communication efforts can be mainly proactive, a word coined by the futurists to remind us to anticipate events and have plans to deal with them. In its application to organizational communication, *proactive* means "issues communication." The job is to identify, define and articulate the major issues that the organization must address if it is to be successful.

What is an issue? Unfortunately, this is something of a dealer's choice, but the dictionary provides one helpful hint by calling it "a matter that is in dispute." In general, an *organizational issue* is any major concern that is likely to have a significant effect on the organization's ability to achieve its goals.

Like reactive communication, proactive communication can be modeled to be more easily understood. Begin the process with an honest and thorough assessment of where the organization is today. The process is a sizing up and can be done in any way management chooses so long as it is objective and reasonably complete.

The probable sources for the assessment of any organization are many and varied (Fig. 2.5). One of the first places to look is at the organization's long-range plan, which can be a gold mine of goals, objectives, risks and exposures if it is well done. This plan should help to reveal where management hopes to take the organization and what management sees as some of the obstacles along the way.

The annual operating plan is an excellent source of where the organization needs and wants to go in the shorter term. Because it looks at a more predictable business environment, the annual operating plan tends to be focused and realistic about the organization's prospects.

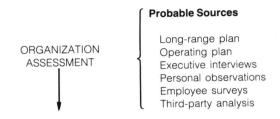

Figure 2.5.

A third excellent source of information for assessing an organization is provided by interviews with senior executives. Ask what they aspire to in their own areas of the business and what they see as the major impediments to getting there, in both the short and long term.

Personal observations of the person doing the assessment also should carry weight as long as the person has been around long enough to have formed some valid impressions. Employee surveys are also useful. The caveat is that they must be administered by an objective third party. They also must be absolutely anonymous so that anyone who fills in a survey form is guaranteed that there will be no adverse consequences for participating.

An objective assessment can also be made by an astute consultant who is hired to look at the business and size up management and employee aspirations and potential. Such third-party analyses, along with unsolicited analyses from investment experts and securities analysts, can be invaluable in examining a large corporation.

The sources for a good assessment are as varied and as broad as the imagination of the people doing the assessing. Everything that helps to capture the reality of the organization's personality, its strengths and weaknesses, should be thrown into the pot. The product should then be a stew that simmers endlessly, with new ingredients added as the organization changes. The last point is important because no living organization stands still, and an assessment, once done, must be modified as time and circumstances require.

The next step in proactive communication planning is to face a question that most organizations tend to ignore—why are we investing time and resources in the communication process? What return do we expect? The assumptions here are usually implicit rather than explicit. We all "know" that we are communicating to recognize people's contributions and to motivate them, we all "know" that we are trying to improve morale through better information, we all "know" that we are attempting to win employee support for business goals and strategy, and on and on. But do we really know?

The task here obviously is to develop a common set of assumptions (Fig. 2.6) about the probable effects of good communication practice in the organization. What are reasonable expected outcomes if someone could magically begin doing all the right things tomorrow? It is vital to articulate these assumptions and to agree what can be expected from the process. This is the time to get rid of unrealistic or impossible views of what communication can accomplish in and for the organization.

Once the fundamental assumptions are developed by the communicator and agreed to by the senior executive of the organization, it is possible, and indeed essential, to begin developing both the program and the content strategies that will be required. In the model of proactive communication (Fig. 2.7), the program strategy is on the left and the content strategy is on the right. They are parallel tasks; the communicator must uncover issues and think about how to deliver them convincingly.

Pretend that the process is mainly serial. When the organization assessment has been carefully and painstakingly developed and the fundamental assumptions have been agreed to, the next step is to develop communication guidelines. They should articulate the role and responsibility of management in the communication process.

The guidelines keep everyone honest by spelling out where communication responsibility lies and how it should be carried out. Ideally, such guidelines should be pronounced from the very top of the organization and endorsed at every key level. At some companies, for example, the guidelines are in the employee handbook for everyone to see as a commitment to the ideal of effective information exchange within the company. They also are the justification for plans and programs to improve the employee communication process.

The next step is to develop the communication program that will move the organization closer to its goals.

Two Tasks in Content Strategy

There are two main tasks in content strategy. The first is to develop a message platform for the key issues to be communicated to particular constituencies. The carefully selected issues become the foundation on which the organization builds its messages.

The task at this point is to select the issues of major importance to the organization, set them up in some kind of priority list, and use them to develop the messages which become the content of every one of the organization's communication programs.

The second main task under content strategy is message execution, and it is here that the proactive communication program either lapses into a tired recitation of pieties and "me-too" positions or becomes alive with

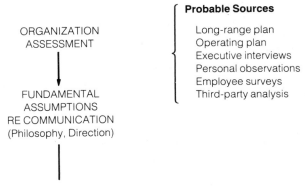

Figure 2.6.

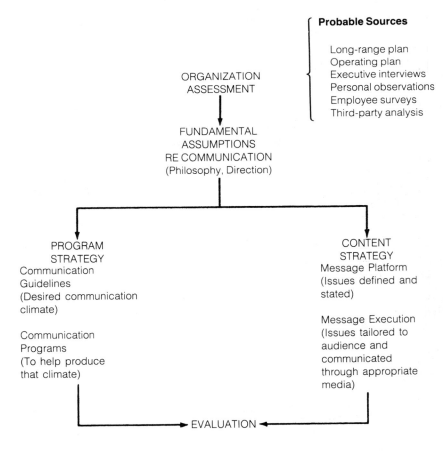

Figure 2.7.

26

honest and gutsy statements and positions the audience can relate to.

The needs and interests of the particular audiences must be considered, whether employees, shareholders, customers, citizens of the community in which the organization does business, or perhaps government regulatory bodies. This process, of course, requires that the communicator determine which issues are important to whom and tailor the message to them.

The final process in the proactive model is evaluation, a difficult process that doesn't normally yield much objective information. Nonetheless, it is imperative for the communicator to use every technique he or she can dream

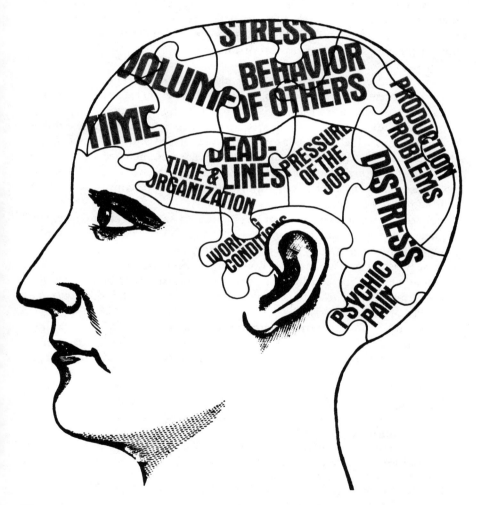

Figure 2.8. Proactive communication lightens the audience's burden by focusing on *why* things have happened or are happening.

up to measure the effectiveness of the process: audience attitude surveys, broad communication surveys, readership surveys, interviews or anything else that can be devised to determine what is or is not working when measured against the original assumptions about communication in the organization.

What are some of the major advantages of proactive issues communication? There are many. The process tends to identify the organization's concerns and priorities and to indicate what management proposes to do about them (Table 2.2). The process is reassuring to employees, particularly because they know what they are experiencing in the way of day-to-day problems. If they never see those things acknowledged as problems or if they hear no talk of possible solutions, they are often anxious. They fear management is simply not on top of things.

A second advantage of the proactive process is that it focuses on the significance of events rather than their mere occurrence. This is extremely important because people want to know what the event means. The event's occurrence is common knowledge, thanks to the grapevine.

A third advantage is that the proactive process tends to provide a frame of reference in which particular events can be placed and explained. "Yes, this may be a setback, but no, it is not a disaster. Remember we told you that one of the tough issues we were up against this year was. . . ." Thus, it is possible to provide a sense of proportion and order to convey the feeling that someone is indeed in charge.

A fourth advantage of the process is that it can be used to anticipate change and provide justification for the change. Organizations sometimes have to take actions that look extraordinary or poorly conceived when viewed in isolation. When the actions can be explained in light of certain issues or needs, they can begin to make very good sense. In the process, people can be prepared to adapt to changes that would otherwise be passively or actively resisted.

Similarly, good proactive communication can help make an organization look like a rational universe in which one's work life has meaning. Given the values and needs of today's worker, this is a significant advantage.

Table 2.2
Advantages of Proactive Communication Planning Process (for Audience)

- Identifies organization's concerns and priorities
- Focuses on significance of events rather than on their mere occurrence
- Provides perspective and sense of order
- Foreshadows change and provides justification
- Fosters "connectedness" of events and sense that one's work life has meaning
- Pressures leadership to match words with actions
- Encourages hope and optimism

Proactive issues, once communicated, are a course the organization will try to steer by. There will be an attempt to match words and actions, and changes will be made deliberately and in response to other issues, not capriciously. The end result of this kind of rational universe is a more hopeful and optimistic work force.

There is an excellent chance that people whose hope and optimism turn out to be well founded will be more productive and more committed. This is a hard premise to prove but common sense suggests that it is true.

What are some of the advantages of proactive communication for the professional communicator?

First, for the communication staff, this disciplined approach to communication carries their effort to organization issues and priorities. The inevitable result is that the communicators get greater attention and support from management because their efforts are seen as valuable to achieving business objectives.

Second, this process helps the communicator to understand his or her job better.

Third, proactive communication influences the content of communication and disciplines the process so that the professional communicator is not merely pursuing the subjects and issues that excite him or her but which may be of little relevance to the health of the organization.

Fourth, because the process requires careful evaluation and analysis of issues, it helps to ensure that communication is an honest process matched to both management and audience needs. Issues are not merely "top down." They also become "bottom up" as the communicator attempts to determine the concerns and information needs of the audience.

There are also significant advantages for management in the proactive approach to communication. For one, communication becomes a manageable process rather than an afterthought or an attempt to explain what went wrong or to defend why something was done. The reactions of various constituencies are anticipated and addressed as the policy or program is being implemented. In short, communication becomes a planned part of the management process.

ROGER D'APRIX, ABC, is the international practice leader for human resource communication consulting with Towers, Perrin, Forster & Crosby in New York. He is accredited by the International Association of Business Communicators.

• 3 •

Assessing and Meeting Audience Needs

Thomas C. Hunter

The extent to which organizational communicators must be sensitive to the expectations, interests, needs and values of their audiences is enormous. It exceeds whatever degree of sensitivity is required in practically any other form of structured communication.

For the most part, audiences of "public" media bring a fairly objective and unemotional set of needs and interests to such communication vehicles. Radio listeners, television viewers, and readers of newspapers and magazines primarily seek information or entertainment. Rarely do they have any special-interest ties beyond that.

Editors of a consumer publication, for example, assuredly must know what their readers want and how they want it "packaged." Beyond providing their readers with what they want, however, the editors hardly need be concerned that their work indicates that the publisher cares about the readers, is personally concerned about the readers' problems, or feels that the readers, as individuals, are important. Organizational communicators, on the other hand, must reflect those concerns, subtly or overtly, on behalf of their publishers—the organizations for which they work. This is true whether the communicator is an employee, a freelancer or an agency representative.

If a commercial broadcast station or a commercial publication is not in tune with and responsive to what a portion of its audience expects to receive from it, that audience segment simply can, and usually will, turn to

31

alternative sources of information or entertainment. That defection certainly is not without its harmful consequences to the medium involved, most notably in reduced revenues if the number of defectors is significant, but the issues and effects involved are rather clear-cut and impersonal. The understanding of them does not call for too great a degree of sensitivity.

The needs and expectations that audiences bring to organizations in which they have a stake are highly subjective and complex. These needs are often emotional and psychological, as with the employee whose sense of self-esteem and personal worth can be affected positively or negatively by the regard in which the employer holds the person and, to a large degree, by how employee communication reflects that regard.

The relationships between an organization and its varied audiences, and the organization's responsiveness to audience interests and needs, are critical to effective communication. Those relationships are born of the special levels of involvement that exist between employers and employees, companies and shareholders, companies and customers, nonprofit organizations and volunteers, health-care facilities and patients, associations and members, service organizations and clients, and on and on.

Based on staff time, production costs and the scope of activities, few if any organizations can or should attempt programs that cater to every communication interest or expectation of each individual with whom they are involved. That surely would create an unmanageable myriad of communication vehicles—conceivably, one for each person. Still, the communicator should seek to find out as much as possible about each person in a given audience.

When asked to explain the key to his ability to produce consistently successful commercials, Chuck Blore of Chuck Blore and Don Richman, Inc. of Hollywood, explained: "We go for a one-to-one with our audience [in order to] understand and touch their basic drives, needs for security, affection." Blore says, "What we do is take 30,000 people, who have 30,000 sets of worries, 30,000 sets of moralities, 30,000 sets of problems and attitudes, and find something that will reach out and touch all of them."

The same task awaits the organizational communicator who expects to be successful; he or she must make every effort to know the audience, with all its needs, expectations, interests and values. The communicator may not always be able to respond. The decision not to respond should be made by choice, however, after knowing and considering all the factors involved. It never should be a "nonchoice" resulting from a lack of awareness of an audience's expectations.

Sometimes, awareness of audience interests can come about unexpectedly. When one company introduced a "Letters" section in its corporate magazine, it anticipated a high response from its active employees, to whom the magazine's editorial content was oriented. The first year, however, retired employees, representing less than 2% of the magazine's total circulation, accounted for more than 22% of the letters to the editor. Obviously, they were a special-interest audience eager to communicate with the company for which they had worked and anxious that the company keep communication channels open to them. From the content and tone of the retirees' letters, it was clear they had strong positive feelings about the company.

Faced with the high response from the retirees, the editors of the magazine considered the possibility of developing a separate newsletter for retirees. There were a number of reasons to do so, aside from the fact that retirees were obviously a receptive audience. Retirees often feel they are cut off from the company and no longer needed. A special communication vehicle, offered out of a sense of corporate responsibility, would help assuage such uneasy feelings. Also, a special publication could supply information to help retirees be effective voices for the company in their contacts with others in their communities.

After weighing these and other considerations involved, including staff time and costs, the editors decided instead to alter slightly the content and slant of the articles in the employee magazine. They did so in a way that reinforced the good feelings existing among the retirees but without jeopardizing reader interest among active employees.

Don't Chance Negative Communication

To attempt to communicate without a deep awareness of an audience's interests and attitudes, and everything else that goes into its makeup, is to attempt to communicate without a clear sense of direction. The chance for communication to be fully effective under such circumstances is merely that—a chance—and the outcome can be worse than not communicating at all. Recipients of misdirected organizational communication can easily conclude, "They not only don't know what corner I'm coming out of, they don't even care."

Consider the effects when organizational communication conveys an evident lack of caring. Employees may begin to approach their work with far less enthusiasm—and a corresponding decrease in their performance and effectiveness. They may seek employment elsewhere. Customers or clients may take their business to competitors who value them and show it. Prospective customers may choose not to get involved with the organization. Shareholders may transfer their investment dollars to companies responsive to their particular needs and interests. Volunteers or donors may seek more appreciative organizations to support. People may begin to regard the organization as an insensitive and unattractive neighbor, one the community can easily do without. These consequences should not each be treated as isolated cases, because one can quickly trigger the others, contaminating all the relations with which an organization may be concerned: employee, customer, community, financial and even government relations.

An employee who senses a lack of concern on the part of the employer, for instance, can lose concern about producing a quality product. As a result, customers soon discover they are purchasing defective products or products that are of poorer quality than ever before. If this lowering of work performance and product quality is widespread, the company can encounter a sales decline of such severity that the financial community no longer regards the firm as an attractive investment. A rash of consumer complaints can lead to escalating demands for stronger consumer protection laws. Meanwhile, there can be a growing awareness among the general public that the company apparently is not concerned about the quality of the products it manufactures. This, in turn, can lead to serious questions about the company's sense of responsibility regarding other aspects of its operations, such as the effects its manufacturing processes have on the environment. The example is extreme, but the point is valid.

Harry Mullikin, president and chief executive officer of Westin International Hotels, once put it this way: "The hotel business operates on saying 'Yes.' Our decisions are made on the basis of 'What does the guest want?'" In other words, what are the guest's expectations and attitudes?

"The essential question," Mullikin elaborated, "is, 'What can be done within the framework of a business in which success is based on satisfying the guest?' The next most important consideration after the guest is, 'What does the hotel employee want?' How can we design a hotel and lay things out so that employees can do their jobs better and more comfortably? Because, if the employee is happier, the guest gets better service, and that then lets us make money to take care of the shareholders. If the guests are dissatisfied and the employees are disgruntled in a hotel in which the shareholders have $30 million invested, we're soon going to have an empty building."

Demographics: The Basics for Understanding

To answer the questions Mullikin raised, the communicator eventually must come to grips with attitudes. Before assessing and dealing with the attitudes of an audience, however, there should be an awareness of its basic makeup—the demographics of that audience. In the case of hotel guests, for instance, are there more men than women? Are they usually vacationers or business people? Do they usually travel singly or with their families? Is the average stay a night or a week? In the case of an international hotel, of what nationalities are the guests?

In general, each group has some needs and interests the others do not. They will guide the communicator in choosing the media to use to convey various messages and what the content and tone of the communication should be. Many communication decisions can be refined by matching demographics against the results of attitudinal surveys. The findings of one extensive research effort indicated that newspaper readers under the age of 30 have a lower attention span and are more visual and less verbal than other readers. The research also concluded that readers are turned off by newspapers that are hard to handle, contain blurred pictures or use stilted, formal or pretentious language. It showed, too, that many readers dislike "jumps" and continued articles.

Assuming that general findings automatically apply to particular audiences can be a serious mistake, though. All readers younger than 30 are not necessarily more visually than verbally oriented—nor, as implied, is everyone older than 30 less visually oriented. The study cited above pertains to readers of commercial newspapers. Had it focused on employee newspapers, the findings might have been somewhat different. Communicators should keep up with general attitude trends, but they should not follow these trends blindly in developing programs for specific audiences. General findings can give strong indications of attitudes that probably exist among comparable audiences, but before addressing them the communicator should determine as accurately as possible whether they apply.

Basic demographics that are important for developing and directing effective communication programs are relatively easy to obtain. Ready sources include personnel records; customer, client and guest lists; patient records in health-care facilities, and student records in educational institutions.

The ease of access to as much information as is available has created a communication problem of its own: invasion of privacy. When this might be a concern, communicators should use extreme care in addressing an audience so that no portion of its members will have reason to feel that others know more about them than they are entitled to know—which is as it should be. When confidentiality is a concern in obtaining demographic information and other statistics, persons with proper access to such records should be the ones to uncover the nonconfidential information helpful for tailoring effective communication.

Demographics often are highly important in achieving communication goals and avoiding communication errors whether aimed at internal or external audiences. An example: A salesperson suggested that his company's employee magazine devote a portion of each issue to publishing product specifications the sales force could pull out and leave behind when calling on customers. Sales personnel accounted for less than 1,000 of a total circulation of more than 15,000. To have followed the suggestion of using the employee magazine for sales information clearly would have meant including material of little interest or value to the majority of readers.

In another instance, a state chapter of a professional association located in a state with two telephone area codes listed the president's number in the chapter newsletter without listing the area code. The editor was not oriented toward the people who needed the area code. Likely interpretation? The status of some members was secondary to that of others.

A national organization started a series of articles in its quarterly magazine, profiling its operations at locations throughout the country, one in each issue. When readers began to ask when the magazine was going to get around to them, the editors did some simple calculations and realized that it would take more than 20 years to cover all 86 locations. Although the audience population at a featured location was pleased when it received the coverage and attention, those at scores of others felt overlooked—and obviously would continue to feel so until the editors could get around to them, years later.

This case is an example of why demographics are important, not only in developing communication but also in monitoring its implementation. A rule of thumb is to maintain in any form of communication a content balance based on the makeup of the audience. Production workers should be able to feel they are receiving treatment equal to that of office workers, men the same treatment as women, field personnel the same as headquarters personnel, and so on, according to the makeup of the audience. Periodic monitoring of the makeup of an audience will alert the communicator to any changes that might occur and indicate, when appropriate, the need for a revision of priorities.

Address the Audience from Its Frame of Reference

A major shortcoming in some organizational communication is the result of managements that insist on addressing audiences—employees, in particular—in terms of what management thinks employee attitudes and interests should be, rather than what they actually are. Communication about employee benefits and economic issues are two prime examples. The following, which appeared in an employee newsletter, is an extreme illustration, but archaic as it is, messages similar to it do surface now and then:

> Every payday you are handed a check for so many dollars and cents. You've earned it; you know you've worked hard for it. It looks pretty good. Do you ever think about the other paycheck? Your company has several extras for you. These may be medical and life insurance, pension plans, parking lots, vacations, holidays, and sick leaves. Even coffee breaks are fringe benefits. But maybe you

would rather see these extras put into cash that you can hold in your hot little hand. Let's pretend you decide to do this. You asked your company to cancel all your benefits and add all the money to your paycheck. You feel so much richer. But this feeling doesn't last long. You arrive at the company parking lot and are stopped. You're told that this is one of those fringe benefits you've given up. So you have to find another place to park, which costs you money and a long walk to get to work. You really need that cup of coffee at your break. Sorry about that, but no benefits. Remember? You suddenly feel a little sick. Better not do that; you can't get sick now. You gave up all the company insurance. And you didn't take out any on your own because it was so much higher for an individual than under a group plan. You're really in a fine mess. You go home at the end of a frustrating day and spend a restless night wondering how you could have been so stupid. You wake up with a migraine headache but no paid sick days. So, off you go with the feeling that life is getting very complicated. You remember that feeling of security you used to have. It came from the thought of that pension or profit-sharing plan that was almost like compulsory savings. You didn't ever manage money too well, but the company was taking care of it for you. Guess you'd better make some changes and make them fast.

Now, aren't you glad we were just pretending? It was a little scary, even though you knew it wasn't true. But it did make you realize those little extras aren't so little after all.

It is hard to imagine that the person who produced this article gave much thought to employee attitudes regarding benefits and the ways they are communicated. Employees hardly ever consider a parking lot a benefit. When told that it is, they most likely will react with feelings ranging from ridicule to resentment.

Consider other serious ramifications of such an article when matched against the following attitudes people have voiced:

An advertising executive reacted to the addition of each new benefit his agency offered by describing it as "just another fishhook in my back to tear away that much more flesh if I ever get up the nerve to leave." A staff consultant described benefit packages as corporate "bondage systems" that keep employees anchored to jobs they don't care for. A regional sales manager reacted to her employer's describing as a benefit the money it put into pension plans: "Baloney. That's a straight-out employment cost for them." A secretary said about her payroll savings plan, under which the company matched dollar-for-dollar the funds employees deposited through payroll deductions: "Terrific. Now all I have to do is go out and get a part-time job so that I can afford to sign up for it."

To publish the preceding article for employees holding these viewpoints is not only useless, it creates an adverse reaction. It does not matter whether these employee viewpoints are *right* or *wrong*; that's the way they perceive things. An organization cannot effectively communicate about benefits as "extras" when employees regard them as rights to which they are entitled.

What possibly could have been the advantage to the Illinois company that apparently decided to set the record straight and, in its annual report to employees, wrote that while employees "earned" $65 million in wages in 1978, they "were paid" $16 million in benefits?

Obviously, there must be communication about employee benefits. They are part of the package that encourages workers to join an organization and stay with it. Organizations, however, should never communicate about benefits in a paternalistic tone; people resent that. How much better, in view of the diversity of employee attitudes, to handle a benefits story the way *Newsday*, the Long Island daily newspaper, did in *Inside Newsday*. First, it described substantive benefits, not parking lots and coffee breaks. Second, it gave a first-person account by staffer Michael Unger, not a management piece saying, in effect, "Let me tell you what we've done for you lately."

A heart attack, open heart surgery and complications after surgery were terrifying enough for me and my family..., but they would have been financially catastrophic were if not for *Newsday's* sick-pay benefits and medical and hospital insurance. Without them, my illness would have left us heavily in debt. More importantly, knowing I had such coverage with *Newsday* was a big relief, a load off my mind, while I was seriously ill. And these vital fringe benefits enabled me to concentrate on getting well without having to worry about huge hospital and medical bills mounting up or how my family would get by from day to day.

I received my salary during the six months I was out of work, part of it directly from *Newsday* and part of it from *Newsday's* insurance carrier, Equitable Life. And the medical and hospital bills were almost totally paid through Equitable, while my wife's separate coverage picked up most of the remainder.

My total hospital and medical bills amounted to about $50,000 between February and June, 1979, and they continued to come in for postoperative care that included participation in a cardiac rehabilitation program. Obviously, with costs like that *Newsday's* fringe benefits become absolute necessities.

Luckily for me, my wife, Amy, handled all of my medical and hospital bills as well as the disability insurance benefits, for which claims had to be filed periodically. But neither Amy nor I could have done it without the concerned and continuing help of *Newsday's* Employee Relations Department. So, here's a special thank-you note to *Newsday's* terrific Rembert Brown, Barbara Zielinski and Sue Hickey in Dan Mannix's department, and to Pat Stewart of Editorial who made sure my paychecks were mailed to my home.

When the hospital costs really started mounting up, the *Newsday* Blue Cross coverage was excellent. For example, the bill for the shortest of my four hospital stays...at St. Francis Hospital in Roslyn—two weeks for the open heart surgery—was for a little more than $14,600. Of that amount, just $70.50 was not paid by Blue Cross. Equitable paid the medical claims with dispatch after Rembert Brown helped my wife file those insurance claims and other more complicated forms. He and Sue and Barbara in Employee Relations made my wife's task much easier. They and Pat Stewart in Editorial really went out of their way to help on a personal basis.

And in a large and growing company like *Newsday*, it's nice to know that can happen.

The two employee benefits articles speak for themselves. The second one is an example to follow when employee attitudes about a subject are not known. Always make a supposition as to the most negative attitudes that could exist among an audience and consider them when deciding how best to communicate.

It is especially difficult to anticipate all the attitudes that exist among an audience when dealing with international communication. Lack of awareness of subtle cultural and political differences and sensitivities make it almost impossible for a communicator in one country to relate totally to audience interests in other countries. Some organizations in other countries hire entire staffs of local communicators, people who naturally understand and empathize with the interests and attitudes of their audiences. Few organizations can afford such staffs, however.

Riss Victor, associate editor of the Credit Union National Association's *Everybody's Money*, with editorial offices in Madison, Wisconsin, found a workable solution when it became evident that many of the articles in *EM* didn't apply to its Canadian readers. At first, *EM* had contracted with Canadian freelance writers for occasional articles. This was not satisfactory, however. It seemed that unless every article was researched and written across the border, the magazine wouldn't meet the concerns of Canadian readers. Budget constraints and the desire to maintain editorial control of content kept CUNA from establishing a full-time staff in Canada, so the editor contacted Canadian consultant Don Stewart, who suggested that, instead of originating articles, he would like a shot at "Canadianizing" the United States material. He examined some back issues and pointed out information that could make the articles more pertinent to Canadians. As Stewart noted, "Canadians are somewhat nationalistic and resent US 'arrogance,' particularly when there is an apparent insensitivity to Canadian feelings. Our [then] Prime Minister, Pierre Trudeau, put it this way, 'Being neighbors to the USA is somewhat like being a mouse in bed with an elephant; the elephant's every move, however well-intentioned, is a serious risk to life.'"

The editors of *EM* agreed to let Stewart remove the irritants that annoy Canadian readers. Now they send him galleys of the articles from the United States and he checks information with Canadian sources and does whatever rewriting is necessary. Sometimes Stewart simply changes *state* to *province*, sometimes articles require research and rewriting or editing to give them a Canadian flavor—or "flavour."

Importance of Personal Contacts

Lack of personal contact with audiences severely restricts a communicator's ability to relate to them. The give-and-take that a one-on-one situation affords is especially effective in getting at deep-rooted attitudes, concerns and interests.

Opportunities for informal sensing of attitudes and interests are countless—for example, by really listening to casual comments in the office and plant, during lunch, in car pools, when visiting clients and on many other occasions. Frank W. Considine, president and chief executive officer of National Can Corporation, has remarked that whenever he visits a plant, he sits down at a table and talks to the supervisors. Communicators should be doing the same thing constantly in their areas of activity—always keeping their antennae out to discover what is on people's minds and to ascertain how receptive people are to what is being communicated and the ways in which it is being communicated. As helpful as formal surveys are, face-to-face encounters offer a far greater opportunity for probing and opening up new areas of thought.

When Westin International Hotels opened the Century Plaza in Los Angeles, employee attitudes were unbelievably good. According to President Harry Mullikin, management had gone to great extremes to ensure that. "It was so good," Mullikin says, "we wanted to be sure we wouldn't lose it." So, during its first summer, the hotel took one of the hotel management students it hires each year and assigned him to survey employees to find out what they did and didn't like and what bothered them or didn't bother them.

After hundreds of interviews, management learned that a major source of discontent was due entirely to a lack of communication. The hotel had no parking lot, so before it opened, Westin arranged, for the convenience of the employees, to lease parking space from a company right behind it. The company charged the Century Plaza $10 a space a month, a charge that the hotel passed along to its employees. It never explained to the employees what the arrangement was, however. As a result, the survey revealed, the employees' number one complaint was, "Why should the hotel make $10 a month by charging us for parking? That's not fair." The hotel management immediately explained the arrangement to its employees, and from then on included the explanation in its orientation program for new employees. Once these steps were taken, the complaint disappeared.

"One of the biggest mistakes management makes," Mullikin says, "is to assume that people know the full story. We had done something we thought was nice for the employees, and we assumed they'd know it. But they didn't."

The extent to which an audience's impressions conform to the facts is not the issue. What an individual *perceives* as reality *is* reality to that person—and this is what communicators must be concerned with when addressing their audiences.

THOMAS C. HUNTER is director of public relations for Union Camp Corporation in Wayne, New Jersey, and is editor of its corporate employee magazine.

· Part II ·

GETTING STARTED: ANALYZING AND ORGANIZING THE WORK

◆ 4 ◆

Auditing Communication Practices

Myron Emanuel, ABC

"How am I doing?" is the number one question asked by communicators, far outnumbering the five Ws. And, today, a more important question is being asked by top management: "How are *you* doing?" The answer is sought in a variety of ways: surveys, both formal and informal, homemade and professional; letters and phone calls; corridor and cloakroom conversations; "gut feelings" and astrological charts.

Most of these methods are pretty good. After all, an intelligent person usually can tell whether he or she is on target or off the mark. We don't need a formal survey to tell us that an article or a videotape was well received; an informal telephone survey can do this effectively. Why, then, this sudden and fairly widespread interest in communication "audits"?

An Old and Commonsense Activity

The communication audit is really a new name for an old and commonsense communication activity. Communicators have always tried to assess the effectiveness of their programs, or to examine the relevance of what they were trying to say with what senior management wanted them to say, or to make sure what they were saying was being heard by those they were trying to reach. If they didn't do these things regularly, either of two bad things happened: they found themselves looking for a new job, or worse, they

45

discovered they were working for an organization that did not care about communicating or did not want to communicate.

Today, there is little danger of an organization not wanting to communicate. In fact, all the evidence points the other way. Despite the recent severe recession, communication budgets and staffs have fared no worse than other staff and operating groups. In a significant number of cases they weathered the downturn with hardly an off beat. And in some firms, communication budgets are up and staffs are being increased. Further, senior management is far more involved in communication than ever before, and communication programs and communicators are being scrutinized far more critically because they are now being seen as essential contributors to profit-and-loss statements. This is the reason for the widespread interest ,in the communication audit. It makes good business sense and takes its place alongside other organizational reviews: the financial audit, the benefits review, strategic planning, market research and manpower needs analysis.

A Complex and Time-consuming Process

Despite the pervasive need for communication audits and a long history of attempts to carry them out, the true communication audit has rarely been attempted until recently. One reason is that it is a very complex and time-consuming process. Another is that it involves skills and techniques not always found in the communication process or among those who direct the process. These require considerable knowledge of business and business terminology, easy access to top management, and intimate knowledge of organizational goals and philosophy (including those on the hidden agenda). It also requires expertise in conducting surveys: preparing bias-free questions, administering surveys, leading focus-group discussions and reading and analyzing computer printouts to identify significant patterns and trends among the responses. Finally, all of this must be reduced to an action plan for the long and short term.

Still another reason for the fairly limited use of communication audits is the confusion many people have in distinguishing them from other surveys and audits. In essence, a communication audit is a comprehensive and thorough study of communication philosophy, concepts, structure, flow and practice within an organization, be it small or large, profit or nonprofit, private or public. A communication audit should be able to uncover information blockages, organizational hindrances to effective communication, and lost opportunities. It can expose misunderstandings, help gauge media effectiveness, and provide an evaluation of ongoing programs. It may be broad in scope or limited. It may be used to measure the effectiveness of communication throughout a large organization or in a single division or

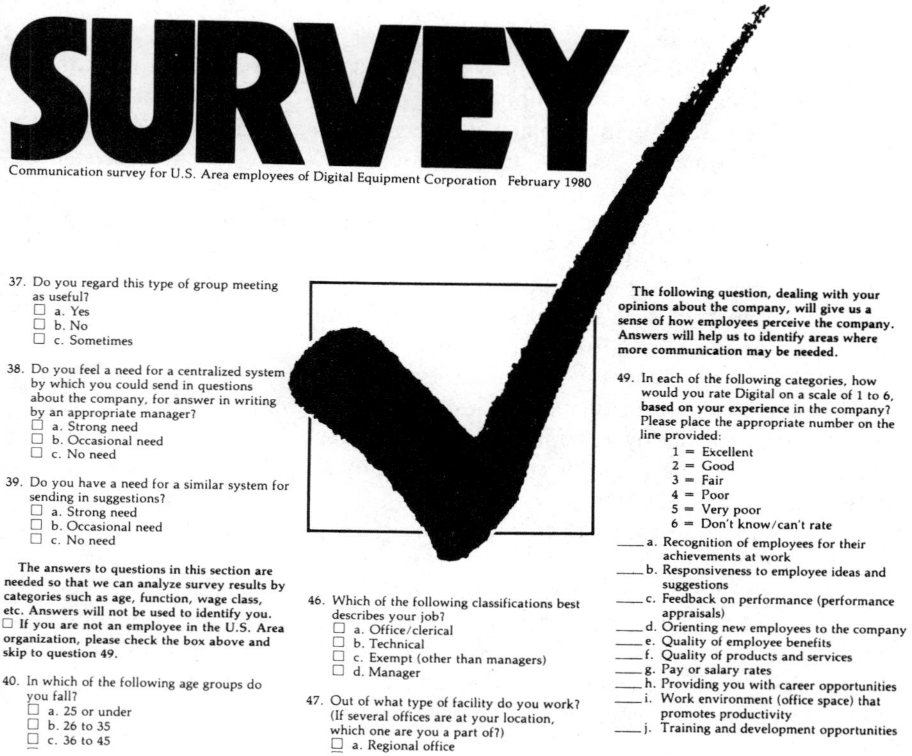

SURVEY

Communication survey for U.S. Area employees of Digital Equipment Corporation   February 1980

37. Do you regard this type of group meeting as useful?
   - ☐ a. Yes
   - ☐ b. No
   - ☐ c. Sometimes

38. Do you feel a need for a centralized system by which you could send in questions about the company, for answer in writing by an appropriate manager?
   - ☐ a. Strong need
   - ☐ b. Occasional need
   - ☐ c. No need

39. Do you have a need for a similar system for sending in suggestions?
   - ☐ a. Strong need
   - ☐ b. Occasional need
   - ☐ c. No need

The answers to questions in this section are needed so that we can analyze survey results by categories such as age, function, wage class, etc. Answers will not be used to identify you.
☐ If you are not an employee in the U.S. Area organization, please check the box above and skip to question 49.

40. In which of the following age groups do you fall?
   - ☐ a. 25 or under
   - ☐ b. 26 to 35
   - ☐ c. 36 to 45

46. Which of the following classifications best describes your job?
   - ☐ a. Office/clerical
   - ☐ b. Technical
   - ☐ c. Exempt (other than managers)
   - ☐ d. Manager

47. Out of what type of facility do you work? (If several offices are at your location, which one are you a part of?)
   - ☐ a. Regional office

The following question, dealing with your opinions about the company, will give us a sense of how employees perceive the company. Answers will help us to identify areas where more communication may be needed.

49. In each of the following categories, how would you rate Digital on a scale of 1 to 6, based on your experience in the company? Please place the appropriate number on the line provided:

   1 = Excellent
   2 = Good
   3 = Fair
   4 = Poor
   5 = Very poor
   6 = Don't know/can't rate

   ____ a. Recognition of employees for their achievements at work
   ____ b. Responsiveness to employee ideas and suggestions
   ____ c. Feedback on performance (performance appraisals)
   ____ d. Orienting new employees to the company
   ____ e. Quality of employee benefits
   ____ f. Quality of products and services
   ____ g. Pay or salary rates
   ____ h. Providing you with career opportunities
   ____ i. Work environment (office space) that promotes productivity
   ____ j. Training and development opportunities

Figure 4.1.

location. Like any audit, its value is increased if it is used regularly. A periodic checkup is good for people, finances and communication programs.

What It Isn't

A communication audit is not an attitude survey, which is the tool that an organization uses to examine employee feelings about the work atmosphere, working conditions, pay and benefits, and so on. Questions about communication may appear in an attitude survey, but they constitute only a relatively small number and are rarely specific to the kind of information a communicator needs. The only function of a communicator's questions in an attitude survey is to serve as a cross-check for attitudinal responses. If such questions are used otherwise—for example, to piggyback a readership survey or probe supervisory communication competence—they will only confuse participants and raise questions in their minds about the true purpose of the audit or survey.

It is *not* an opinion poll, which also has a place in the organizational arsenal of research tools. Opinion polls, apart from their political context, generally focus on specific subjects—for example, cafeteria versus vending machines, flextime versus regular hours, feelings about overtime versus a third shift.

It is *not* a readership survey, which tells you what audiences think of a publication. For example, it cannot tell you whether you should issue the publication at all, or what value it is rendering the organization, or where it ranks as an information source among other competing media, such as the grapevine or the outside press.

It is *not* an issues awareness survey, which tries to gauge employee knowledge of organizational activities and plans. Among the things investigated here are employee *knowledge* of their benefit plans and how they work, or their awareness of specific government legislation or regulation affecting the organization and its future.

It is *not* an economic information or awareness survey, which is designed to probe employees' knowledge of and attitudes toward the economy and how it affects their organization and their jobs. The purpose here is to help strengthen positive attitudes, address negative ones, fill in information gaps, and win employee understanding for organizational goals and activities, particularly where they concern productivity, business direction, governmental regulations and political activities.

It Is "Zero-base" Communication

A standard approach to a communication audit is analogous to the zero-base budgeting process. In effect, you start your study from ground zero, as if you have no program, no communication vehicles, no goals, no staff, no budget. The focus, pure and simple, is on communication of all kinds. But the results of such a study explore all aspects of the organization:

- Organizational goals and philosophy.
- The audience's perception of these goals and objectives.
- The climate for communication.
- The structure of organizational communication, formal and informal.
- The nature and information needs of the various audiences (e.g., management groups, including specific breakdowns for professional, first-level supervision, middle management, sales; hourly employees and their various groupings; nonexempt; plant; office and field). If the study involves external audiences, identify their specific characteristics and information needs, whether they are shareholders, members of the

financial community, opinion leaders, neighbors, media professionals or private interest groups.
- How the communication organization can best meet these audiences' information needs and expectations.
- Where to locate the communication function within the organizational structure so that it can do the most good.

The goal of an audit is to determine which of the organization's philosophies and goals need communication support. It should identify the audience or audiences for these messages and determine their information needs and wants, then establish an organization and pipeline to make sure these messages and information can move freely, efficiently and swiftly in both directions.

When to Audit

There are various circumstances to indicate when communication audits should be done:

- When organizations are aware that their programs lack credibility, are inefficient or ineffective, but find it difficult to uncover or resolve specific problems.
- When there is a need to evaluate a new communication policy or practice. Whether the policy or practice has been announced, initiated or merely planned or conceived, an audit—ideally, conducted by an outsider who has been exposed to various business and communication assignments— can often help avoid pitfalls and make improvements.
- When there is a need to develop or restructure the communication function within the organization.
- When there is a need to develop communication guidelines or budgets.
- When there is a major change in the direction or structure of the communication function.
- When organizations merge or acquire new properties. A careful evaluation of the corporate culture and ongoing communication practices of the firms involved may show that different techniques will be required in each to allay employee fears and suspicions and to develop a positive, cooperative spirit.
- When new personnel practices or changes in the organization are being implemented.
- When there is labor unrest. Often the problems that lead to dissatisfaction among employees are the direct result of poor communication.
- When there are economic crises such as layoffs or cost-reduction programs. Employees are sometimes told *when* this is happening but seldom

why. Knowing the degree of their understanding of management's motives for the cut can provide a basis for explaining it, perhaps even soliciting help in the form of cost-saving ideas and suggestions for improvement. Further, an audit can tell you whether the vehicles and staff you have in place are adequate to the job facing you.

Conducting the Communication Audit

There are a number of ways to approach the communication audit. One that we use incorporates a three-tier probe:

1. Intensive interviews with senior management.
2. A comprehensive probe, often a survey, of the employee audience.
3. A critical review and evaluation of employee communication practice, structure and materials.

The result should be a clear picture of what senior management wants to say to employees, what employees want to hear and know, and how effectively the communication organization is meeting these needs. This research effort should produce material to create short- and long-term strategies, communication plans and action plans for a communication program to meet these needs. It should indicate how the communication organization should be structured, what media you need, what you should be saying to which audience or audiences, and how to manage an upward communication program.

Executive Interviews

Step One should be a series of one-on-one, intensive discussions with the senior officers of the organization. When we conduct these interviews, we always include the CEO, the chief operating officer, all the other senior officers (executive vice presidents, senior vice presidents, division presidents, etc.), and *anyone* else who is in a position to make and enforce corporate policy. The questions we ask are direct and blunt. We probe organizational goals, problems and challenges, with particular emphasis on the organization's strategies, goals and direction. We ask for candid assessments of the communication process, organization and effectiveness. We rarely discuss media, personalities, or methods. What we are after is the personality and culture of the organization as reflected in senior management, their concerns, and the key messages management wants to send out to win employee understanding and support. Our assumption is that there is no existing communication program—that we are starting from scratch.

Without question, this aspect of the audit should be conducted by an outside organization. It would be difficult, if not impossible, for an employee (and a subordinate employee at that) of the organization to extract the kind of information needed. Much of the information gleaned in these interviews is incorporated in the next step—the target audience survey.

The Audience Probe

The next step is to go to the audience (in this case let us assume it is an employee audience). Here we will find out what they know about the organization, what they don't know, and what they "know" that is wrong; how they receive their news and information and how they prefer to receive it; what they think of the information (is it credible, pertinent, timely, understandable?); how they evaluate the various media, and which subjects are of greatest interest to them and which turn them off. Other topics brought up in the executive interviews often provoke additional questions that should be asked.

There are many ways to conduct such a survey:

- *Telephone interviews.* Generally these are unsatisfactory for such an investigation.
- *Individual interviews.* These are ideal but prohibitively expensive in terms of time and money.
- *Printed "check off" questionnaires.* These are the most cost-effective and provide a statistical benchmark against which you can measure future progress. But questionnaires have a number of drawbacks. Many people feel oversurveyed and claim they're bored by such surveys. Further, the responses you get are specific to the question you ask, if you don't ask the pertinent question, you can't get the pertinent answer. In other words, questionnaires leave little room for uncovering the unexpected or unmasking a serious concern that may be unknown to you. Unless questionnaires of this type are administered on site to everyone, or are returned by everyone in your sample, your response rate may be less than adequate. If it's a mail survey, you're at the mercy of the postal service or of employee indifference, distractions or forgetfulness.
- *The card-sort survey.* In essence, it's another way of doing the statistical survey, but the technique seems to fascinate participants and helps overcome the boredom factor. Participants are given a "deck" of cards with statements printed on them. The cards become the "answers" and responses.
- *Focus-group discussions.* These are almost as good as individual interviews. The essential factor here is an experienced and "neutral" group

leader, who is able to assure participants of confidentiality, keep the discussion on track and be firm about keeping nonstop talkers in check. A drawback to this method is a lack of statistical data: your information is subjective in nature—what the people said or what the group decided. One way to counteract such a drawback is to select the participants by a sampling method that reflects closely the employee population.

- *A combination of the statistical survey and the focus-group discussion.* This approach offers the best balance of cost-effectiveness, appeal, valid statistical data, flexibility, and in-depth probing. This technique was one that Sperry Corporation found useful and informative. Employees from throughout the organization assembled in conference rooms at their work sites in groups of 20. Because of a modified random sampling technique, a very small sample of the total employee population was sufficient for the study. Each group consisted of peers—supervisors in their own groups, hourly people in their groups, managers in theirs. The first part of the allotted hour was devoted to the card-sort survey, which provided the statistical base required for the benchmark. The remaining time was devoted to a candid discussion, which often brought out points not covered in the formal survey and provided insight into geographic and divisional differences and special concerns. It brought to the surface many rumors and so-called "facts" that the ensuing communication program could address.

General Motors, in a 1982 communication audit, first conducted a survey administered on site to a computer-selected random sampling of its employee population. Then, a few weeks later the company conducted focus-group discussions with employees at carefully selected plants.

The results of a survey or investigation should give you a report of how employees or members view the communication environment in your organization, what they want and need, how well your messages and those of top management have been received, and how well or poorly employees and members' messages and questions move up the line.

The Critique

The final research step is to examine the organizational structure and communication vehicles, formal and informal, to see how well they are meeting the organization's expectations and employees' and members' needs. Publications, bulletin boards, memos, slide and video presentations, and the like are examined for content, appearance, frequency, pertinence, credibility and readability. Meetings of various kinds are examined. The grapevine and other informal communication networks are scrutinized.

The product of all this research effort is a mountainous and mind-boggling collection of interview notes, computer printouts, group discussion notes or tapes, publication critiques and evaluations. From this, a coherent picture of the communication process in your organization should develop.

- What messages does management want to send?
- What messages does management think it has sent?
- Through what media did the messages travel?
- How fast or slowly did these messages flow through the communication pipeline, and with what degree of accuracy or distortion?
- Where are the blockages? How selective are the blockages—total? Did some messages get through?
- How did employees or members understand the messages?
- What do they want to know?
- What do they feel they need to know?
- Is what management wants to say of any interest to them?
- Is what they want to hear of any interest to management?
- If there is a gap here, how wide and deep is it?

A thorough analysis of the research should give you the data and authority to create a set of communication policies and guidelines responsive to management's expectations and employees' or members' needs. For example, in a major nationwide survey of Xerox Corporation employees (through focus-group discussions), Joseph A. Varilla, the company's director of corporate communications, developed the following statement. Because top corporate management was involved early and heavily in the survey by way of lengthy executive interviews, they endorsed these policy guidelines *in toto* and made sure that the policy statement carried their names.

1. Responsibility for the success of the Xerox communications program is vested in all Xerox managers.
2. Communications leadership in any Xerox organization is the responsibility of that organization's senior management.
3. Each manager is responsible to his or her manager and to his or her people for communication of information on the state of the business, the tasks and goals of the organization, and the progress of the work organization's programs.
4. Each manager owes it to his or her employees to pass their concerns and questions upward and to press for timely and responsive answers, if answers are not immediately available.
5. Each manager is responsible to his or her people for candid communication on the individual's performance and career aspirations, and for resolving misunderstandings of Xerox policy and its application.

	ATTITUDE SURVEYS	COMMUNICATIONS AUDITS	AWARENESS SURVEYS	READERSHIP SURVEYS
	Also known as "organizational climate" or "environment" surveys, "employee relations" or "human relations" audits or surveys; can measure feelings about a wide range of subjects, or zero in on just one topic— benefits, for example.	Focus exclusively on what an organization (or any part of an organization) is doing to communicate with a given audience; may also include a review of all media being used.	Assess employee knowledge and attitudes regarding specific issues; "economic awareness" survey measures understanding of the firm's business; "health awareness" survey (C&M, July/August 1979) determines understanding of national health insurance, health care cost containment.	Simplest survey type; unlike Communications Audit, cannot provide broad-based communications information.
SOME REASONS WHY...	- To assess employee understanding and/or acceptance of personnel policies and practices - To assess training needs - To measure morale and identify causes of employee discontent - To provide management with an objective overview of organizational characteristics - To check on supervisory effectiveness - To identify specific problems in individual demographic groups - To establish benchmarks - To measure progress against previously established benchmarks	- To find out how well communications programs are working - To diagnose current or potential communications problems or missed opportunities - To evaluate a new communications policy or practice - To assess the relationship of communications to other organizational operations on corporate and local levels - To help develop communications budgets - To develop or restructure the communications function within an organization - To provide background for developing formal communications policies and plans	- To identify areas of special employee concern - To assess current levels of knowledge on a specific issue - To pinpoint gaps in knowledge - To gauge attitudes toward a specific issue as input for a possible communications program - To evaluate the effectiveness of a current communications program	- To find out if readers are receiving publications regularly - To evaluate the impact of content on readers - To assess readers' perceptions of the quality of publications - To get reactions to or ideas about a possible new publication - To develop a list of topics that would interest readers - To provide background for developing an annual plan and budget for publications
SOME TIMES WHEN...	- Major reorganization - Merger or acquisition - New management team - Business downturn (layoffs, cost reduction programs, plant shutdowns) - External events (unfavorable publicity, lawsuit) cause concern - Upcoming union negotiations		- Issue spotlighted by current events (e.g., oil company prices) - Knowledgeable spokespersons on issue needed by management - Policy shifts (organizational or national) affect the firm	- Flagging interest in existing publications - Planned changes in publications - Development of publication budgets - Circulation of "underground" publications
SOME THINGS TO EXPLORE...	- Physical working conditions - Basic job satisfaction - Personnel policies and practices - Pay and benefits - Working relationships with others - Attitudes toward management - Communications	- Management's communications philosophy - Messages being sent - Messages being received - How messages are being received— real and preferred favorably? uniformly? - Sources of information— real and preferred - Quality and effectiveness of current media	- Economic facts of the business - Productivity - The organization's role in a national or local issue/event - Pay and benefits - Personnel policies and practices	- Content - Readability - Distribution - Graphics - Frequency - Format
SOME POSSIBLE PARTICIPANTS...	- Senior executives, divisional managers, middle managers, professional employees, salaried employees, sales and field personnel, first-line supervisors, foremen, rank-and-file employees			- Anyone who receives the publication(s); survey should be administered so that nonreaders also have input

Figure 4.2. A Guide to Employee Surveys.

6. Employees' self-esteem, as well as the quality of work life, can only be protected through continuing interpersonal and intergroup communication between them and their manager.
7. It is the responsibility of the senior manager of each Xerox operating unit to maintain an appropriate employee communications media program for the organization.
8. In their communications with their people, all managers have an obligation to be forthright and timely in discussing objectives, results, problems, difficulties and opportunities.

Each organization, of course, must develop its own policy guidelines based on its own philosophy, personality and needs.

Communication Plans

Two communication plans generally evolve from an audit: a long-range plan, tied rather closely to the organization's long-range business plan, and a short-term plan, tied to the organization's current fiscal-year plan but also incorporating and addressing the employees' or members' information needs and desires uncovered during the audit.

The long-range communication plan, of necessity, has to be general because it conforms to the organization's strategic goals. For example, an insurance company may establish as one of its long-range goals an earnings growth rate of 9% annually, compounded. Further, it may decide that half this growth will be achieved internally—through work efficiencies, more and better equipment, reassignment of key personnel and groups, and so on. The other half will be achieved through acquisition. The long-term communication plan must flow from this, and the communication organization must be ready to prepare the employees for major shifts in personnel and work assignments, new methods and procedures, cost cutting, and even layoffs. It must keep quiet about negotiations concerning acquisitions (for obvious legal and financial reasons) but have all the information ready to release if and when an acquisition is announced.

The short-range communication plan is very detailed. It flows from the specific findings of the audit and lists the subjects to be covered, the specific audience for each of these messages, the communication methods that will be used to cover these topics and audiences, the way feedback will be obtained, and the personnel and budget required to carry out these assignments.

The budget is always the last element to be developed, which is as it should be. The reasons are these:

• The organization has determined that there was a need for a communication audit.

- The audit was conducted with heavy involvement of senior management—through extensive interviews with them. Further, their views and questions were carried forward into the employee survey. In other words, they've been on board from the beginning.
- Communication guidelines and policies were hammered out to conform to organizational philosophy and policy and these were approved by top management.
- Communication plans, long- and short-term, were developed and approved by top management.

Therefore, the budget to support the operation is almost a by-product of all these steps. In fact, if management buys the new communication program, it almost automatically buys the budget. That, among all the other benefits, is one of the great dividends of the communication audit.

Communication audits help establish benchmarks and indicate directions the communicator should follow. They should be done every two years because organizations change. The communicator should reexamine audit results and proposals stemming from them quarterly to monitor operations against goals.

MYRON EMANUEL, ABC, heads Myron Emanuel Communications, Inc., in New York. He is accredited by the International Association of Business Communicators and was named a Fellow of IABC in 1975.

Example: Why Outside Consultants?

The use of outside consultants is often a touchy subject with organizational communicators. A substantial number feel that calling in a consultant is an admission of failure or weakness. Typically, they say, "We don't have the budget for it" or "Our firm doesn't believe in outside consultants."

These comments are ridiculous. Any medium-to-large firm depends on consultants, often of many different kinds. Legal departments always have outside legal counsel, often on retainer. Finance departments retain outside auditors and accounting firms. Most firms have outside actuaries. Benefits departments almost invariably use outside consultants to establish or alter benefit plans and to design and prepare employee annual benefits statements. Compensation departments use consultants for a variety of purposes. Production, marketing and engineering departments are deeply involved with consultants. And they *all* have the "budget" for it. If you have no budget for a communication consulting service, obviously you are doing a perfect job, or you are not aware of what help is available to you, or your management doesn't think communication is worth more than they are now paying.

How would you go about selecting a consulting firm? Dick Coffin, a vice president of TPF&C, makes these suggestions: Look at the field, check reputations, talk to friends and check professional organizations such as the Association of Consulting Management Engineers (ACME). Get a list of the four or five most likely candidates. Send them a request for a proposal, defining the nature and scope of the assignment and what is expected of the consultant. Ask direct questions about fees and timing and request written proposals. Then meet with the candidates to test their understanding of your problem and your organization or industry. Are they interested? Have they done their homework carefully? Ask if they are selling you canned solutions or programs. These rarely work well though the world is full of consultants trying to make your problems fit their solutions. Beware of consultants who have the solution to your problem at the first meeting.

Two tests of a good consulting firm are its client list and repeat business. Get references and follow up on them. Ask if they have ever been sued by a client. In larger firms, ask about the ratio of consultants to support staff (e.g., research people, administrative assistants, creative directors). Some run very thin. Keep in mind, however, if your project doesn't require a nationwide string of offices, or a major research library staff and a host of peripheral staff, then a small organization or a top-flight, independent consultant will be more cost-efficient.

Ask about costs. Confirm verbally the quotes in the consultant's proposal. If supplier costs are involved, check on markups. Ask that the consultants include their perception of expected results of a project in the proposal.

Mike Emanuel

◆ 5 ◆

Chartering the Communication Function

Thomas A. Ruddell, ABC

Being a communicator without a well-defined, management-blessed "charter" is like driving an automobile without a license. You can do it, but at risk of being stopped and penalized. The penalty for the "unlicensed" communicator can be a job that's (a) frustrating or (b) short-lived.

Your employer-granted "license" to practice communication in return for a paycheck must be much more than a high-sounding commandment nailed to the office wall or a power-doling paragraph in your job description. Your roots as a professional communicator should run deep into the culture and doctrine of the organization for which you work. You should have a firm understanding and be a leading advocate of the philosophy and values that guide the organization. Your communication plans and goals/objectives should tie in directly with those of the organization. You should operate under communication policies that are understood and accepted above you, below you and on all four sides.

Understanding the Mission

A poll of people attending a major conference of communication professionals showed that only 40% of the businesses, government agencies and nonprofit associations represented had well-defined statements of mission

59

or purpose. As many as 34% said their organizations had no such statements, and the rest said they weren't sure. Of those reporting the existence of some sort of mission statement, no one thought it had been communicated effectively.

Communication professionals are expected to help build commitment to the organization and its activities. How can this be done effectively without focusing on the very reasons that the organization exists? A good place to start getting a grasp on the organization's mission is in its history. You will almost certainly find that your organization grew out of some visionary's grand design. Maybe it was the ferocious-looking gentleman with celluloid collar and bearded jowls who glowers out of a gilded frame at people passing through the front door. Perhaps this visionary's grand design was far-reaching, like that of the American Telephone & Telegraph Company: "We will build a telephone system so that anybody, anywhere, can talk with anyone else in the world quickly, cheaply and satisfactorily." Or maybe the grand design was very simple: "We will build the world's greatest mousetrap."

Whether far-reaching or simple, chances are this vision continues to influence the purpose of the organization for which you work. The employee audience is especially important when communicating the organizational mission or purpose because, in the long run, such communication can have an effect on productivity, job satisfaction and loyalty to the organization. It's like the old story of the three stone cutters. When asked what they were doing, the first responded, "Swinging this damn hammer." The second said, "Cutting stone." But the third, looking proud and happy, replied, "Helping to build a magnificent cathedral."

Other audiences are important, too. Stockholders, customers, association members and others can harbor more positive feelings about the organization if they understand its purpose.

Summing up the essence of an organization in clear, concise, memorable language isn't easy. A statement explaining that an organization is dedicated to the "maximum effectualization of resource utilization pursuant to the optimization of remunerative operational parameters" will die in a bottom file drawer, unwept, unhonored and, of course, greatly unsung.

Like the visions of the stone cutter's cathedral, a good mission statement should contain a contribution to the world. Too often, mission statements focus on what can be extracted from the world rather than on what can be contributed *to* the world.

"Make money" is a clear, concise, two-word mission statement. It doesn't do much, though, to rally support among unionized factory workers, cost-conscious customers, people who live next to plant smokestacks, or tax-hungry legislators.

Consider, for example, the missions of two utility companies:

Utility A	*Utility B*
"The basic purpose of Utility A is to perpetuate the company, rendering needed, satisfactory products and services and earning optimum, long-range profits."	"The basic purpose of Utility B is to meet each customer's on-going need for economical and reliable electric service in ways that merit the trust and confidence of the public."

If you work for Utility A, you may have a little trouble becoming excited and inspired by a statement that puts survival in the forefront, sets only "satisfactory" as a standard of excellence and seeks from customers the biggest profits for the longest period of time. But if you work for Utility B, chances are you could be something of a "mission missionary." There aren't many corporate purposes better-regarded than meeting the needs of people—especially when the people are considered as individuals. And there isn't a standard of excellence in business that's much higher than meriting the trust and confidence of the public.

An organization that meets the needs of people and has their trust and confidence will survive. And it will be profitable.

Of course, the evidence points to very few organizations having good statements of mission or purpose. If you find yourself in that position, consider it an opportunity rather than a problem. One of the greatest contributions a communicator can make to an employer is to help audiences focus supportively on the purpose for which the organization exists.

Helping to develop an effective mission statement can be an exciting and challenging task. It will demand of you first-rate:

- Analytical skills to help identify correctly the fundamental purpose of the organization.
- Diplomatic skills to help consolidate inevitably varying views of the organization and what it's trying to accomplish.
- Writing skills to bring together the few right, memorable and understandable words.

If you're successful, you may come up with something like these mission statements:

Dayton-Hudson Corporation: "To serve as the consumers' purchasing agent in fulfilling their needs and expectations for merchandise and services."

The International Association of Business Communicators: "Improve the ability of communicators to help organizations achieve their goals."

The easier the statement is to remember and the more closely its values line up with those of its audience, the better it will be. Through communication, the mission should become a strong part of the organization's culture.

This makes your role as a communicator especially important. You must use your various tools of communication continually to breathe life into the purpose of the organization and its contributions to the world.

Developing or refining an organization's mission statement rarely is delegated to a communication staff, however. It's a task that is handled best by a team of senior-level people, but should include someone with communication expertise. If you are the in-house expert on communication, your role might well include:

1. Getting the process started by identifying the need.
2. Working with the team in the development or revision process, possibly serving as facilitator in constructing the language.
3. Providing background materials to outside consultants if they are retained.
4. Developing communication plans and strategies to carry the results to various audiences.
5. Integrating the end product into all communication activities.

Having a clear statement of organizational mission or purpose and making sure your audiences know about it and understand it should be an important part of your communication activity. A sense of organizational direction is critically important. As the Roman philosopher Lucius Seneca said centuries ago, "When a man does not know what harbor he is making for, no wind is the right wind."

Plugging into Philosophy

A credible statement of mission or purpose is important but it should not stand alone. It should be backed up with a clear explanation of the organization's philosophy or underlying values.

John F. Kennedy's declaration that America "will put a man on the moon by the end of the decade" was a wonderfully succinct statement of mission, even as he turned to his staff and told them to work out the details. The dedication of the scientists, engineers, technicians and astronauts who made it happen (and the taxpayers and congressmen who made it possible) was rooted in values, beliefs and traditions that went far beyond the words of an American president.

So it is—or should be—with organizations of all kinds. The people who run them, work for them, patronize them and support them should have a clear idea of what the organizations stand for. You should ask: Does this organization *have* stated values? What values are only implied? If you work for a consumer products company, what are its beliefs about the price and quality of mechandise? If your employer is a hospital, what standards are set for patient care? In an investor-owned company, what values are placed on dividend payout vs. earnings reinvestment? In any organization, what sort of philosophy applies to the professional growth of its members or employees?

That an organization, in this case a business, should have well-defined and well-practiced values and beliefs was so important to Thomas Watson, Jr., chairman of IBM, that he wrote a book called *A Business and Its Beliefs.* In it, he said, "I firmly believe that any organization, in order to achieve success, must have a sound set of beliefs on which it premises all of its policies and actions." He said that success depends on adherence to those beliefs and that in facing up to the challenges of a changing world, an organization should be willing to change everything *but* those deeply held beliefs and values.

"The basic philosophy, spirit and drive of an organization have far more to do with its relative achievements than do technological or economic resources, organizational structure, innovation and timing," Watson wrote. Philosophy, spirit, drive. They're contagious in successful organizations. The contagion spreads through communication, and professional communicators should be principal carriers.

How do you communicate an organization's beliefs? There are no rules, but here are a few suggestions:

Get them in writing. If a summary of the organization's mission and philosophy hasn't been developed, help develop one. Remember, such documents should be easy to read and fairly general. With employees as the most important audience, language and style should be understandable and attractive to everyone from the chief executive officer to the night watchman.

Get them talked about. Far more communication takes place through an organization's informal channels than through the formal ones. Encourage discussion by using formal channels to make organizational philosophy a hot topic.

Make good use of media. Publications, videotape, posters, advertising, special events. You can use practically any medium to bring about greater understanding of what the organization believes in.

Use symbols and slogans. Easy-to-remember graphics and slogans can help reinforce a values message. Du Pont makes widespread use of its slogan, "Better Things for Better Living." Mack Trucks distributes coins to quality-conscious employees, coins bearing Mack's famous bulldog trademark and reminding recipients that "YOU make the difference." Some organizations run contests with prizes for those who submit slogans that best reflect their values and beliefs.

Reinforce the legends. Use the words of the founding visionary to reinforce the organizational heritage. If a key value is superlative service to customers, publicize employees who have gone "above and beyond" to provide outstanding service. If there's a strong belief in innovation, reward the innovators for the fruits of their labors. Make heroes of those who epitomize the organization's beliefs. Create role models.

Guide newcomers. Since many orientation programs for new employees are developed and conducted by communication professionals, or at least are supported by the communication department, it shouldn't be hard for the communicator to make the mission and philosophy a strong part of a person's first-day experience. Here's an excerpt from the corporate business philosophy of Pennsylvania Power & Light Company. It's printed on a pocket-sized card given to all employees and widely distributed to other audiences:

- We will be an institution that is humane, responsible and contributive to the betterment of society, with special emphasis on our service area. We will not compromise safety, public health or environmental quality in carrying out our mission.
- We will maintain an open and full disclosure policy with customers, investors, employees and others affected by our business.
- We will support the development and application of sound governmental policies that we believe to be in the best interests of our publics.
- We will create and maintain a work environment that attracts and retains capable people, encourages self-development and enables them to take pride and satisfaction in their work.
- We will strive to earn a fair return on the capital provided by investors, maintain a sound credit standing and have the financial strength required to raise capital at reasonable rates.
- We intend to be a well-run, responsive, cost-effective company. We will measure our performance by regularly comparing it against the best that others achieve under similar conditions.

Sometimes expressions of corporate philosophy are reduced to a few memorable words that serve as guiding principles. Armstrong World Industries, for example, established a platform of consumer trust many years ago with the words "Let the Buyer Have Faith." Sherwin-Williams declares that it exists "not just to produce paints, but to contribute to more colorful living." Hallmark Cards communicates widely its guiding value that "Good Taste Is Good Business." And Anheuser-Busch raises a glass of Bud and proclaims, "Making Friends Is Our Business."

Goals and Objectives

Communication for the sake of communicating is superfluous. Communication for the achievement of organizational objectives is imperative. That's important to remember because communicators sometimes get so carried away with the arts-and-crafts nature of communication activity that they forget the very management-centered nature of the communication function.

There are "shape-of-the-table" arguments over the terms "goal" and "objective." Many people use the terms interchangeably. Some say you develop goals to achieve objectives, others say objectives are written to support goals. For our purposes, though, let's side with those who say the following:

- A goal is a clear statement of intent to solve a significant problem or achieve a significant result within a specific time frame.
- An objective is one of the action steps through which a goal is to be accomplished.

In any event, most organizations have some kind of process to establish both short- and long-range targets. It may take the form of a Management by Objectives (MBO) program or Management by Objectives and Results (MOR), or simply be a list of desired achievements. Whatever the form, you should get a copy, become familiar with it and find ways to establish direct links between organizational goals/objectives and communication goals/objectives.

If, for example, the organization's most important goal for the coming year is a 30% reduction in operating costs, your top goal shouldn't be to publish 12 issues of an expanded four-color magazine in hopes of winning a coveted Gold Quill Award. Your goal should be to support the cost-reduction effort. One of the supporting objectives could be development of a communication program to generate understanding and support. Your communication goal could be to develop and carry out that program, and your objectives might include such things as recognition for innovative cost reduction and regular progress reporting for all employees.

What better "charter" for communication than to have the top communication goal tied directly to the number one organizational goal?

Here are five more examples of how communication goals/objectives can be linked directly to organizational goals/objectives:

If the organization's goal is to...	Then the communication goals/objectives could include...
Bring a new facility on line by March of next year	Support the development effort by recognizing milestones and the people who achieve them.
Add 100 nurses and medical technicians to the hospital staff within 60 days	Help attract good people by publicizing the opportunities and presenting the hospital as a good place to work.

Close the 200-employee regional headquarters in East Snowshoe by the first quarter of next year	Mount a comprehensive internal and external communication program to generate understanding and support among employees and others in the East Snowshoe region.
Achieve 10% market penetration for a new product during the first year	Support marketing communication efforts by rallying the sales drive employees, shareowners and others with a stake in corporate success.
Reduce the year-to-year fleet accident rate by 50%	Make safe driving a dominant theme in future issues of the organizational publication and other organizational media.

The goals/objectives development process can take many forms. If the organization has a well-established process, stick to it as closely as possible. In any case, you should try to abide by a few fundamentals:

1. Make sure whatever process you intend to use has the blessing of management before you start.
2. Make sure your goals address significant organizational problems, concerns or issues, avoiding the temptation to puff up your paperwork with routine activities—and risking your credibility in the process.
3. Include specific target dates for your goals and objectives.
4. Put plenty of "reach" and "stretch" into them. Don't denigrate your capabilities by assigning yourself cream puffs when the organization is gnawing on raw beef.
5. Make your goals and objectives measurable. They're of little value if you can't figure out whether or to what extent they've been achieved.
6. Review progress regularly with those who are involved or who have an interest.
7. Maintain flexibility. Remember that it may be necessary to make mid-course corrections if you are to attain maximum success.
8. Be certain that specific responsibility for the accomplishment of each activity has been assigned and is understood.

Sample Goals/Objectives Layout

Corporate Goal

By the end of this year, reduce the weekly average reject rate in the widget production process to no more than 7 per 1,000.

Included Among Objectives to Carry Out the Corporate Goal

Within the next 30 days, develop and implement a communication program to support the reject reduction effort.

Communication Goal

Support the corporate goal to reduce the widget reject rate by developing in the next 30 days and carrying out through the remainder of the year a comprehensive communication program.

Included Among Objectives to Carry Out the Communication Goal

- Draft the communication plan and gain management approval to proceed within the 30-day time limit.
- Run a three-part series on reorganization of the Quality Assurance program in the March, April and May issues of the *Wily Widgeteer*.
- By the end of March, set up a special bulletin board program to give employees rapid feedback on changes in the reject rate.
- Produce in time for the production control supervisors' annual conference a sound/slide show explaining the importance of the reject reduction program.
- By May 15, design, produce and deliver to each plant superintendent 2,000 "I Reject Rejections" T-shirts.

Communication professionals have a way to go in formalizing goals and objectives. A survey by the International Association of Business Communicators showed that only 58% of communicators polled said they have any kind of written goals or objectives. Of those who do, 93% said they dovetail with those of the organization. More than 80% said they were applied regularly to communication programming and given periodic performance measurements.

Department Missions and Job Descriptions

Now that you're well tied into the organization's mission, philosophy and goals/objectives, don't overlook two other important aspects of your "charter" to communicate: the specific mission, mandate or charge given to the organization's communication function, and a job description spelling out your duties and responsibilities.

Having an agreed-upon departmental mission (or "sub-unit charter") is more important to the communication function than to some other staff groups because communicators tend to work across all organizational lines and everyone in the organization is engaged in communicating.

Whether your mandate from senior management comes in the form of a department mission statement, is contained in your job description, or in a letter from the boss isn't important. What *is* important is that agreed-upon documentation exists, authorizing you to engage in a well-defined range of communication activities—or giving you a broad mandate.

Here's a mission statement that spells out three important activities for the corporate communication department of a large company:

> Help the company earn the trust and confidence of its publics by conducting effective employee communication programs, by providing top-quality professional services to client departments and by offering sound communication counsel to management.

Here's the statement of purpose accompanying the job description of a public affairs director:

> To ensure society's continuation of the Company's franchise to operate constructively and profitably by:
> 1. Defining from time to time the company's obligations to society.
> 2. Coordinating corporate resources, both human and physical, to meet those obligations.
> 3. Influencing insofar as possible society's expectations and requirements of the company.

This statement covers overall responsibility for the communication officer of a nonprofit agency in Canada:

> ...will be directly responsible to the executive director for the development of agency-relations programs, information sharing and public relations of the Centre.

Your job description should cover at least these three important areas:

1. Your accountabilities, including duties, responsibilities and prerogatives.
2. The operating framework of your job—title, position to which it reports, and positions for which it has direct and indirect responsibilities.
3. Results expected from your work, along with some means of measurement.

As an example of results being expected, a northeastern United States telephone company prefaces the body of its job descriptions with "Performance is good when. . . ." There are 14 end results expected of the division public affairs manager, including these:

> Performance is good when. . .
> • Policies and programs designed to promote and maintain favorable relations toward the company on the part of its various publics are formulated and executed

- Press relations, including media contacts and the preparation and distribution of all general and local news releases is properly administered and supervised
- Contributions or donations to public welfare organizations are administered in accordance with division and corporate policy.

Item 14, by the way, is simply that "performance is good when..." the preceding 13 items "are accomplished within budgetary limitations."

Some words of caution about all of this: Whatever instruments you have as your operating mandate, make sure they have support throughout the organization. Your career will not be enhanced one bit if, as has happened, you type up your own mission statement, job description or whatever and stick it in a file, to be drawn like a sword at the start of the next turf battle—almost as foolhardy is getting your mandate approved by the chief executive officer and assuming it will be accepted automatically by everyone else in senior management.

A poll of professional communicators at an international conference showed that 58% worked under some sort of formal management mandate or "charter." About half said their mandate was reviewed at least annually. A greater portion, 68%, said they have written job descriptions, but a third of those respondents said they weren't satisfied with them.

Communication Policies

The most challenging part of your "charter" to communicate may well be developing and maintaining effective policies covering your organization's communication activities.

Plugging into the organization's mission, philosophy and goals/objectives gets you going in the right direction. Getting your mandate from management via a departmental mission, job description or whatever helps you know how far you can go in that direction. Communication policies seek to get everyone in the organization going in the same direction when it comes to relating to internal and external audiences.

Communication policies should be helpful, "living" documents. They should provide quick guidance to any employee: the distant office manager suddenly faced with media relations tasks, the superintendent who wants to start an employee newsletter, the newly hired communicator who wants a good rundown on how things generally are handled, or the old-timer who simply can't remember which department to contact on a legislative matter.

To be effective, communication policies should be brief, well-organized and general. They should be far removed from the thick policy manual. Robert Townsend gave us ample warning about policy manuals in his hard-hitting book, *Up the Organization:* "Don't bother. If they're general, they're useless. If they're specific, they're how-to manuals—expensive to prepare and revise." He went on to say that only "goldbricks and martinets" read policy manuals, the former to avoid work and the latter to frustrate and punish the creative and adventuresome. "If you have to have a policy manual, publish the Ten Commandments," Townsend concluded.

He raises some notes of caution, but very few chief executive officers today would agree that the best policy is no policy, whether to cover communication or anything else.

A Conference Board paper on "Managing Corporate External Relations" notes that "time and time again corporate executives indicated that the critical factor in achieving effective external relations is the strict observance of corporate policy and the goals the corporation has set for itself in relation to its publics." Policies to guide internal communication are every bit as important.

Of course, policies can never take the place of strong values systems in organizations. Several best-selling books on excellence in management make a strong case for informal approaches to policy, calling for the long-term development of strong values systems to guide "the way we do things around here."

It's a rare organization, though, that can operate a fully effective communication process while relying solely on corporate culture to produce consistency of message and unity of effort. Simple, well-written policies covering important aspects of communication can be of considerable value, and they can save a lot of grief in day-to-day operations.

Developing such policies isn't easy, nor is gaining organization-wide acceptance. After all, communication involves everyone in an organization. It crosses every departmental line—up, down and across, effectively or ineffectively. It flows in and out of the organization to various publics, for better or for worse. Every employee communicates. Every manager has some communication responsibility. Several functional areas may have accountability for some communication end results, and there may be fuzzy lines of responsibility drawn between them.

So it's not too surprising that while communication professionals tend to agree that policies are needed, only about a third of those surveyed say they work in organizations that have them. Two-thirds of that third concede that the policies are not well communicated or understood.

Types of Communication Policies

There are two broad categories of communication policies:

1. General statements that may be linked to the organization's overall philosophy, principles or values.

2. Operating policies that may serve as extensions of the communication department's charter or as senior management's means of delineating communication responsibility.

General statements can take many forms. Union Carbide, for example, embraces this approach within its formal corporate policy:

> It is the Public Relations Policy of the Corporation to make every effort to attain public recognition of the character and capability of Union Carbide Corporation, and its contributions to the quality of life, and thereby to gain public support for its activities.

The policy gives comprehensive definitions of the company's publics— customers and suppliers, stockholders and the financial community, employees, plant communities, government officials and legislative bodies, and the general public.

General Electric sets this tone for its employee communication efforts:

> Over the years, employees have learned that they can rely on the accuracy of management statements, and this credibility is a valuable asset jealously guarded by all who bear responsibility for communication with employees.

General Electric states six supporting principles: maintaining accuracy, avoiding exaggeration, separating facts from opinion, correcting misstatements quickly, avoiding inappropriate use of company informational materials, and clarifying the company interest in communicating on public issues.

TRW takes a directional approach in its internal communication policy, spelling out principles for upward, downward and lateral communications for plants, divisions and subsidiaries; for group and executive vice presidents, and for the corporate staff and CEO.

Linkage between communication policy and corporate principles is right up front at CIBA-GEIGY:

> Our information policy is based on the Corporate Principles and the Principles of Leadership and Teamwork. It aims actively and continuously to build up and foster reciprocal understanding and trust between the company and its employees, its investors and the general public.

CIBA-GEIGY's policy consists of ten concise, well-written principles that fit on two sides of a single sheet of paper—with plenty of white space. They exemplify the kind of positive communication climate the company seeks to create.

Operating Policies

Specific operating policies can be a lot harder to lock down than general statements rooted in the organizational values system. Such policy statements can take all shapes and sizes and consist of varying amounts of detail. There's no such thing as a "model" communication policy that can fit all organizations, but here are some general characteristics of a good one:

- It's a collection of individual policy statements rather than a heavy, straight-through text.
- Each statement fits on a single sheet of paper, preferably loose-leaf for simple updating.
- The statements are well organized by subject, easy to refer to and easy to read.
- Each policy contains these five elements:
  1. A guiding principle on which the policy is based.
  2. A clear statement of the policy itself (preferably in one or two sentences).
  3. A delineation of who (by job title) is responsible for what's covered by the policy.
  4. Some general guidelines to help people abide by the policy.
  5. Sources of additional information.

The spirit of all such policies should be one of helpfulness and flexibility. If you've got responsibility for developing operating policies, you'll gain greater acceptance with broad, flexible statements and guidelines that recognize the wide-ranging nature of organizational communication than with heavy-handed "thou shalts" and "thou shalt nots."

Let's say you're about to tackle operating policy development for the mythical Z Corporation. Here are some examples of what you might include:

	DISCLOSURE
Principle:	Actions may be above reproach, but if people think information is being withheld, they won't be above suspicion.
POLICY:	*We will take the initiative in providing information of significant aspects of the Z Corporation's business that may reasonably be considered of public interest.*
Responsibilities:	Ultimate authority on disclosure matters rests with the chief executive officer. The vice president-corporate communication will work directly with senior managers in carrying out this policy and will audit the company's "track record."

Guidelines: [Cover such areas as these:
1. Who should bear the burden of proof in deciding not to disclose something of interest to the public.
2. Potential problems from withholding information simply to avoid embarrassment to the company.
3. Recognition of a possible conflict between full disclosure and individual rights to privacy.
4. Relationships to government regulations covering disclosure of certain financial and other types of information.
5. Avoiding "no comment" responses, especially on matters already on the public record or about to be.]

References: [Let people know where to look for related policy statements. Cite appropriate government regulations and where to find them. Give one or two phone numbers for quick contact with company disclosure experts.]

BULLETIN BOARDS

Principle: Of all internal communication media, nothing so effectively can provide for rapid, frequent and accurate information as bulletin boards.

POLICY: *Bulletin boards of approved design will be provided in an easily accessible place in each work location throughout the Z Corporation.*

Responsibilities: The manager-internal communication has overall responsibility for the Z Corporation's bulletin board program. The senior manager in each area with a bulletin board is responsible for having the board maintained, assuring prompt and proper posting of corporate materials and developing and posting appropriate local materials.

Guidelines: [Include helpful hints for managers and the people to whom they delegate responsibility to take care of the boards. Give examples of what sorts of things may be appropriate for local postings and what may not.]

References: [Provide sources of further guidance and the telephone number of someone to call for supporting services.]

CORPORATE IDENTITY

Principle: A company's image and the team spirit of its people are enhanced by the unity and strength of its corporate identity efforts.

POLICY: *The symbols through which our internal and external publics identify Z Corporation will be applied in a consistent manner in keeping with high standards of design and production.*

Guidelines: [Include some examples of how the logo, colors, slogans, etc., should be used in publications, on signs and vehicles, on souvenir items, etc.]

References: [Cite the company's trademark manual or other policy statements and, again, provide sources of guidance and support.]

Other policies could include communication planning, overall availability of support services for various types of communication, language and style in written materials, the organizational approval process, handling communication on matters in litigation, communicating during negotiations with bargaining units, internal mail classifications, news media relations, news release preparation and delivery, attribution of released information, proper backgrounding of materials for release, correction of erroneous information, and communication on legislative matters.

Who Should Develop Policy

For most organizations, communication policy will be most effective when it originates at the top. This is especially true for principle-based, broad statements on communication. At General Motors, for example, communication tenets were developed by a committee of the Board of Directors. In many other organizations, such philosophical material emanates from the chief executive officer or the senior management committee.

The top-ranking communication manager quite often has the task of drafting such materials, however, and it isn't unusual for a vice president-corporate communication to play a leading role in developing the organizational mission statement and general operating philosophy as well. Involvement in producing operating policy on communication, however, could fall to just about anyone on a communication staff.

Development Steps

Specifically *who* develops policy is not as important as *how* policy is developed. Since every communication professional probably will become involved in policy development at one time or another during a career, you should know that seven steps are essential to the process:

1. *Analysis.* Thoroughly investigate the need for the policy and set some realistic objectives for policy development.
2. *Formulation.* Select the topics to be covered based on the needs. Gather suggestions from people who will be affected by the policy. Draft the documents.
3. *Approval.* Get the drafts approved by the appropriate people in the management structure.
4. *Communication.* Get the new policy known throughout the organization. As necessary, provide some training in its use.
5. *Interpretation.* Be prepared to handle the inevitable questions and calls for exceptions.
6. *Acceptance.* Just because your policy has been approved and communicated doesn't mean it will be accepted. Take whatever additional steps are necessary to build acceptance, including a trip back to the drawing board.
7. *Control.* Determine how effective the policy is under conditions of use. Monitor compliance. Identify problem areas. Keep revising. Remember that operating policies should be "living" documents designed to help, not dead documents designed to hinder.

Summary

When you've finished the policy development process and your concise, clear-language masterpiece is in use, there are several end results you should have accomplished. You should have produced something in which principles of organizational behavior are spelled out, clarified and supported. You should have provided significant help to people who have a stake in the communications of the organization, giving them sound guidance with plenty of flexibility to use their good judgment. Most of all, like everything else covered in this chapter, you should have contributed something through which the process of communication in the organization is improved and the content of communication materials and efforts is enhanced.

THOMAS A. RUDDELL, ABC, is vice president of corporate communications for Tampa Electric, Tampa, Florida. He was chairman of the International Association of Business Communicators in 1982–1983, and is accredited by the association.

◆ 6 ◆

Organizing and Budgeting Techniques

Jim Haynes, APR

Everything an organization does or does not do communicates something about it. Since organizations are made up of people, everything any person within the organization does or doesn't do communicates something about the organization as well.

An organization's reputation, or "identification," is based on its actions, operations, public policies and statements, products, services and financial results. Equally important is the way the organization and its representatives are *perceived*—the way the buildings look, the telephones are answered and the organization's print materials look, as well as the logo and the letterhead. *Everything* communicates something about it. Because everything and everyone related to an organization are parts of the communication effort, communication is a team effort. Successful, effective communication is achieved only by planned, coordinated, professionally executed efforts.

Planning for Success

To organize all the elements essential to successful communication, the professional communicator should carefully assess the organization's needs; analyze goals and audiences; carefully apply specific, targeted media and messages, and then present the entire program in a written communication plan. Only when communication assists the organization in achieving specific objectives is the communication function recognized by top management as a successful, essential part of the organization. In preparing the communication plan, it is appropriate and essential for the communicator to begin with a clear understanding of top management's goals for the entire organization. Fig. 6.1 illustrates how organizational objectives related to numerous management considerations determine communication objectives which "drive" strategies, audience definitions, media selection and messages.

Once you understand organizational objectives and begin developing communication objectives that will help the organization's management accomplish goals, it is a good idea to meet with vice presidents, middle-management personnel and department heads. This step is important because a communication program must have widespread support to be workable. By incorporating suggestions from throughout the organization, and by serving as communication consultant to those people and helping them with specific problems, you will be paving the road to the success of your communication program.

As you prepare communication objectives, remember that progress toward a goal must be measurable; otherwise, objectives are worthless. Having immeasurable objectives puts you in the same situation as runners in a race without a finish line. All too often, communication "objectives" are wishes rather than goals, since there is no provision for determining when the "objective" is accomplished (see Chapter 4).

Consider the possibility of hiring an outside consultant to work with you as you meet with top management and write the communication plan. Even if your experience qualifies you to do all the work yourself, having an outside "expert" will often lend credence to your recommendations. Locate a competent consultant with background in the area of your interest. You'll probably find that his or her specialization and objectivity will make significant, innovative contributions to your program or project.

Writing Message Statements

In addition to establishing objectives for what you want to accomplish, it is worthwhile to write a precise statement of what you want to *say*. Ask yourself, "What would I communicate to everyone if I had only one sentence to use for the communication?" The answer to that question can become your basic message statement—a statement that contains the essence of your total communication message. The basic message statement should be used in the annual report, in brochures, as a final paragraph in each news release, and in other communication.

Figure 6.1. Communication by Objective

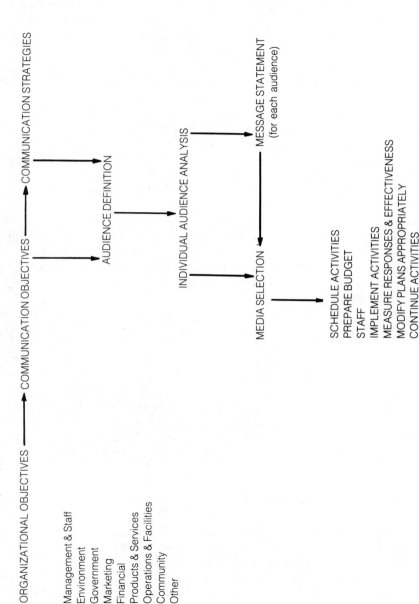

After you have a workable basic message statement, work on "customized" message statements for each audience and for each activity directed to them. If you analyze your employee publications, you should be able to summarize the thrust of your communication efforts in a series of phrases like these:

- Our organization rewards loyal employees.
- Our benefits programs are outstanding.
- This is an interesting and challenging place to work.
- We encourage employees to continue their education and develop leadership/management potentials.
- Our management team is composed of personable individuals dedicated to leadership within our industry.
- Research and development keep us ahead of our competition.

By writing a series of such statements (which *must* be honest), you establish criteria for evaluating ideas for future articles and photographs. If a potential article or photo doesn't help communicate one of the statements, it's probably not worth using. By restricting the number and complexity of the messages you convey, you can assure that the most important messages are effectively communicated.

After you understand your organization's objectives and have established communication objectives, defined audiences and established message statements, you can begin to determine which media will be most effective in reaching each target audience (see Chapter 8). Unfortunately, many communicators select media without understanding objectives and audiences. That process is as risky as having a physician prescribe medication without diagnosing the illness. The result will be effective only by chance. Every medium of communication should be analyzed and evaluated in terms of the organization's objectives and the medium's capabilities relative to audiences, message statements and, of course, staff and budget.

Preparing the Communication Plan

The written plan is a "road map" that is essential to measuring progress toward objectives for a specific project or an ongoing program. If the plan is written after consultation with top management, their expectations of communication performance will be more realistic. Having the written plan approved by management allows you to devote staff time and budget to important activities, protecting you from unrealistic requests from division and department heads who often want "extras" from your budget.

Every communication plan is structured differently, reflecting the needs of the organization and its people, but the following topics should be considered for inclusion in the plan:

- *Background.* This section provides the communicator with an opportunity to "play back" in writing a discussion of his or her understanding of how the organization reached its present situation. Generally it is worthwhile to include a brief description of the organization and its management. By writing such a discussion, the communicator cements his or her own understanding and offers it to the organization for correction or confirmation.
- *The present situation.* Where is the organization now in terms of its overall situation and its communication program? The first part of this section might discuss what makes the organization unique, its position in its field and in its community, and so on. Include both negative and positive factors, utilizing information from discussions with top management and department heads.
- *Discussion of the communication process.* This section may be included when the communicator determines that the people within the organization do not have professional communication training and do not understand the communication process and the function of public relations. Discuss the importance of communication and outline the process, perhaps utilizing a "model" of communication.
- *Why a communication plan?* In some organizations, one or two people are interested in establishing an organized communication function, while others are cool or even hostile to the idea. This section of the plan should explain why there should be an organized communication function and the importance of the communication plan in accomplishing that goal.
- *Message reinforcement.* This is an optional section for those organizations in which the people do not understand the need for consistency in the communication process. It gives you the opportunity to make a pitch for a unified "identity" program within the organization and to emphasize the importance of repeating, with variations, one basic message statement over and over again.
- *An introduction to the plan.* This section gives the professional communicator the opportunity to discuss the philosophy represented in the plan—reasons for the thinking contained in the plan.
- *Objectives.* Relate the organizational objectives and discuss how the communication program will contribute to them. List the main objectives of the communication program. List and discuss intermediate goals that will assist in accomplishing the main objective.

An objective is the *end result to be achieved* and ordinarily relates to a target audience. Statements of objectives should begin with active verbs, such as "achieve," "increase" or "reach."

- *Rationale.* Explain *why* the end result is needed. Well-written statements usually begin with the preposition "to," followed by action verbs: "to improve," "to provide."
- *Strategy.* Discuss *how* you recommend the plan be implemented. You may, for example, develop a strategy to position your management as experts in specific fields, to support the organizational objective of building confidence in your management among employees and specific other audiences. To differentiate strategies from objectives and rationales, begin statements of strategy with a preposition, such as "by" or "through," followed by a gerund (ending in "-ing") or a noun: "by creating," "by providing," "through the direction of." You may need more than one strategy to deal with a comprehensive program. In some cases, the development of strategies helps identify key audiences; in other cases, a particular audience is a "given" and strategies are developed to communicate with, or involve, that audience.
- *Basic message statement.* Present the central message to which all the activities in the plan will contribute. In writing this message, ask yourself, "If I had only one sentence to reach all my audiences in this program, what would that sentence be?"
- *Audiences.* Analyze your audiences or constituencies carefully. Use demographic information and research to pinpoint specific audiences. "Employees" and "shareholders" are far too broad as categories.
- *Audience messages.* Write a one- or two-sentence message for each audience—a brief summary of exactly what you want to communicate to each group. Obviously, these statements must complement the basic message statement and reflect each audience's needs and predispositions.
- *Activities, responsibilities and budget.* List the activities designed to accomplish each objective, the person or persons responsible, the timing (completion date), and the estimated cost of each activity. Sometimes it is not possible to include all this information; include as much as possible.
- *Research and evaluation.* Describe fact-finding and formal research that will be conducted and how it will be used. If you do not plan to conduct formal research, change the heading to "Measuring Effectiveness" and include information on the techniques you will use to determine how well you accomplish your objectives.

Fig. 6.2 provides a framework for developing objectives, strategies, audiences, messages, activities and channels of communication (media). It should be pointed out that the sequence of planning varies; sometimes an objective dictates audiences, and strategies then are developed to reach those audiences. In other cases, an activity like an annual open house is a "given," and objectives, strategies and other elements must flow from that activity. Fig. 6.2 should be used as a flexible planning tool. All seven

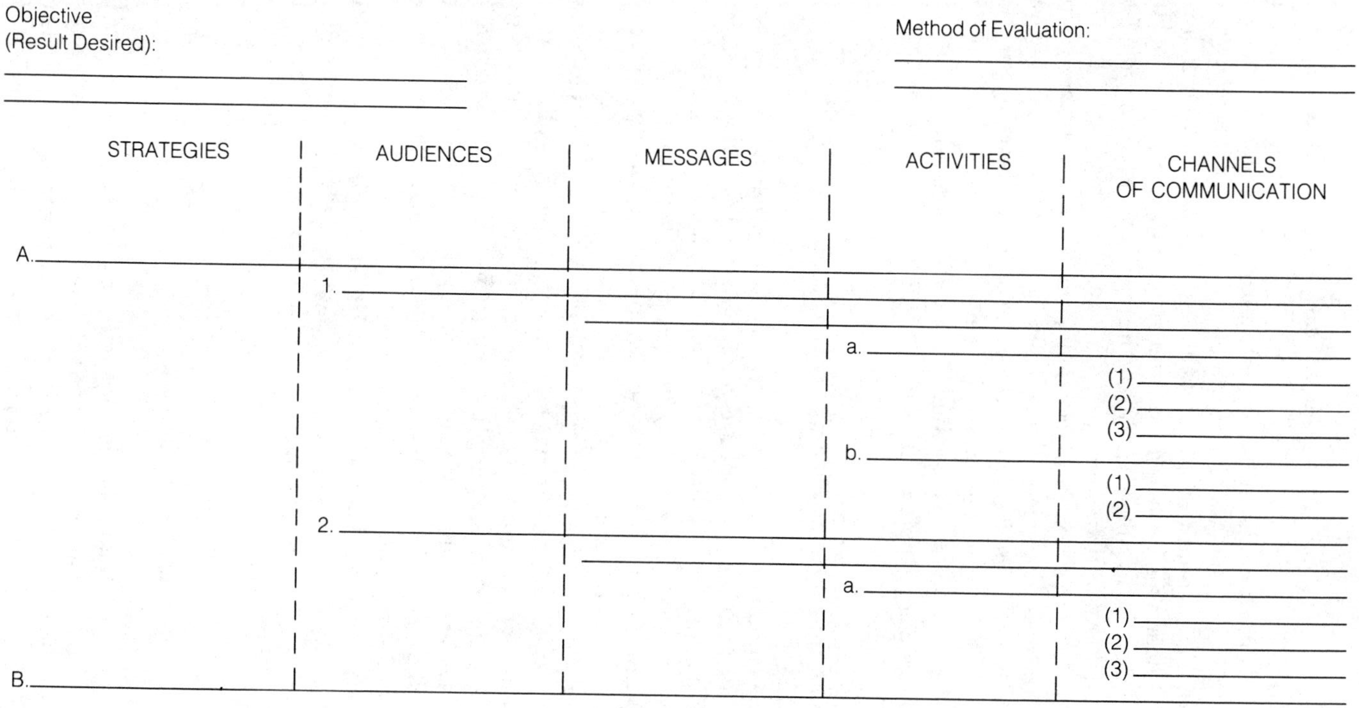
Objective
(Result Desired):
Method of Evaluation:
STRATEGIES
AUDIENCES
MESSAGES
ACTIVITIES
CHANNELS
OF COMMUNICATION
A.
1.
a.
(1)
(2)
(3)
b.
(1)
(2)
2.
a.
(1)
(2)
(3)
B.

Copyright 1983 by Jim Haynes, APR

Figure 6.2. Communications Planning Worksheet

elements presented should be considered early in the public relations planning process.

Notice that in Fig. 6.2, "Method of Evaluation" is shown opposite "Objective." This emphasizes that each objective should be related to evaluation. That is, an objective should include specific information on how its accomplishment will be measured, and the timeframe involved. For example, "To increase membership by 6% during the next four months" is much more measurable than simply, "To increase membership."

Measuring effectiveness involves comparing data on membership, attendance, awareness, knowledge, sales, readership, profits or other factors *before and after* action and communication take place. Working out the method of evaluation during planning is essential to worthwhile measurement, and studying alternative methods of measurement can help in the evolution of strategies (approaches) which are more effective.

The Communication Plan as Communication Tool

In preparing a communication plan, remember that the executives to whom you present the plan for approval are your audience. Look closely at their backgrounds and interests before you complete the plan. A large percentage of management executives, especially in business, come from the ranks of engineering, law and business administration and probably have never examined how the process of communication works.

As you prepare your plan, be sure to comment on your efforts to obtain management input and how the plan supports management's objectives for the organization. Be sure the plan looks like the reports and documents that executives are accustomed to seeing. Engineers, for example, have particular formats for project scheduling. If your company president is an engineer, he will relate well to your schedules if they are in this familiar format. Go to an engineer to find out what is most appropriate.

If you are presenting a budget, be sure your format follows the standard budget style used by vice presidents and division heads. Ask your accounting department about the format of typical departmental or divisional budgets, and follow it.

Presenting the Communication Plan

Once your communication plan is complete, you'll need to present it for approval to your organization's chief executive officer, the management committee, the board of directors, or some other appropriate group. Have copies for each person at the meeting, but avoid handing out any copies until your presentation and request for approval are completed, or you risk losing control of the conference as people leaf through the printed plan, lose interest in what you are saying, and ask questions on topics you intended to cover in a sequence. Keep the copies in a folder until you are ready to distribute them.

If you need illustrations, use flip-charts or photostatic enlargements of typed information for small groups; for ten or more participants, overhead transparencies or slides should be used.

In programs involving numerous activities, you may find useful a format similar to the one in Fig. 6.3. In this presentation, projects are numbered to simplify cost control. Activities that were described in detail in the main plan are reduced to captions, and a "macro" schedule is presented. In this type of program, there is a tendency to overstate production capabilities and schedule too many activities for completion at one time. This type of presentation helps keep expectations reasonable and sets up a step-by-step sequence for design, writing, typesetting, photography and final production. This type of schedule should be used only in presentations; more detailed scheduling is necessary for production and cost control.

Communication Budgeting by Objective

The simple secret to success in originating and managing a communication budget (and any other budget, for that matter) is to decide what's worth doing and what's *not* worth doing. Once you have decided what's worth doing, list these activities in order of descending importance. After obtaining cost estimates for each, you have a budget for one project.

What about a budget for your communication department? Let's take a look at how to go about it, using a "zero base" technique that will allow you to budget according to the relative importance of your communication objectives. Your communication objectives were designed to support organizational objectives, so this technique will assist you in securing management approval for communication activities.

After you have studied your organization's objectives and determined how communication can assist in their accomplishment, do the following (see Fig. 6.4):

- List all your audiences in descending order of importance.
- For *each* audience, list the communication media and activities you plan to use during the next 12 months to reach that audience. Again, put in order of descending importance.
- Indicate what it costs to use each medium one time.
- List the number of times during the next 12 months you plan to use the medium (e.g., how many newsletter issues will you print?).

JOB NUMBER	ACTIVITIES	SCHEDULE
		• FEB • MAR • APR • MAY • JUN •
CF 1	Initial conferences & planning	▬▬
	Prepare budget & contract	▬▬
CF 2	Study recommendations from 20 ESCs	▬▬
CF 3	Study other states' programs	▬▬
CF 4	Become familiar with Texas Ed. Agency	▬
CF 5	Visit ESCs in Regions X and XIII	▬
CF 6	Develop graphic design concept	▬▬▬
CF 7	Accommodate insertion of local phone #s	▬▬▬▬▬▬▬▬▬▬▬▬▬▬▬▬▬
CF 8	Capitol News Conference	▬▬▬▬
	Radio news release	▬
	TV news film	▬▬
CF 9	Materials for news conference	▬▬▬▬
CF 10	On-site consultation & assistance	▬▬▬▬▬▬▬▬▬
CF 11	Television public service tapes	▬▬▬▬▬
	Television public service slides	▬▬▬▬▬
CF 12	Radio public service tapes	▬▬▬▬▬
	Radio public service scripts	▬▬▬▬▬
CF 13	Sponsored newspaper ads	▬▬▬▬▬
CF 14	16mm film	▬▬▬▬▬▬▬
CF 15	Posters for Independent School Dists. .	▬▬▬▬▬▬▬
CF 16	Bumper sticker artwork	▬▬▬▬
CF 17	Door-to-door handout art	▬▬▬▬
CF 18	Statement stuffer art	▬▬▬▬
CF 19	Austin workshop for ESC personnel	▬▬▬▬▬
	Public information handbook	▬▬▬▬▬
	Artwork for handbook	▬▬▬▬
	Implementation checklist	▬▬▬
	Letter to law enforcement personnel	▬▬
	Model materials for mass media	▬▬
	Visual aids for workshop	▬
	Model "take home" materials	▬▬
	Model announcement for ISDs	▬▬▬
CF 20	State-wide publicity follow-up news releases (2)	▬▬ ▬▬
CF 21	Reports, conferences, presentations and travel	▬▬▬▬▬▬▬▬▬▬▬▬▬▬▬▬▬
CF 22	Complete manual for future use	▬▬▬▬
CF 23	Brochure for direct mail use and for use with film	▬▬▬▬▬▬
	Planning for Phase II	▬▬▬▬▬▬▬▬▬
	Proposal for Phase II	▬▬▬▬▬▬

Figure 6.3. Activity Schedule Format

86

Audience: I. _____

A. Media Activities: B. One-time cost: C. Times per year: D. Annual Cost:

1. _____ 1. _____ 1. _____ 1. $_____
2. _____ 2. _____ 2. _____ 2. $_____
3. _____ 3. _____ 3. _____ 3. $_____
4. _____ 4. _____ 4. _____ 4. $_____
5. _____ 5. _____ 5. _____ 5. $_____
6. _____ 6. _____ 6. _____ 6. $_____

Audience I Total Cost . . . . $_____

Audience: II. _____

A. Media Activities: B. One-time cost: C. Times per year: D. Annual Cost:

1. _____ 1. _____ 1. _____ 1. $_____
2. _____ 2. _____ 2. _____ 2. $_____
3. _____ 3. _____ 3. _____ 3. $_____
4. _____ 4. _____ 4. _____ 4. $_____
5. _____ 5. _____ 5. _____ 5. $_____
6. _____ 6. _____ 6. _____ 6. $_____

Audience II Total Cost . . . . $_____

(Continue with Audience III, etc.)
Add overhead expenses after combining totals for all audiences.

Figure 6.4. Budgeting

87

- Multiply the number of times by the one-time cost, to reach a total cost for the year for each medium.
- Do the same thing for each communication medium, audience by audience.
- Add up the total cost for the year for *each* audience, dropping out the costs for media that repeat from one audience to the next. (A newsletter might be distributed to several different audiences; include its basic cost only once, the first time it appears. Add printing and postage costs for each additional audience for which it is used.)
- Add *all* the totals for all the audiences. Add to your total the cost of overhead expenses that cannot logically be appropriated to the cost of communication with individual audiences. Overhead items will vary from organization to organization but will include such expenses as salaries, staff benefits, rent, utilities, equipment and supplies. The total is your *desired* communication budget for the year.

If the total is too big, you have two choices: eliminate audiences, starting at the bottom of the list with the least important audience, or eliminate media, starting at the bottom of the list for each audience. Be sure to make a comparison with present expenditures. Organizations that have never prepared an overall communication budget are often surprised to learn how much money they have been spending on ineffective materials and activities!

Once you have determined how your budget will be allocated, on the basis of audience and media priorities, reassemble it for accounting purposes. Most organizations have standard budget classifications that must be used for budgets of all departments so that accounting can be computerized. If such is the case in your organization, you will be provided a list of such categories and will have to live with them as best you can.

Project Budgeting

To produce reliable budgets for major projects, break the project into categories and establish separate cost estimates for each category. For a printed piece like an annual report or an employee publication, the categories might include:

- Concept development and design
- Layout (thumbnail sketches, rough comprehensive, or tight "comp")
- Writing and editing, including travel, research and interviews
- Typesetting and photostats
- Photography and illustrations, including travel, models, prints and retouching

- Mechanical art
- Printing, including color separations, negatives and proofs
- Distribution (labels, envelopes, postage)

Refuse to "guess" at estimates in advance of agreement on design. When someone asks how much a brochure will cost before it is designed, respond that an accurate figure can be determined only by submitting the completed design to typesetters, photographers and printers for written estimates. If *they* want to "guesstimate," let them, but avoid the temptation to do so yourself; it can do nothing but produce misunderstandings.

Try to complete the design a week or more ahead of the presentation for management approval. Submit the design sketches or comp to qualified printers, photographers and typesetters and obtain written estimates. If you're using in-house services, obtain written estimates of the number of hours and related interdepartmental charges you can expect. If you're using outside people for design, mechanical art and photography, get written estimates for each. Add to the totals an amount for supplies, travel and retouching. Then add a 10% to 15% contingency for expenses you cannot anticipate: additional photography, overtime, typesetting, and the like. Prepare a written cost estimate (a better title than "budget" since "cost estimate" implies it is subject to refinement) for each category.

If any decisions that affect total costs, are made in the presentation conference (or at a later date), indicate that the changes will cost additional money. Document decisions made in the meeting with a memo, sending copies to those present and any others who may be involved, and request revised cost estimates once the changes have been incorporated into the design. Design changes (e.g., addition of photos, changes in paper quality), delays in meeting deadlines and increases in quantities are the principal reasons that projects exceed cost estimates. Eager-to-please communicators too often simply say changes can be accommodated, failing to note that any change will affect total costs and time of delivery.

Even without computer support, project costs can be monitored easily. If you establish functional categories for your project budget (design, writing, editing, etc.), you can use these categories to monitor or report the project's budget status. To do this, use a four-column accounting ledger and list functional categories as captions, leaving several inches of space between the captions. Beside each, post in the first column the functional cost estimate. At the end of each month, post total costs for each function in the second column and keep a "cost to date" total in the third column. In the fourth column, post a current budget balance. With this system, you will be able to prepare reports to management at the beginning of each month. It increases confidence levels and prevents end-of-project "surprises."

Of course, any time a change is made, you will need to document in writing what was changed, who made the decision, and what effect the

Expenditures:	Jan	Feb	Mar	Apr	May	Jun	6 Mo. Totals	Jul	Aug	Sep	Oct	Nov	Dec	12 Mo. Totals
Staff:														
Salaries														
Benefits														
Expenses														
Part-time help														
Office:														
Space Cost or Rent														
Utilities														
Equipment:														
Maintenance & Repair														
Purchases														
Rental														
Communications:														
Telephone														
TWX, Etc.														
Messenger service														
Postage														
Production:														
Design services														
Typesetting														
Photography														
Printing														
A/V														
Paid Media														
(Other)														
TOTALS														

Figure 6.5. Typical Administrative Budget Format. This is an "administrative" budget format. While codes of accounts are normally used in organizational budgets, this format reflects the general characteristics of budget and expenditure reports found in many organizations.

change has on cost estimates and on the project schedule. If the change is minor, you can post the costs related to the change to the category established for "contingencies." If it is a major change, you may need to revise your total budget. (See Fig. 6.5.)

Monitoring Budgets

Monitoring budgets, especially in a large organization, can be more difficult and time-consuming than preparing the original budget. Usually, the organization's accounting department will provide a computer printout showing actual expenditures compared to budgeted amounts in each category, by account, for the previous month and for the year to date. Some will also indicate the amount and percentage under or over budget for each category. Unfortunately, such reports are of little help to the communication manager attempting to keep costs for each project in line with budgets.

If your organization does not provide computerized cost control services, try the following:

- Establish your own departmental code of accounts, related to projects rather than functions. Use a numeric code containing a two-digit year indication followed by a three- or four-digit project code. Set up a code-control log and designate sequential code numbers for projects as they are begun: the first project in 1985 would be assigned code 85-0001, the second would be assigned 85-0002, and so on.
- Write the project code number on each invoice for each project.
- Set up a personal computer file or file folder for each major project (e.g., monthly employee publication, annual report, audiovisual presentation) and "category" folders for other projects (e.g., news releases). Then, as invoices arrive, post your departmental code on them and file a copy of the invoice in the appropriate folder. Run monthly totals to make sure project budgets are kept in line.
- In large organizations with in-house service functions, such as graphic design, typesetting, photography and printing, inter-departmental charges can make your budget difficult to monitor. However, the departmental codes described above can be used to keep charges in line with budgets and to prevent unauthorized charges. Implementing the plan will require the cooperation of the accounting department.

Be sure to reach agreement with the accounting department staff so that no interdepartmental charges will be made to your budget units unless the department charging your budget uses one of your project-control codes. Then, as you assign work to the service organizations, agree in advance to the total amount of time and materials to be involved and give them a project code number to use. Their charges can then be included in the monthly reports from the accounting department, or you can request from each of the service departments a report on what charges they are making to each of your project code numbers.

Even more precise control can be obtained by issuing a written purchase order for every commitment related to a project. One copy of the purchase order can be sent to the supplier and a second copy can be used to post anticipated charges to a project cost control sheet. As invoices from suppliers arrive, they are posted to the same sheet. In this manner, the project director can determine whether any outstanding charges remain to be billed and posted.

The status of costs should be reviewed weekly, and reports to management (or clients) should be made at least monthly.

Communication Department Staffing

An appropriate organization and level of staffing for communication should be an expected outgrowth of the development of the communication plan. The plan focuses on the organization's needs and gives specific direction to communication activities designed to contribute to those needs.

While the plan is being developed, it is logical to group similar functions and estimate the number of person-hours per week needed to perform each function. Obviously, if the requirements estimated for any one function exceed 40 hours a week, more than one staff position may be necessary. Perhaps a staff "section" of several people may be appropriate. (More detailed information on staffing is presented in Chapter 7.)

Building Management Confidence

Top management controls the destiny of communicators. Our positions within the organization, our salaries, professional development expenses and operating budgets must all be approved by them. It is obviously in our best interest to understand management's needs and how communication can assist in accomplishing their goals. Communicators should treat management as their most important audience. To do so, study the demographics, backgrounds and predispositions of the people at the top and prepare a communication approach most acceptable to them.

Management often is confused about what to expect from communicators, who must gain management's respect by consistently *acting like managers*, demonstrating that they can plan and budget and control and report with the same precision and professionalism that management expects from every other department within the organization. The alternative is to limp along, day after day, decade after decade, complaining about how hard we work and how little respect and reward we receive for our efforts.

The reality of your situation may be that by understanding your organization, knowing your management as people, and involving them in the communication process you manage, you can work more effectively and play a more important role in your organization. But you cannot do so haphazardly; you must be organized.

JIM HAYNES, APR, is assistant dean for professional programs in the College of Communication at The University of Texas at Austin. He is accredited by the Public Relations Society of America.

✦ 7 ✦

Staffing the Communication Department

Linda Peterson and James R. Dodge*

Historically, people who performed communication functions for organizations were a cadre of Flying Dutchmen. In whose country should they reside? Traditional ties with personnel and employee relations landed them in personnel, industrial relations and any number of related departments. Anyone who could write or shoot pictures or fish the organization out of a mess after the mess was made was likely to be found in the public relations department, often a publicity department. The recognition that communication has an important part to play in policymaking, as well as in managing publicity and crises already at hand, led to a parallel discovery that communication has many vital audiences and services.

Responding to change, more and more organizations are both segmenting and centralizing their communication efforts. The new look is a corporate communication department, headed by a senior executive vice president. Within the department, work is likely to be divided into functional areas that meet different audience needs. Public affairs, for example, includes lobbyists and legislative analysts, consumer and/or customer relations for organizations that deal directly with the public, and regulatory relations for organizations subject to government regulation. Press relations typically is staffed by people able to meet media demands

* The authors acknowledge the assistance of Graham Allen, ABC, in preparing this chapter.

and, in large organizations, maintain contact with the media. The staff might be subdivided into print and electronic specialties. Organizational communication, recognizing employees as an important constituency, includes both all-employee and targeted groups such as union-represented, management and retirees. Financial relations targets communication for both shareholders and members of the financial community, such as analysts and investment bankers. Advertising might fit into communication or marketing departments.

Organizations with very special communication needs are breaking with traditional lines to meet those needs. Pacific Telesis, for example, uses an "account executive" concept. Communicators with reporting relationships in the public relations department are assigned as "special counsel" to major operating divisions of the company. The marketing department has an in-house communication expert, someone equipped with communication skills who is especially attuned to the needs and problems of the marketing organization, to provide communication tools to help solve operating problems there.

Obviously, these organizational descriptions fit best with medium-to-large corporations. Small companies, nonprofit agencies, governmental bodies, and privately held corporations with few employees and little or no general public contact or exposure have somewhat different needs. They tend to be staffed with generalists who can perform a variety of communication functions.

The Smaller Shop

While the small shop typically has a small budget, it has big duties. The practitioner generally conducts a broad-brush program that includes the vital elements of public, stockholder, government and employee relations, which can make for a varied and stimulating workday. Once adjusted to the long hours, endless interruptions, and frequently frenetic activity, few such communicators would trade their jobs for anything less. There's nothing quite like the satisfaction earned from meeting the creative and professional challenges this kind of balancing act presents.

Kay Staib is one such communicator. She stepped out of a large corporate department to become communication manager at American Express Canada, Inc., where she was handed the responsibility for creating a complete communication program with a staff of one. A year later she was happily managing an innovative, demanding employee communication program and a stream of community relations projects while putting the finishing touches on a public relations plan.

"While the hours are longer and the pressures are more intense, I'm having more fun here than I did at any large company I've worked for," Staib says. Easy access to top management and shorter turnaround times for policy decisions figure prominently in Staib's satisfaction. "I've accomplished more here in 12 months than I could in several years at larger companies. When I present an idea to management, I get an answer on the spot. It is very refreshing."

Deborah Demer, corporate communications manager at Hexcel Corporation, a diversified manufacturing firm in San Francisco, credits her communication-oriented CEO and a rapid review process with enabling her to manage investor relations, financial communication, media contacts, employee communication and corporate contributions effectively, with the assistance of a part-time secretary and occasional use of freelance writers and designers. "If management was not as open and responsive as it is, my productivity would be cut in half," she says.

While supportive, accessible management is essential for success in any communication department, regardless of its size, it is crucial to the lone communicator who must move quickly and simultaneously on a variety of projects. But the communicator must also bring something special to the task. As Frances Permanter, community affairs director at Capital Cablevision in Jackson, Mississippi, puts it, "I have to be more flexible here to adapt to schedule changes and unexpected developments. My work is less specialized. I'm more of a communication generalist."

Permanter has found "that little things that crop up during the day often are the most important matters at the moment." While she keeps major projects going, she also allows time each day "to take care of the little things."

These communicators agree that the essential qualities their jobs require include the ability to plan, a willingness to adjust priorities in a rapidly changing environment, a full complement of basic communication skills and, above all, the ability to understand and work with many types of people.

The small-department communicator operates much as an agency entrepreneur does, serving many "clients" and interacting with people at all levels—for example, top management, assembly-line workers, media representatives, suppliers, government officials and stockholders—while shepherding projects from concept to completion. For extra hands and talent, the communicator sometimes turns to outside sources for design and production services and, when the budget permits, for writing and photography. But the bulk of the task work, as well as the planning and managing, falls to the communicator. This is an attraction of the small shop for the complete communicator.

The Larger Operation

The department's organization and the way it fits into the overall plan of the institution are as individual as fingerprints. Organization charts, with all the intricacies of dotted and straight lines indicating who reports to whom, are necessary, to be sure. The structure and the staffing that supports it should all be aimed at getting and keeping access to top-management decision making. The communication staff should be organized to provide solutions to operating problems, rather than simply perpetuate communication vehicles.

This means, for example, that the senior member of the department should be part of the officer policymaking body, whether it is an advisory group, a formal policy review committee, or simply an informal network. The organization he or she heads needs to be structured to provide good, current information on the state of the environments, both internal and external.

Giving communication people the opportunity to break role, to join an inter- or intradepartmental problem-solving team, forces them to think outside the mold. If it's interdepartmental, it has the advantage of exposing the communication professional to line organizations (and vice versa), enabling that person to see, firsthand, mainstream problems of the business. If it's a multidiscipline intradepartmental team, it can expose a print person to other media or a "management communicator" to the problems and techniques of communicating with blue-collar workers. All these opportunities protect senior members of the communication department from isolation and from a sense of being outside the main concerns of the business. They get good, current information and a staff comfortable in any organizational environment.

Organizations are organizations, and even creative people fit into categories. When it comes time to match people to jobs, it's useful to keep in mind each job and what it requires. We will look later at interviewing and hiring people for positions in each category. First, let's examine the kinds of persons found in the various levels of the communication department.

Donald F. McLaughlin, director of media relations at AT&T, identifies three layers in a typical communication organization. First, there are the craftspersons or practitioners. Most professional communicators start here, either directly from school or from an allied field—newspapers, television and radio, advertising, marketing or teaching. Craftspeople, McLaughlin says, are those who "do" for a living. They are primarily writers, photographers, designers, illustrators and assistant editors. They may have some administrative duties, but essentially they are producers.

The next level or layer includes creative/administrative people. They are likely to have the title of editor or manager and are likely to be both doers and supervisors. They are still involved in the craft—supervising a publications staff, editing a magazine and managing its staff, running an audio-visual shop—but they are also charged with supervising people, programs, or both.

Next comes the creative/administrative/executive layer. This is usually occupied by persons who have a strong craft background, have supervised both creative and administrative types, and have made the move to management. McLaughlin says that the men and women at this level can do more than turn out good copy and nifty layouts and effectively supervise an amalgam of others doing the same. They also have sufficient interpersonal communication skills, deductive reasoning ability, knowledge and savvy to convince others in the organization—horizontally and vertically—that what they're doing is making or saving money for the organization. Their titles range from director to department head to vice president. In large organizations, each division may have many people in these levels. There may be writers and senior writers in level one; supervisors, administrators, managers and editors in level two; and directors, assistant vice presidents, vice presidents and executive vice presidents in level three. In small organizations, one or two persons may handle all the tasks.

Why do these layers matter? Concern with them doesn't mean an obsession with pigeonholing people and their capabilities. Rather, knowing what kinds of skills a job requires—professional, technical, administrative, managerial—makes filling it with the right people less risky. If you're after a practitioner, for example, you are probably concerned primarily with professional credentials. Can he or she write, interview, edit, design, shoot pictures? If you're after an administrator, can he or she motivate, manage, guide, relate to superiors and subordinates? If you're after a director, can he or she translate top-management concerns into communication solutions? Does she or he see communication programs as management tools, deploy resources—time, money, people—to get the best return on investment? Can he or she lead an organization?

There's a myth that implies supervising creative people is somehow so different that none of the rules that apply to supervising "regular people" fit. Nonsense. There are some tricks for establishing and maintaining an environment in which creative people can flourish, but before they get pulled out of the hat, the tried-and-true rules about managing people need to be functioning:

- *Define responsibilities.* Not knowing what you're supposed to do, when you're supposed to do it, and who you're supposed to do it for are leading causes of anxiety and dissatisfaction. Job descriptions do not have to be couched in stulifying institutional language. They should describe the job and the expectations that go with it.
- *Establish methods to measure.* People like to be paid for what they do, not for how they smile at the boss. Creative jobs are not unmeasurable, especially if they are based on a well-developed set of departmental and corporate objectives and are well defined. Dale McConkey's *MBO for Staff Managers* is a good introduction to organizing staff (as opposed to line) management jobs.

- *Don't make unnecessary rules.*   Aside from providing the basics—decent salaries and work areas, and the opportunity to grow—the secret to managing creative people probably lies in the maxim of the Bauhaus designers: less is more. Flextime, relaxed dress codes when there's no public contact, time for thinking—all of these recognize the non-assembly-line aspects of the creative process. Of course, that doesn't mean releasing "blocked" writers to Big Sur, the Poconos or the Laurentians for unlimited periods of time.
- *Create an open, nonthreatening atmosphere.*   With highly motivated, independent subordinates, the one who bosses best probably bosses least. The manager should function as a facilitator, providing access to information and resources up and down the organization, setting a climate as free as possible of secrets, threats and reprisals. While these are good rules to follow for running almost any organization of independent people, they are especially critical rules for supervising creative people. Nothing maims or mutilates the creative process as badly as the conviction that the products always have to "play" to a certain audience. Managers need to play politics, of course, but political considerations shouldn't color the beginning, middle and end of every creative process.
- *Encourage intelligent risk-taking.*   Caution breeds expectability and its first cousin, boredom. No two communication problems are alike, and if a communication staff is going to come up with innovative solutions tailored to specific problems, they shouldn't be hamstrung by convention and tradition. If they are, a computer can probably be programmed to generate the solutions. That doesn't mean the manager should suspend critical judgment—garbage in, garbage out, to borrow from the computer people—but at the brainstorming, problem-solving stages, nonevaluative acceptance keeps the juices flowing. The time for "reality testing," criticism, and fine-tuning comes when the field has been narrowed. Subordinates should feel comfortable raising any idea, no matter how crazy. Ideally, their first thoughts should be, "I wonder if..." not, "Oh, no, the boss will never go for that."

The manager, in other words, is there to make problem solving easier, to encourage a certain amount of risk-taking, and to act as facilitator.

Interviewing and Hiring

To find, interview and hire the best people, begin with job specifications. These are more than job descriptions. They detail exactly what the group needs to accomplish and what kind of person it will probably take to achieve the results.

There are two kinds of job specifications—the make-or-break and the nice-to-have. If the job opening is for a writer, make-or-break is a proven ability to write. Nice-to-have might be a degree in economics, journalism, animal husbandry or chemistry—whatever seems appropriate for the organization. It is important to distinguish between the two categories of specs. To determine what they should be, look at the organization's objectives, review job responsibilities, consider past and current job holders, and think about possible changes. Ask the boss, ask peers, and think about what product or program the candidate may need to turn out a month after he or she is hired. Then prepare the specifications.

Once the job specs are defined, develop questions designed to elicit the information needed to make a decision. For example, if making speeches will be a part of the job, the manager should ask: "Have you given speeches before? What kinds of groups? How do you get ready for one? May I see a copy (or better yet, a videotape)?" Later on, the hiring manager might want to arrange for final candidates to give mini-presentations.

Of course, the questions need to relate directly to the level of the job. In other words, if the opening is for a craft professional, writing samples, recommendations, reputation, and so on will probably suffice. If the job is for an administrative/craftperson, the extra credentials and experience for managing need to be explored. For the third level, the director or senior manager, all the above plus the services of an executive search firm might be called into action.

Entire books have been written on the fine art of interviewing. In all, these key points emerge:

- *Have an agenda.* Know what information you need and ask questions to get it.
- *Ask open, probing questions.* Who, what, why, how? Can you give me an example? How would you do that differently now?
- *Give the candidate time to talk.* Don't cut off responses.
- *Keep control.* The interview should be a two-way process, but the manager needs to control the flow.
- *Remember the law.* Questions must be directly related to job performance.

After each interview, summarize key points. Make lists of items that need further exploration, people to talk with, work samples to review, and so forth.

Role-playing, case studies and writing tests can be useful. If, for instance, the candidate would serve as company spokesperson, the interviewer might ask, "Suppose the Environmental Protection Agency announces that one of our local mills is under investigation. I'm going to play the role of newspaper reporter and ask you to answer some questions." Or, the interviewer might pose an ongoing problem—for example, inade-

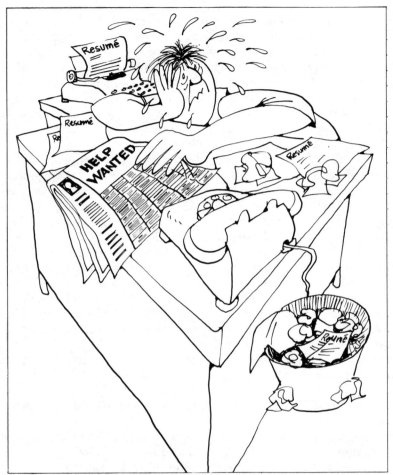

Figure 7.1. Matching the right communicator with the right job avoids both personal and managerial headaches.

quate horizontal communication at middle management—and ask for the candidate's thoughts on the subject.

Finally, the interviewer might leave the candidate with data and typewriter and ask him or her to come up with a feature article or news story, or both, on a designated topic. All these techniques are legitimate if they relate to the job opening. They are useful if the interviewer has the expertise to evaluate them.

Once a decision to hire has been made, it is important to present the job offer in as much detail as possible. The job, its responsibilities, salary, benefits, and opportunities for growth need to be explained fully. The job candidate should be encouraged to discuss them.

Promoting

Given the right people in the right places in the right environment, how do you recognize who should move up and when? Identifying potential and developing it merits more space than this chapter can devote to it. Still, since it is so critical a part of a manager's job, it is worth identifying a few signposts that point to potential.

Work of the complete subordinate arrives on the boss's desk without loose ends. Research is thorough, the work is well developed and accurate. Obstacles are anticipated and follow-up and contingency plans are built in.

"The catalyst" can bring a group together and can persuade others to do things without arousing hostility or resentment. He or she can resolve conflicts and is a credit-giver rather than a glory-grabber.

"The decision maker" is willing to make decisions and accept their consequences. He or she doesn't shoot from the hip, but gathers information and makes a good, defensible decision without running to the boss for guidance at every step.

Once potential is identified, it's the joint responsibility of boss and subordinate to develop it further. Task force assignments, "opportunity" assignments that stretch talents and abilities that need further growth, and evening classes are possibilities they should discuss. Together they should decide what is appropriate to pursue.

If the subordinate is a craftsperson, interested in making the transition from doer to manager, supervisory and managerial skills can be developed with "acting" assignments—filling in for the boss. If the subordinate wants to climb the next rung in the specialist ladder or develop another craft specialty, classes, self-development programs, or "apprenticeship" arrangements might work out best. Whatever the goal, the development process has to be a joint effort, with the boss providing resources, and opportunities and feedback and the subordinate doing the rest.

Firing

This being not the best of all possible worlds, from time to time the right person might not end up in the right place. Then what? If the manager has done a good and conscientious job of establishing expectations and performance standards and then measured by those standards, the most painful variety of separation—the surprise—should never take place. Exit interviews should never include a scenario of the departing subordinate protesting, "But I thought I was doing so well."

Performance appraisals or reviews, held at least quarterly, are more than an ounce of prevention. They let people know exactly where they stand, where problems exist (if they do), and what the boss is prepared to do to help the subordinate measure up.

While the content of boss-subordinate conversations surely does not need to be formalized, the structure or system for dealing with performance problems probably should be. Borrowing a leaf from union-management relations, here are four steps to follow:

1. *Counsel.*   This is the first "we've got a problem" conversation. After the informal chats fail, it's probably a good idea to begin by describing the problem and asking the subordinate for ideas on how to solve it. Does he or she know how the job should be done? Maybe the problem is training. Is it a lack of interest? If the work is dull, maybe the boss can do something. If not, it might be an early warning signal that a job search could be coming. Is it an interpersonal problem? Perhaps some friendly advice from the boss or someone else will help. The key is getting the subordinate's ideas and commitment for solving the problem.
2. *Warn.*   If step 1 doesn't produce improvement, the problem needs to be examined. The boss needs to restate expectations and the subordinate needs to know what the consequences will be if improvement doesn't result.
3. *Job on the line.*   When 1 and 2 fail, the subordinate needs to know it's "shape up or ship out" time. Obviously, the boss needs to keep documentation on this conversation and should have supporting material (e.g., assignments and performance appraisals).
4. *Dismissal.*   Sometimes it happens, though probably not often enough. If there's a poor match between job and employee, in the long run there will be less trauma and ego damage if job and incumbent come to a parting of the ways. If the steps described above are followed, the separation can take place with minimal damage to the individual and the organization. Don't belabor the parting. Get it over with.

Career Pathing

Having the right people in the right place at the right time doesn't mean maintaining the status quo. People change, jobs change, organizations change. For some reasons, this is a tough concept to swallow, so traditionally, organizational communication has been a business of job hopping. Professionals move from job to job, from organization to organization, because they don't see a career path where they are.

That path doesn't have to be up, but it does have to lead *somewhere.* Even in a three-person department there should be opportunities for growth within the job, within the group. Developing a game of "musical jobs" just to keep people fresh probably isn't terribly effective, but a certain amount of cross-training, joint problem solving, and sharing administrative tasks develops people and keeps the wolf of boredom away from the door.

Using Outside Suppliers

The masthead of a West Coast company magazine recognizes its staff of 4 full-time regulars and lists the creative contributions of 22 writers, illustrators and photographers from the "outside." Behind the scenes of entire communication departments, a small, relatively unsung, but assignment-hungry corps of designers, illustrators, writers and photographers comes forth as needed to become the "unseen" members of the staff. Communicators today regularly call on their reserves to augment the in-house regulars to accomplish what cannot be done inside, and to rechannel disrupted work flows and soothe ruffled budgets.

It follows, of course, that outside help cannot be deployed indiscriminately. Experienced communication managers hang on to projects that are best handled in-house and farm out projects outsiders can accomplish just as easily. They bring in outside support when an extra-special touch is required that can't be found on staff, and when it seems smarter, from a budget or deadline standpoint, to call on a specialist whose expertise will get a project off the ground faster and cheaper.

The services of consultants and outside creative suppliers fall into two major camps. The first is more *cerebral*—communication audits, evaluations of ongoing programs, counseling on organization and staff decisions, and problem solving. The other is more *creative*, with the emphasis on "doing" rather than "thinking." *Cerebral services* include *audits*—what you're doing, how well you're doing, what you should be doing; *program and project evaluations*—do they measure up? *counsel*—on modifying existing programs or establishing new ones, organization and staff changes, budget and cost control measures, identifying audiences, targeting messages, and matching audiences and messages with media. *Creative services* include project management (taking over the whole thing), research, conceptualizing, organizing, supervising production and creative efforts, writing and editing, coordinating production, and any combination of the above. What consultants do is bring their ideas, their interests, and their time to all or any of the above services to produce the results you need.

Getting the most out of outside creative service is an art; the following dialogue is not. Word Smith, a communicator is giving Lynn Smith, a photographer, the business. What is *said* is in quotes. What is *meant* is in parentheses.

"Ah, Lynn, you're just the person I wanted to see." (Actually, I called three photographers and you were the first to get back to me.)

"Really." (If he's got another of those company picnic gigs, I'll slit my throat.)

"Saturday is our annual Hayloft Jamboree and Greased Pig chase, and. . . ." (If she cuts it with this, she gets the rafting-the-Colorado piece.)

"How do you want to handle it?" (So, I won't slit my throat, but please, some ideas.)

"Give it a photojournalistic approach. You know, shoot it as it happens and give me a good selection of prints for the *Bulletin*." (I'll leave it up to her and hope it comes out okay.)

"Check." (Hey, I've got carte blanche. This guy's all right.)

"And, now. . .ahem, hum, er. . . ." (What's your day rate?)

Six weeks later, Lynn delivered the assignment—a thigh-thwacking, embarrassing selection of prints showing the company's principal officers in the mud in what appear to be bleary-eyed, compromising embraces with slickered-up pigs—great for the *National Enquire*, but not for the company *Bulletin*. Moreover, Lynn, whose specialty is sports news, used a motor-driven shutter and, as was her style, shot up 20 roles of film from which she made 75 prints for a total of $295, which, to Word's surprise, was tacked to the normal day-rate charges.

Later, over lunch with his colleagues, Word defended the tardiness of the latest issue of the *Bulletin* by placing the blame squarely on Lynn; her failure to meet the deadline (it was left purely to chance), her sense of news (conditioned, no doubt, by her sports news background), and her ability to exploit the dollar (the business arrangements were self-consciously kicked aside).

The real problem was that Word Smith didn't know what he was buying and didn't know how to manage the project. Word's success could have been guaranteed if he had known more about outside services and how to deal with them.

To Market, to Market

It's wise to plan ahead for those occasions when outside creative talent is needed. Develop lists of photographers, writers, designers and illustrators and assess their special strengths before the time you need them.

Portfolio showings are the primary means of getting the seller together with the buyer. In metropolitan areas with large communities of creative people, communicators often have set times of the week or month for portfolio sessions. Ganging them, so to speak, avoids scattered interruptions and establishes a framework for comparing style and approach among the portfolios.

Assessment of style is the most important factor. Sports photography is hardly appropriate for covering a facilities dedication, nor is landscape or travel experience necessarily going to pull off a tough candidates' night assignment. The same goes for writing, design and illustration. Some creative suppliers are flexible, however. A certain illustrator, for example, might make the transition from hard edge to watercolor wash with ease. The portfolio will show the degree of the artist's flexibility.

As the interview session (usually about 30 minutes) comes to an end, important questions should be addressed: fees, rights to the creative product, contracts and purchase orders, for instance. Don't leave anything to chance. Hammering out details of an assignment begins with a thorough understanding of the objective of the assignment and a healthy appreciation of the style and operating philosophy of the sponsoring organization. The process ends with a detailed schedule of deadlines and fees. If clearances and releases are to be handled by the supplier, it should be with the understanding that the ultimate responsibility for them still resides in-house.

Outside creative suppliers have well-developed conditions on which they base their fees. Writers, once paid by the word, are shifting to day or project rates. Photographers charge by the hour, day and even half-day. Illustrators charge according to the complexity of the product and its end use. Designers' fees are based on the size and complexity of the project; production fees, on the basis of time and material. But virtually all will work against a bid if asked. Many will negotiate charges if a project interests them enough and the deadline is not tomorrow. Often a fee will hinge on how and where the work will be used. Advertising art, for instance, usually commands higher fees than editorial art.

Even after a fee schedule is negotiated, communicators are often buffeted by the unexpected. Fees might not include per diem and travel expenses, film and processing, stats, special-order typography and authors' changes. Growing numbers of photographers and artists will accept a commission only on the basis of one-time use.

Having completed the business arrangements, the creative supplier begins the assignment. The communicator and the supplier should maintain continuing contact throughout. The writer completes the research and submits an outline and, perhaps, a sample of how the section or piece should be styled. The illustrator submits tissues showing concept and technique. The designer comes to an understanding of the objective and works with the communicator to select and organize materials for emphasis and editorial thrust. If there's time, the photographer might submit a selection of Polaroid prints.

As the project moves along, the communicator exercises judgment and discretion and indulges hunches. A gnawing doubt is never ignored; flexibility to turn a project to accommodate serendipity is allowed. Creative forces can be unleashed, but under the control and guidance of the individual in charge.

Editors and communicators sometimes use outside talent for specified work. One who is strong at research, for instance, might be commissioned to do the legwork. A good organizer might take a cut at the first draft; a graceful writer might style a manuscript.

The emerging breed of organizational communicators is relatively unfamiliar with illustrators, especially those who move primarily in advertising circles and are used to heavy art direction. After their first encounters with them, communicators quickly develop the savvy needed to get results.

Matters of determining format and blending with other elements often require involvement of designers. Will it be flatwork? (The separation cost is then borne by the printer.) Or will it be done on color overlay? (Then the artist should be paid extra.) Thus, communicator and designer should work together to direct the project.

Working with photographers is especially risky when dealing with the unknown over long distances. Remote assignments call for both rigid art direction, to assure that minimal standards are met, and enough flexibility to take advantage of the delightfully unexpected or the photographer's own special skills and insights that might bring a marginal assignment to life. Photographers like to be worked hard when sent out on location. They usually don't object, when asked, to shoot for the files during waiting time or during the hours between the completion of the assignment and dusk.

Ideally, an editorial designer reads and has a sense of what the piece is all about. Good editorial designers are fairly new to the scene. They understand the essence of the content and play to it. They should get involved early and stay on the project until the final press check. Editors with design sense also are growing in numbers. They understand the power of visual images and the economies of playing to them.

The community of "outside" suppliers has become more than just a luxury affordable only by the big and the well budgeted. The flexibility, the extra measure, the economies and efficiencies the small creative entrepreneur brings to the communication environment have earned him or her a permanent and much regarded position on the "unseen" staff.

Now, about *Your* Career

One of the most important responsibilities of a professional communicator is personally charting a clearly defined career path, a path marked with short- and long-term goals for regularly measuring professional growth. Easier said than done? Agreed, but success comes most often to those who know where they are going and who carefully plan their journey.

If you haven't already done so, set aside some quiet time to think seriously about what you would like to achieve in your communication career, what pinnacle you ultimately hope to attain, what title, for instance, you would like to hold as you approach retirement. Perhaps you aspire to the presidency of a major trade association, or to a vice presidency in a Fortune 500 corporation. Or, maybe your dream is to be a senior communication officer in the armed forces, a member of a large communication staff, or a partner in a consulting firm.

Whatever your ultimate goal, fix on it and plan your strategy for achieving it. Keep in mind, however, that people being what they are—changeable—you may have to exercise some flexibility along the way.

Typically, professional communicators spend their early years acquiring and sharpening basic communication skills in specialized jobs—as a news or feature writer for a company publication, an audiovisual assistant, or a staff member of a speakers bureau. With a little seasoning and some skills development, the young professional moves up to editor, media contact, or film producer, acquiring experience in program planning and budgeting along the way.

As the professional grows and wins the respect of superiors, the career path sometimes veers more in the direction of management, away from the functional roles that attract most communicators to the profession in the first place. When this happens, many communication practitioners face a difficult choice. "Do I give up what I like most to cross the bridge into management, or do I sacrifice advancement to stay with what I know and care most about?" For many, it is a soul-wrenching decision. Others never look back.

As you set about sketching your personal career plan, take time to talk to some communicators you admire, communicators who have achieved some of the success that you aspire to. Find out from them how they got where they are and what skills they needed to get there.

Take an honest look at yourself. Analyze your own strengths and weaknesses. List the professional skills that you do not yet have but will need to reach your goal. Then draw up a timetable for acquiring those skills. If you work for a corporation, your employer may have a plan for reimbursing you for job-related educational expenses.

The booklet, "Communication Careers Professional Development Guide," prepared by IABC lists competency requirements for typical career levels, step-by-step, from college graduate to senior corporate officer. It can help you formulate your career plan.

Once you have a plan, use it. Revise it annually, or more often if necessary, because time and experience will help you sharpen your focus on who and where you want to be.

A third and vital element in your pursuit of the brass ring is knowing whom to call when you need information, advice or moral support. Every successful person has a well-developed and meticulously maintained network of contacts that he or she can call on for help in solving a problem, finding an employee, choosing a supplier, or getting a job. Who knows whom is often the critical factor. Quite often, it isn't the immediate contact who provides the assignment, but a contact of the contact's. Networks, like outer space, have no limits.

The importance of networking has led some major firms to instruct their newly hired junior executives in the fine art of discovering, nurturing and maintaining contacts. The process is a mutual arrangement of giving and getting, of helping one another become more effective in business.

Effective networkers never let old contacts get cold. Even as they change jobs and move to new locations, they keep in touch to keep relationships alive, not just when they need something. Their contacts are of all ages and walks of life. They aren't necessarily friends, for networking has very little to do with how people feel about each other. However, your network may well produce many lifelong friendships.

So, how do you make your network work more effectively for you? Here are some of the fundamentals:

- First, list *all* of your contacts. Don't leave anyone out. Everyone you know has a network that they could plug you into; it builds from there.
- Develop a description of the kinds of people, professional groups, suppliers, etc., who could be important to you in achieving your career goals. Focus on building that aspect of your network.
- Be systematic. Make network maintenance part of your daily routine. Set goals, such as making five new contacts a week, having lunch three times a week with contacts to build relationships and exchange information, setting aside an hour a day for network phone calls, and going to evening meetings three or four times a month to meet and maintain contacts. This may sound calculated. It is. Your network serves you in proportion to the effort you put into it.
- Have a clear purpose. Know what you want when you ask a contact for information or meet a new contact for the first time. Be sure that you understand what the other person needs so that you can reciprocate. Networking is a two-way street.
- Follow up when a contact puts you in touch with a new contact, or offers advice. It is frustrating to offer help and have it ignored.
- Keep good records. Start a card file, phone log, address book—whatever works for you. Use it faithfully to record names, dates, key bits of conversation and useful personal data.
- Respect confidences.
- Report back to those who have helped you. They'll feel good about it and you've maintained the contact.

- Be businesslike.
- Deliver on your promises.

Networking is an exciting and rewarding part of business life. Your network can put you into the mainstream of information and technical assistance, and help you avoid the pangs of isolation that can befall any hardworking professional. Best of all, it can provide a shortcut to the career goal you seek.

LINDA PETERSON and JAMES R. DODGE are principals of Peterson & Dodge, a San Francisco communication consulting firm.

Example: American Express Canada

When American Express Canada, Inc., conducted an employee attitude survey a few years ago, the results clearly called for an internal communication overhaul. Kay Staib, ABC, was hired to do the job.

Using the company's survey results as well as guidelines gleaned from an international survey of corporate communication effectiveness, conducted in 1980 by Towers, Perrin, Forster & Crosby, Staib focused her efforts on the communication "hot spots" targeted by each. Initially, she concentrated on face-to-face communication as a means of getting quick results and meeting employee preferences. Staib won management's support for a three-times-a-month "Let's Talk" session that brought 15 randomly selected employees together with the Chief Executive Officer. During these hour-and-a-half sessions, they discussed where the business was going, where it has been, problem areas, and any other subjects that employees cared to bring up.

After the sessions, the employees broke into discussion groups where they came to grips with case study questions posed by Staib along the line of "If you were the boss, what would you do about this situation?" According to Staib, this exercise brought important issues and unseen problems to management's attention.

Monthly staff meetings are held in all departments by managers who are supported by training and instruction on how to conduct productive meetings. It's not uncommon for senior managers to drop in on these meetings as they evaluate and assess their effectiveness.

Other communication activities include:

- *Expressline,* a program through which employees can communicate a work-related concern, problem, or question confidentially and receive a timely and substantive response, was implemented for employees who feel they cannot discuss a particular concern with their immediate supervisor.

- An active bulletin board program to keep current information flowing to the staff.
- Brown bag luncheons featuring presentations on a variety of subjects, from work-related issues to personal growth and better living.

All of these activities are closely tuned into corporate goals and objectives. And to keep them there, Staib sits in on functional strategic planning sessions. She studies the annual plans of each of the departmental vice presidents and annotates items where she believes her department can be supportive.

Feedback flows from the very bottom of the organization all the way up to the executive suite. In fact, employees evaluate their managers, managers their vice presidents, and the vice presidents evaluate the CEO. And these evaluations are taken seriously to the extent that firm plans are expected from those who need to make improvements.

Staib credits her CEO and his management team for much of the success of her program. "Management believes in communication and lends its enthusiastic support to make it work," she says.

The success of the American Express Canada program really is tested regularly in a company-wide communication survey that becomes Staib's planning guide for shaping her program for the following year.

Linda Peterson and Jim Dodge

· Part III ·

SELECTING AND USING VARIOUS MEDIA AND METHODS

◆ 8 ◆

Matching Media with Audience and Message

Camille Emig

Years ago, if an organization even thought about internal communication it probably resulted in a directive to start a "house organ." An editor was recruited, maybe from personnel or secretarial ranks, and he or she then started looking for a printer and for people who could provide information on babies, bowling scores and retirements. Although somewhat exaggerated, unfortunately in many cases this scenario was not far from the truth.

Part of the reason for the changing role of the business communicator—from "house organ editor" to communication specialist in areas from writing to videotape production—has been the expansion and sophistication of the media the professional uses. Years ago there was good reason to call the person "house organ editor." In most cases that's exactly what he or she was. Today the communicator has tools with which to work, everything from magazines and employee annual reports to closed-circuit television and telephone information systems.

Print: An Overview

Although there has been a dramatic expansion of media in recent years, print is still the most widely used. But it too has undergone many changes in content and format. No longer are there only company magazines or newspapers; paycheck stuffers, magapapers, employee annual reports and posters are all being used effectively to communicate with specific audiences. The descendants of the "house organ" rival daily newspapers and general-interest magazines in professional expertise and interest.

The "company publication" has deep historical roots, with evidence of forerunners of today's publications dating back to eleventh-century Chinese feudal times. Today there are thousands of business and organizational publications of various formats.

Magazines remain a popular print medium. From organization to organization, the size, number of pages, use of color and illustrations, frequency, audiences and purposes differ greatly. Internal publications are usually aimed at an organization's employees or members and contain a variety of articles, from those on company programs and policies to others on the hobbies or life styles of employees. They usually seek to inform, recognize employee or member contributions to the organization, motivate and show employees that their organization is a good one to be associated with. Some internal publications are also distributed to selected external audiences.

The *Ralston Purina Magazine*, for example, is a three- or four-color bimonthly for about 27,000 employees and friends of Ralston Purina Company. It contains company- and people-related articles and uses photos liberally. Its editor is convinced that this format best reaches its diverse audience because a magazine can be viewed at leisure and shared with family members.

At Bell Atlantic, a quarterly corporate magazine reaches 80,000 active employees and selected outside audiences. *Atlantic Bell Magazine* (formerly *New Jersey Bell Magazine*) is four-color and contains company news and articles on issues within or outside the company that are of interest to employees. The company uses a number of media to communicate to its employees, but the magazine allows in-depth, philosophical discussions of items that may be announced as news in other media.

The Review is an external magazine published in English and French by Imperial Oil Limited, Toronto, for about 75,000 "thought-leaders" in Canada. The four-color quarterly publication is an opinion forum that has had articles relating to social and cultural topics as well as such current issues as energy.

An external magazine with far different objectives is *Team Talk*, published by Anheuser-Busch, Inc., for its beer wholesalers. The four-color bimonthly shares marketing ideas among the brewery's 900-plus independent distributors. Its articles deal with brewery marketing programs and wholesaler accomplishments, all aimed at providing information that can be used to make the wholesalers' businesses more successful and, bottom line, to sell more product.

Some magazines are designed to reach more than one audience. Although its primary audience is 46,000 employees worldwide, *JD Journal*, published by Deere & Company, is also sent to retirees, dealers, selected

Figure 8.1. Part of the communication process is matching the medium with the message. Magazines, comic strips or audiovisuals can all be used to reach specific audiences.

opinion leaders and friends. Normally 28 to 32 pages, the four-color publication was started in 1972 as the first worldwide communication vehicle for the company. The editor uses the magazine format because he believes it is the best way to communicate about the company to its multiple audiences in an interesting and exciting way, and to emphasize the company's concern for quality products and service.

The second most popular print media used by business communicators are the newspaper and magapaper. Most organizational newspapers are tabloid size (11 × 15½ inches) and feature short articles in a format similar to that of a daily newspaper. The magapaper is a combination newspaper and magazine that contains a mix of news articles and longer features and uses photos liberally. The design is more in the magazine style. Sometimes there is a fine line between the newspaper and magapaper.

A good corporate newspaper is the *ArcoSpark*, published for Atlantic Richfield Company employees. It has a special monthly edition for retirees. The publication contains company and industry-related news and articles about employees and their jobs. The editors chose the newspaper format because they wanted a timely, topical publication that could compete well with other publications employees read.

Most magapapers are published less frequently than newspapers. *Today*, distributed to employees, staff and volunteers of Methodist Hospital in Brooklyn, and to select community members, is bimonthly. It contains a mixture of human-interest articles and news affecting the hospital, such as hospital cost information. The editor chose this medium because of its visual effectiveness and attraction.

The Reda Pump Division of TRW produces a monthly magapaper for its 2,500 employees worldwide. It is news-oriented but includes special inserts on topics that need more depth. The magapaper format uses a bold, dramatic design and graphics.

Borg-Warner Corporation uses the magapaper format for its quarterly management publication, *Perspective*. It was started in 1980 to expand the information being communicated to managers in a monthly newsletter. In recent years, more publications directed specifically at the select manager/supervisor audience have been started.

The fastest-growing print medium in business and organizational communication is the newsletter. Usually smaller than the newspaper, less formal and quickly produced, the newsletter's popularity can be attributed in part to the need to reach audiences already bombarded with information. Newsletters usually contain short, newsy items and are designed so readers can quickly go from cover to cover, usually only four or eight pages.

AE Management Journal was started in 1982 to provide supervisors at GTE Automatic Electric (now GTE Network Systems) with information on key issues and company programs, offer advice on improving communication, and focus on interesting and thought-provoking articles on a broad range of subjects. The publication goes to approximately 1,000 supervisors monthly. The newsletter format was selected because the editor wanted a publication that is informal, easy to produce and less expensive than some other media.

A form of the newsletter, the news sheet, is used by Borg-Warner to communicate news on a daily basis to headquarters employees. The *Daily Bulletin* ranges in size (8½ × 11 inches or 8½ × 14 inches) and length (one or two pages), depending on the amount of news to be communicated. It is distributed through the mail system.

The Reda Pump Division has two weekly newsletters. *Intake* goes to all 2,500 employees; it contains information about the company. *Management* is sent to managers and supervisors. It contains news briefs, case studies relating how managers solve problems and tips and how-to articles for supervisors.

A variety of other printed materials—paycheck stuffers, special informational brochures, employee handbooks, annual reports, posters, mobiles and even T-shirts—are described in other chapters.

Publications Are Not Alone

Audiovisuals

Although print is still the most frequently used medium in organizational communication, the trend is to expand into other media. It's not surprising to find that in a world dominated by visual communication, audiovisuals

Figure 8.2. The same medium can be used for different audiences.

are growing in importance. In most cases, their use is an expansion, not a replacement, of the print media.

Video is one of the fastest growing audiovisual media in internal communication. It was traditionally used in training, education and safety areas, but now it is more frequently used in other communication areas, especially employee communication. Many video productions are highly credible, have immediate impact and communicate a sense of being "newsy." SmithKline Beckman Corporation in Philadelphia has one of the oldest corporate news programs in the United States. The weekly five- to seven-minute employee news programs, started in 1971, are produced in-house on tape. They are aired for employees in lobbies and lounges.

Reda Pump Division's quarterly video report features a company executive or director who discusses the state of the business. It also contains other news items of interest to employees.

Ralston Purina produces a video magazine to complement its publications. It contains management and marketing stories, human interest segments and information on other topics of interest to employees, such as benefits. Introduced in 1980, the quarterly production reaches employees at 88 locations in the United States.

Some communicators combine audiovisual media to create multi-image presentations—slide and sound and film in one presentation, for example. These also are sometimes referred to as "multimedia," although that term could also include print. Chapter 12 describes audiovisuals more fully.

Face-to-Face Communication/Feedback

Face-to-face communication and feedback programs can take on a variety of forms, from interpersonal communication between two employees or members to organized systems that allow employees to ask questions and receive answers. Such programs are founded on the premise that you cannot have communication when only one party is doing the communicating.

Obviously, there is a need for the downward flow of information that is generally provided through the various print and audiovisual programs. But people are demanding more, so many organizations are using face-to-face programs (discussed more fully in Chapter 13) and feedback programs (described in Chapter 19) more frequently. Most organizations recognize that these programs are not a solution to overall poor internal communication, but they can contribute to a healthy communication environment.

Most face-to-face programs use meetings of some type, which can include any number of people and are an excellent way to combine face-to-face communication and feedback.

Borg-Warner has regular meetings to bring different levels of management together and a yearly operational meeting that focuses on company goals and operating trends. Information is exchanged and questions are answered by top management at the annual meeting. The Chairman's Meeting is held every other year. It focuses on company philosophies and long-range direction to encourage a feeling of togetherness and sharing. Borg-Warner's communication staff believes that the Chairman's Meeting has had a great impact on the company, which has undergone substantial changes in recent years.

At Atlantic Richfield, meetings are held with the president and small groups of employees to encourage feedback and demonstrate the company's willingness to communicate openly. It also holds "brown-bag" lunchtime meetings, when employees can get information from speakers and slide presentations and through questions and answers.

Since 1974, Anheuser-Busch, Inc., the brewing subsidiary of Anheuser-Busch Companies, has held annual employee communication meetings at its breweries. Members of top management, including the chairman of the board, travel to 10 sites around the country for the meetings, which vary from year to year from a business-only meeting to a combination business-entertainment format. One year an employee-only meeting is held at the brewery for a slide presentation, followed by employee questions and answers. Another time, employees can invite a guest for a multimedia informational presentation, followed by dinner and entertainment.

A number of organizations are sponsoring programs that psychologists call "sensing sessions," management-employee meetings that involve voicing opinions, asking questions or simply complaining. Programs vary from company to company, but their major purpose is to provide both management and employees with information and feedback. Reda Pump Division invites a sample of employees to meet and to make comments and ask questions, which are recorded. These are then taken to the appropriate departments and the responses are given back to the sensing group.

"Comment"-type programs allow employees to ask questions anonymously about the company. A special form is used and only the program coordinator knows who asked the question. It is forwarded anonymously to the appropriate person in the organization, who returns the answer to the coordinator, who sends it on to the employee. This type of program encourages employee feedback and, in addition to answering employee questions, can provide management with important information about employee concerns. Speak-up programs are covered more fully in Chapter 19.

Other Media

In addition to print, audiovisuals and various forms of face-to-face and feedback programs, a variety of other media are available to the business communicator. The bulletin board is one obvious communication vehicle—

most organizations have them. But the key to using them effectively is having a program that puts the communicator in control of the boards, as is explained in Chapter 11.

A communication vehicle we all use frequently also has a niche in the internal communication area. Many companies are using the telephone to communicate with their audiences on everything from medical benefits to strike information. An instant communication device, the telephone can give fast access to company news, help quell rumors, answer questions and zero in on needs, ideas and gripes, as described in Chapter 11.

Another way to communicate information to large groups of people is through informational meetings. These differ from the meetings already discussed in that their purpose is to communicate information only and not receive feedback, although some feedback does result through questions and answers. These meetings are usually attended by large groups of people, and feature a slide-and-sound or multimedia presentation.

A new technology, teleconferencing, is now being used to bring groups of people in various geographic locations together for a "meeting." A teleconference can include one or more presenters or speakers transmitted to the receiving locations. It also can transmit audience interaction; people at the various locations can be seen or heard by the sending location.

Media Work Together

Most of the media and examples discussed in this chapter were, in a sense, taken out of context because, in most cases, media aren't used alone.

For example, the media used by Atlantic Richfield—a weekly newspaper and various meetings—are only part of its internal communication program. It also includes a twice-a-week management newsletter, telephone feedback programs, slide and sound programs on an as-needed basis, video programs for employees, a bulletin board program and printed booklets or brochures that fill various communication needs. Likewise, the Reda Pump Division of TRW, in addition to the employee and management newsletters, employee magapaper, video report and face-to-face meetings mentioned, produces a newsletter every other week that focuses only on people, has a bulletin board program, and handles other special publications (such as a cookbook of employee recipes) and special events (such as a "county fair" for employees).

At Borg-Warner, the management magapaper, daily news sheet and meetings are part of a corporate communication program aimed primarily at management employees. Other components are a monthly newsletter for managers, a program that summarizes news releases and outside information about the company and a communication consulting service. Each division has an employee communication program.

Tailoring the Message

After reviewing the media available to the communicator, it is easy to see that the job has become complex. Not only are there more media available to get the job done, but the nature of the job itself is more complicated. The "house organ editor" has become the communication professional charged with meeting needs or solving problems with organizations. No longer can he or she use the old "let's run an article in the company magazine" formula to solve the many communication problems facing organizations today.

In deciding which media to use, internal communicators must know what they want to communicate, why they're communicating, whom they're communicating with, and what results they hope to get from the effort. It means having goals and objectives, and the strategies to achieve them. The importance of having written communication plans for any program or project was emphasized in previous chapters. Communication goals and objectives must be meshed with management's goals and objectives, and they must have management's stamp of approval if they are to be effective.

Once plans are established and approved, the communicator can tackle the problem of what to do to achieve the planned objectives. Because communication is a two-way street—there is no communication if the message is not received—an in-depth knowledge of whom you're communicating with is a key factor in deciding what to communicate. As discussed in Chapter 3, knowing your audience—their values, needs and interests—is an essential step in tailoring your message.

There are a number of ways to get to know your audience. Every organization has records that can provide demographic information (e.g., age, sex and years of service). Attitude surveys, communication audits and readership and media-use surveys can be conducted.

A survey of your audience is not going to give pat answers on the kinds of information to communicate, but knowing your audience's perceived needs will help in making the decision on the message content and how to deliver it. You can apply a marketing strategy to communication and segment your audience. For example, there may be a need for special communication to management employees, but information of interest to supervisors may not pertain to production workers. Your audience can also be segmented by division or geographic location, in addition to job responsibility, because people in different company locations and operating areas have different information needs.

Once you've done your research and analysis of the audience and its needs and meshed this information with the organization's communication objectives, you are at the point at which you can begin making your decisions on the media you will use.

Choosing the Media

The choice of which media to use is not a guessing game. Using print because "that's the way it's always been done" or video because "it's the thing to do" just are not valid reasons for choosing either.

There is no magic formula. It takes an analysis of the advantages and disadvantages of each medium, meshed with the decisions you've already made about what to communicate and to whom. Look at the strengths and weaknesses of each medium in three key areas: effectiveness in communicating your message and meeting your goals, distribution and budget considerations.

Advantages and Disadvantages

Print media are lasting—written messages can be retained, filed, passed on and referred to later. Print media are also "traditional"—people are accustomed to reading magazines, newspapers and books. Reading often helps people retain certain kinds of information and can reinforce information previously communicated verbally.

Among the print media, each type also has its own attributes. Magazines can handle longer, in-depth information. They also have the "keep me" characteristic and people have the tendency to save them and share them with others. Newspapers and newsletters provide information for the "skimmer." They allow readers to be more selective in their reading choices because they offer a wide variety of shorter items from which to choose. The growth of the newsletter has been partially attributed to the squeeze on readers' time. Very often newsletters are read while magazines and even newspapers wait for time that may never come.

On the other hand, printed pieces can take a long time in production, limiting the ability to communicate real news. Any printed material competes with a vast amount of other printed materials (commercial newspapers and magazines) and with radio and television. The fact that it is printed, and therefore appears permanent, makes management cautious about putting certain information "in concrete," which can make it difficult to obtain information and approvals.

The audiovisual media's biggest advantage is the ability to make an impact on audiences by reaching two senses, sight and sound. The ability to use sight, sound and *motion* can give immediate impact and leave long-lasting impressions on an audience. Audiovisuals have credibility among audiences that are accustomed to television.

Disadvantages include equipment and distribution problems that are more pronounced than are those with print. In addition, the information is "gone" once it is viewed, it cannot be reviewed easily.

Different audiovisual media also offer various advantages and disadvantages. For example, video can be produced much more quickly than film, and lighting requirements are somewhat less stringent. It also is very suitable for news-style programs. On the other hand, film still offers the highest quality and is better than video for large audience viewing on large screens.

Face-to-face communications are recognized as the most effective form of communication. They practically assure receipt of the message and usually result in immediate feedback. On the other hand, they reach smaller audiences and require more time and effort to implement, and to solve logistical problems.

Bulletin boards offer a means to get information out quickly (a news item can be typed, copied and mailed in hours) to a variety of locations. If properly placed and attractively done, bulletin boards can corral a quantity of "readers," but they cannot assure that the message will be received by all the audience.

Telephone information systems also provide a quick way to get news out, but they require the employee or member to take action (use the phone) to get the message.

Generally, most communicators use print as the basis of their communication programs, and audiovisuals, telephone, face-to-face programs or other media to complement the print work. The use of print and audiovisuals has been increasing in recent years, as has the use of more types of face-to-face programs. It's unlikely that any one medium will replace the others.

What Will It Cost?

Let's say you've done your homework. You have your objectives, you feel that you have a thorough knowledge of your audience or audiences, and you know what you want to communicate. You've analyzed the advantages and disadvantages of the various media. You have one more decision point before finalizing and beginning to execute your program—cost.

All the research, analysis and planning in the world is useless if the communication program or project doesn't have the resources needed to accomplish it. Sometimes you may be able to sell the program on its merit and obtain the budget you need; at others, you may have a set budget and must work within it.

What does it cost to produce a four-color magazine? A black and white news sheet? A video news program?

There are many variables to consider in answering any questions about what a specific medium will cost. With print, the frequency, quantity, size, paper, design, use of color and art, and means of distribution are key factors.

With audiovisuals, the length of a video production and whether it is produced in-house or with outside services, or the number of slide projectors and screens used in a sound and slide production, greatly affect the total cost.

Although it is extremely difficult to pinpoint the cost of using a specific medium without having the exact specifications, some generalizations can be made.

Print: Generally magazines are the most expensive to produce, followed by magapapers, newspapers, newsletters and news sheets. But a four-color magapaper could cost more than a two-color magazine.

Audiovisuals: Film is usually the most expensive audiovisual medium, followed by video, and sound and slide programs. But a 30-projector, five-screen slide program could cost more than a 15-minute video production. One big cost to consider with audiovisuals is hardware: cameras, playback equipment and the like. For example, if you need to communicate company-wide and have 100 locations, the cost of buying the playback equipment for viewing a video production could be prohibitive. Over a number of years, however, the investment may be worth it if your goal is immediate communication and you replace another medium not meeting this objective.

Cost-effectiveness is the key. Comparing costs of the various media is usually like comparing apples with oranges. Dollars spent should not necessarily be the yardstick by which to measure effective communication. It's better to spend $5,000 and achieve your goals than to spend $2,500 and accomplish nothing.

Summary

A knowledge of the media available—what each medium can do, which can get your message to the audience when, where and how you want it communicated and in the most cost-effective manner to achieve your goals and objectives—is prerequisite for the communicator who must match the media with the audience and message. It's not an easy assignment, but it's necessary to ensure the most effective communication program or project possible.

Yes, the business communicator has a much tougher and more challenging job than the "house organ editor" he or she succeeded—but few business communicators would trade places.

CAMILLE EMIG is associate director, Corporate Communications, Anheuser-Busch Companies, St. Louis, Missouri. She has served on the executive board of the International Association of Business Communicators.

Example: Atlantic Richfield

Atlantic Richfield Company's employee communication staff faced a new challenge when it reported for work January 2, 1979. The centralized Atlantic Richfield organization that had existed only a few days before was gone. In its place, with less than a month's notice, was a new organization, consisting of eight separate companies under the ARCO corporate umbrella.

The staff was aware that each of the eight companies would want to establish its own identity, and that each of the eight individuals now heading up these companies would have ideas about communication. It was one thing, after all, to be dealing with the vice president of the North American Producing Division; the staff would now be dealing with the president of ARCO Oil and Gas Company—the same individual, but perhaps a whole new outlook toward communication for his or her company.

The months that followed brought no drastic changes in employee communication's media efforts. *ArcoSpark*, distributed weekly to more than 70,000 employees and retirees throughout the world, continued. Other established publications continued. Field offices, staffed by employee communication personnel in Dallas, Denver and Philadelphia, continued to report directly to corporate headquarters in Los Angeles.

Atlantic Richfield's overall communication objectives did not change. Put simply, the company believes that informed employees who take pride in their company, their jobs, their fellow employees and themselves are better workers—and are better able to contribute to the profitability of the corporation.

Ongoing efforts to meet this objective have included reshaping a multifaceted communication program to respond to the specific needs of a changing organization.

The department uses *ArcoSpark* to emphasize company identities, through such subtle methods as boldfacing individual company names in the "Around the Country" news summary, and through consciously balancing coverage according to a *pro rata* share of total employee population. Readers of *min*, the management information newsletter, were surveyed and their comments and suggestions have helped make it an improved publication. Articles in *mgr*, a management journal, examine individual company units for the benefit of all the corporation's managers and supervisors.

Telephone information programs at numerous locations provide employees with an outlet for their opinions to be heard and their questions answered. Bulletin boards continue to be effective means of communication, and lunchtime forums and panel discussions, with occasional film and video highlights, promote personal face-to-face communication.

Atlantic Richfield's individual companies had some of their own communication needs too. Anaconda Industries, which resulted from the consolidation of several smaller units, needed a booklet to tell its employees about their new company. Several of the companies joined together to produce a booklet for MBA recruitment, with employee communication coordinating the project. Others were having difficulty in relocating employees to Los Angeles so a booklet, *Look at L.A.!*, was prepared.

The response continues. ARCO Coal Company now has a new employee information booklet, and a benefits summary for all Anaconda companies is off the press. Anaconda Copper Company's executives will be introduced to employees through a videotape and ARCO Chemical Company has a quarterly publication to keep employees informed about activities that are not appropriate for *ArcoSpark*.

Dave Orman
Manager, Employee Communication
Atlantic Richfield Company

◆ 9 ◆

Publications: What's in the Package

Joan Kampe and Lyn Christenson

In the 1980s, as more and more information is transmitted via computers, the value of publications to an organization needs to be reexamined. What information do people need and want to receive? What is the most appropriate medium for communicating? Have we, in fact, entered "the electronics age?" Do people still read, or have we become increasingly reliant on other forms of communication?

Despite heraldic achievements in video teleconferencing, cable television and a host of new technologies, publications continue to offer organizational communicators a very viable means for "getting the word out." Certain advantages are clear. Publications can be read according to the reader's schedule, not that of the meeting organizers or the video schedulers. Publications issued on regular schedules offer a broad format for comprehensive explanation and analysis. They also offer permanence and efficacy in delivering precise messages to large and often geographically dispersed audiences. Finally, there is both practicality and psychological comfort in having something you can hold onto, file or send to a friend.

Trends in Publications

During the past decade there was an obvious shift in organizational publications, away from the purely entertaining articles and toward those with more meaning and substance. Specifically, editors concerned with producing meaningful publications began to take a sharp look at content.

Editors who clung to the "safe" topics of the 1960s and earlier and who failed to accommodate to the tremendous changes going on around them found themselves decidely out of step with reader interests and needs. In short, editors who failed to recognize the very real human issues that concern their audiences—"Where is my organization going? What's my role and what does it all mean in the larger context of my life?"—found themselves out of touch with the real needs of their readers.

Enlightened editors, on the other hand, looked at the changes affecting organizations and saw them as opportunities to revamp their publications, making them more timely, honest and relevant and at the same time meeting the interests and preferences of their audiences. That is, in an effort to provide greater meaning to the events affecting the organization, it is essential to avoid the trap of becoming "too corporate" and insensitive to the human side of the organization.

Principal Kinds of Organizational Publications

Organizations use four main kinds of publications: newspapers, news-letters, magazines and magapapers. These vary in appearance, cost and complexity—and also objectives.

- *Newsletters.* Simplest, fastest and least complicated of all periodical forms, newsletters are produced by rank amateurs and seasoned professionals. Smaller and with fewer pages than a newspaper, the format of a newsletter is generally more flexible and the writing brief but not rigid. They are particularly appropriate for meeting information needs of smaller or specialized organizations and audiences.
- *Newspaper.* Somewhat more complex than newsletters, these often look much like city newspapers, carry hard (often late-breaking) news and features, and use illustrations sparsely. Quick to produce and economical, newspapers are often used for timely news to supplement less frequently issued magazines.
- *Magazines.* These generally contain carefully selected material targeted to a specific audience. Using a feature treatment, interpretive writing, and liberal inclusion of photos and art, they are generally produced less frequently than other publications—monthly, bimonthly or quarterly, as a rule.
- *Magapaper.* A hybrid of newspapers and magazines (also called *newsines*), magapapers combine the feature approach of a magazine with newspaper design. They are, in many ways, newspapers straddling the fence between news and information and feature and in-depth treatment.

According to a recent survey conducted by IABC, 31.5% of organizational

Figure 9.1. Audience needs determine frequency and format of a publication. Atlantic Richfield's *ArcoSpark* is a weekly tabloid reaching employees worldwide; Chase Manhattan Bank's *Chase News* is a monthly for staff at the bank and its subsidiaries.

publications are magazines, 12.5% are newspapers, 8.5% are magapapers and 39.5% are newsletters. The other 8% are hybrids of these formats.

Because they are fastest to produce, newspapers and newsletters are used to bring current news to organizational audiences. Because they are often the least expensive of the common kinds of publications, they can be used by virtually every organization, from the small company that relies on the newsletter as its sole publication to the large corporation that publishes newsletters and newspapers as local or regional supplements to widely distributed company publications. Magapapers frequently look much like newspapers but combine news coverage with magazine-style features. Thus, an editor who does not want to produce a magazine can still provide expanded coverage of important issues. Magazines vary from black-and-white to full color and from coverage of a small college to coverage of a corporation with operations around the world.

Whatever the format, organizational publications share one goal: to focus on key issues of the organization, interpreting and humanizing significant policies and activities and putting them into perspective for employees, members and others. Often, too, individuals are singled out for helping the organization achieve its objectives.

Determining the Publication's Contents: The Editor's Role

Once the purpose of the publication has been established, the next step in organizing the publication is to review the areas of emphasis. These could be the organization's business results, employee relations, cost control and the importance of individual initiative. Next, determine what standing columns or sections will be required. For example, if one of the publication's objectives is to provide recognition for employees with long service or members with consistent affiliation, it would be appropriate to include a section called "Anniversaries." Or, if another of the publication's objectives is to provide recognition for individual achievements, a section may be included on milestones within the organization, such as promotions, community achievement awards, speeches presented or patents earned.

If another of the publication's objectives is to explain business results, it may be appropriate to include a message from the chief executive officer. To produce such a column, the editor can interview the executive or the executive may write the copy. To make such a column credible in any organizational publication, the contents must reflect the genuine commitment and reactions of the executive. The column loses a tremendous amount of value if it is passed down the line to a junior staff person to prepare. After all, the purpose of such a column is to open up communication with the leader of the organization. If the leader fails to participate, the column is relatively meaningless.

Similar columns—medical advice, for example—in organizational publications elicit the greatest interest when they discuss topics that interest the readers, not simply the initiator of the column. The editor must consider every aspect of the editorial content, asking, "Of what interest is this to my readers?" Of course, organizational politics often dictate that certain topics be covered in a publication. In these cases it is probably preferable to meet with those in management who want a particular topic covered, then identify what it is they want to accomplish by examining the topic in the organization's publication. From there, look at other publications and seek creative ways to present material.

One way of assuring the relevance of your publication's contents to your readers is to conduct periodic readership surveys. From such surveys you can find out everything from who's reading your publication to what they think of its design. In addition, you can determine what segment of your audience you're not reaching and isolate problem areas in the publication.

But structuring the survey and handling the logistics involved are not simple matters: questions have to be prepared that elicit valuable responses, a sample of employees has to be chosen scientifically, an introductory note familiarizing recipients of the survey with its purpose must be written, and someone has to take care of the mailing.

When the completed surveys are returned, compilation of responses and interpretation of data begins. Responses must be organized and analyzed for their meanings: unorganized data is of little help to anyone. It's best to be prepared to do your homework when it comes to survey preparation, and many fine books are available. An excellent guide, "How to Conduct a Readership Survey," is available from Ragan Communications. Outside contractors can be used to structure and conduct your survey or to interpret your results.

Editors at McKesson Corporation's *Direction* magazine have adapted a survey orginally developed by Xerox Corporation. The survey is sent to 1,400 randomly selected employees after the publication of each issue. Questions include: "How often do you read *Direction*?" "How thoroughly do you read it?" "For whom do you feel *Direction* is written?" and "Do you like the appearance of the magazine?"

The survey also asks specific questions about articles that appeared in the previous issue of the magazine, and space is provided for any additional comments respondents might want to make. Questions about respondent demographics are asked in order to facilitate the breakout of data according to subgroups within the company.

Survey responses have shown that readers are interested in such topics as future company plans, benefits, company products and services, financial results and legislation affecting the business. They have also shown that fewer employees are interested now in such subjects as employee hobbies and service anniversaries. Such information helps the editors plan future issues that are relevant to employees.

Whatever the specific results of any readership survey, the information should not be used to *dictate* coverage in the magazine. It should *guide* coverage.

Localize the News

Inserts tailored to a region or local area are frequently useful in publications of large organizations. They can range in subject matter and appearance from a few paragraphs summarizing local news events to several pages cataloging annual benefit program changes. Inserts allow publications covering a large geographical area to be personalized for each region within that area. They also may be an economy measure, since the insert that combines photos and several kinds of news may make separate publications at each location unnecessary.

A multidivision company, for example, may produce a tabloid newspaper for employees at several locations. The other pages may contain information of interest company-wide, such as corporate news, benefits changes and employment opportunities. Perhaps several different divisions want to communicate with their employees about how an issue affects their unit of the business, or about news of interest to only a segment of the corporate-wide audience. In that case, a separate insert fills the bill. Special inserts also can treat benefits, business results and other topics requiring in-depth explanation.

Gathering the News

Once the issues affecting the organization have been clearly spelled out and objectives for the publication have been formalized, the next step is to create a system for gathering information. Say, for example, the following issues have been clearly identified as "most important" to a company: (1) business results, (2) employee relations, (3) social responsibility, (4) employee safety and health, (5) affirmative action, (6) energy conservation, (7) cost control and (8) individual initiative. Who are the newsmakers within the organization who can serve as your news sources?

Begin to keep abreast of business results by cultivating relationships with the senior decision makers. Meet with them on a regular basis to review their problems, priorities, concerns and exposures. Read the financial reports and planning documents compiled for senior management. Certainly, the more information you have access to, and the greater trust and rapport you are able to establish with your organization's decision makers, the greater the likelihood that your publication will accurately reflect the business climate.

In simplest terms, this means establishing "a beat." Who are the best sources of information? In a corporation, look to the executives who oversee the daily operations of each business unit. In organizations where getting an appointment with such a person is almost as difficult as buying a ticket to a sold-out athletic event, consider second-string news sources. Contact "the rising stars" who report to the busy executive. Consider similar opportunities in nonprofit organizations.

For information about employee relations, include people in the organization who are responsible for managing the area. For example, look to the personnel staff for assistance in reporting and interpreting issues related to labor relations, safety, affirmative action, employee benefits and wages and salaries. Certainly such contacts are a two-way street: you keep abreast of what's happening in your organization and the people responsible for implementing programs stand a substantially better chance of telling their story accurately in the organization's publications.

As your organization develops greater and greater awareness of social responsibility, look to the people charged with administering programs in community relations. Similarly, look for those who are conducting programs for cost reduction, energy conservation and other issues affecting your organization. Be as creative as possible as you draw up your lists of news sources.

Creating a Correspondents' Network

That's only half the story. Once you've identified your "beats" and those people who can keep you abreast of the major issues affecting your organization, how can you develop material that is warm, lively, human and responsive? For example, if you're interested in communicating about safety in your organization, how can you approach the topic in a manner that is meaningful and interesting to your readers? How can you find an employee or group of employees that will give you the personal angle on which to

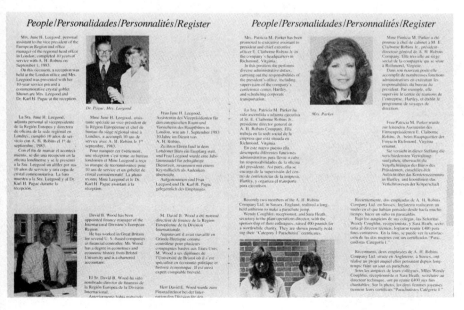

Figure 9.2. *Round Robins International* is a digest-size quarterly published in English, Spanish, French and German. It is distributed to employees of A. H. Robins, its subsidiaries, branches, distributors and other affiliates worldwide.

build an entire story? Many organizations have found the solution in developing a network of correspondents. Such a string of reporters allows the editor to emphasize the people in the organization and to focus on company issues in human terms. To pretend that the creation of a reporter network will solve the problems of "What's going on in our Memphis office?" or "Are there any employees with newsworthy interests in the Supply Department?" would be an exaggeration, but it is one more technique in the editorial bag of tricks to stimulate interest and involve readers in your publication. Clearly, this also is a two-way street: readers in far-flung locations receive recognition and the editor gets good story leads.

The mechanics of establishing a correspondents' network are simple and straightforward. At McKesson Corporation, a San Francisco-based corporation with operations in nearly 300 locations in the United States and overseas, the editorial staff of *Direction* magazine sought the assistance of the manager at each facility in selecting a correspondent. Using a form letter with a tear-off portion on which the manager was to indicate the name and work telephone number of the selected correspondent, the editorial staff outlined the desirable qualifications: someone with "a nose for news" and a sensitivity toward the interests of all employees, not just an immediate circle of friends. The letter served as a means of involving the manager and eliciting support for the correspondent's activities.

For editors whose publications are circulated at a single location, the selection process is somewhat simpler. Sometimes correspondents can be chosen by the editor, though it still makes good sense to involve a correspondent's supervisor in the selection process in order to keep him or her "in the loop."

A good cross-section of correspondents clearly increases the odds of producing a diversified list of story possibilities for a publication. For that reason, correspondents should be selected from among secretaries, plant workers, cafeteria workers, truck drivers, fork-lift operators and marketing managers, or their counterparts in other types of organizations. Be sure to find correspondents who reflect the socioeconomic mix that is today's business environment. Employees from all levels and backgrounds contribute to the success of an organization, and their viewpoints should be reflected in the company publication. The most successful organizational and company publications value input from all employees. But take care not to thrust the responsibility on someone who is already overburdened and who really lacks enthusiasm and interest for the assignment.

Once the correspondents have been selected, compile a set of clear instructions for them. One of the best ways to familiarize them with their role is to produce a brochure or handbook outlining their responsibilities. For *Direction* correspondents, for example, the editorial staff distributes a brochure that is divided into sections: *Let's Take it from the Top* (a description of the magazine that emphasizes the role of the correspondents),

Newsworthy Events to Watch for and Report, The Human Interest Angle of Feature Articles, What to Do with Your News or Feature Idea Once You've Found It, Why Accuracy in Reporting Counts, A Word About Round-up Stories, What Direction *Can't Use, Photographs that Enhance Your Story Idea, Where to Dig for News, A Word About Deadlines, What If Your Story Doesn't Run?* and *Now That You've Got It All Together.* Such a brochure should do two things: provide a summary of what you're trying to accomplish with the publication, and describe specific topics that are inappropriate. If correspondents are to write the articles, explain how it can be done. If they are to supply information, explain how that information will be used.

The *Direction Correspondents Notebook* includes a comment about the importance of timeliness in reporting events. "Story ideas with a time limit, unless they're received well in advance of the season, are not appropriate. For example, Christmas stories, no matter how heart-warming, would lose their appeal in the Spring issue. But if your group has a holiday tradition, such as organizing a Christmas food drive for the elderly, alert us at least two months in advance." Such a brochure can add prestige and professionalism to the role of the correspondent. In effect, you're saying to these people that you take their role seriously enough to prepare a special brochure.

To complement the *Direction Correspondents Notebook*, the editorial staff also created a *Direction Correspondents Newsletter* to solicit leads for specific upcoming feature stories in the magazine and to single out individual correspondents for recognition. For example, through the news-letter, correspondents have been alerted to find co-workers who use the corporation's tuition assistance program, people involved in their local communities, and those who participate in physical fitness projects.

It is critical to be specific. To ask correspondents, "Any news this month?" is fruitless. They require specific instructions because they're generally not communication professionals and are performing other functions in the organization. "Keep it simple" are probably the strongest bywords. Requests for suggestions about people to include in stories may occasionally result in very little response from correspondents. For example, instead of preparing a feature article on the health hazards associated with smoking, the editor of one publication asked correspondents whether there had been a "Stamp Out Smoking" campaign at their work facilities. Only one correspondent responded, but from that lead a story on the decision to prohibit smoking at a company warehouse was developed.

Editors who have difficulty eliciting meaningful story leads from correspondents should consider adding correspondents if it is a case of too many people being covered by too few reporters. At the same time, the editor may need to review the guidance, direction and feedback provided to the network of correspondents. Some organizations recognize their correspondents by listing them on the masthead of the publication. Company product samples, Christmas gifts and wall plaques that designate someone as a correspondent are appropriate thank-yous. Editors recommend using as much flourish as you can afford.

If you receive inappropriate material, acknowledge it by explaining to the correspondent why the material won't see print. Perhaps the item is of interest to a small, local audience. Return it with a suggestion to post it on an area bulletin board. If it is something of interest to one segment of your readership that is perhaps served by another publication, such as a local unit's newsletter, route the material to the alternate publication. But be sure to acknowledge the effort; unpaid, unrewarded volunteer correspondents won't persist without recognition.

By taking the initiative to seek out story leads from people in the organization and from a network of correspondents, the editor maintains sharper control of the contents of a publication. Instead of reacting to requests for "a story on energy conservation," for example, you can produce a warmer, livelier story about employees who are clever energy conservers. It's one way to avoid stories that are dull, boring and unread.

How Some Organizations Get the Word Out

The purpose of *JD Journal*, the worldwide employee magazine of John Deere & Company, is "to inform employees of the company's goals, policies, accomplishments, needs and concerns in an honest, readable manner. In so doing, employees and their families gain a sense of belonging to the same corporate family, that their good work does make a difference, and that they work for a good, responsible, successful employer that cares about their interest and is worthy of their efforts." Other goals of the *JD Journal* are "to create goodwill for the company among outside readers by conveying to them the kind of company John Deere is and how it's meeting its business, social and human responsibilities," and to "stimulate thought and dialog among employees and outside readers, broaden their interest and keep them abreast of current issues that affect them and John Deere."

How can publications professionals carry out their goals, and demonstrate to senior management that they can help solve the major problems of the organization? At Methodist Hospital in Brooklyn, the public affairs staff offers three steps for focusing management's attention on the role publications can play:

1. *Investigate.*   Determine what problems management sees as crucial and judge where communication skills can best be applied to do something about them. Trust and respect are gained by taking on the difficult challenges.

2. *Know the character of management.* Know its prejudices, its objectives, its interests.
3. *Identify the organization's opinion leaders.* Who can help? Who can hurt your efforts? Cultivate those who can help. Work to make believers of those who would prefer that you be an employee of some other organization, or not working at all.

Employee communication needs in hospitals and other medical institutions parallel those in other organizations. At Methodist Hospital, Public Affairs Director Bob Chandler uses *Today* as the principal communication vehicle for reaching 20,000 persons, including employees, the medical staff, and various community opinion leaders. Chandler selected the magapaper format for bimonthly *Today* because it emphasizes visual attractiveness and can include believable photos that motivate people to pick it up and read it. "A hospital is not like any other business," Chandler says. "The words and illustrations carried in hospital publications should believably portray the special relationship between people. The focus should not be on doctors, patients, CAT scanners, beds, policies or new programs. Publications that communicate should focus on what a nurse did for a patient, what the association administrator thinks the new Blue Cross reimbursement rate will do to operating costs. Publications should present reality. And editors should let them."

Reality, human relationships and the hospital's role in the community were all graphically portrayed by a front-page *Today* feature on a new expectant parents' handbook, "Life Begins at the Methodist Hospital." Opened with the touching photo of a mother holding her brand-new daughter (also the cover of the new brochure), the article described Methodist Hospital's obstetrics services. Other *Today* articles have spotlighted free medical care offered to people on limited incomes; staff members' impression of work with geriatric patients, and the care and planning that go into an important, but frequently criticized, part of hospital stays—the meals.

Chandler says it is important to keep in mind that employee publications often do double duty with other audiences. "The employee publications may be more folksy than other publications, but should not be so folksy as to be wholly irrelevant to other publics." Many other persons see employee publications, he points out, and "by generalizing publications a bit, making certain sections relevant for more than one audience, the hospital can increase contact or exposure to its various publics."

At Exxon USA, the public affairs staff meets with management to identify the major issues affecting the organization. They set communication goals that are tied to the issues and then plan story possibilities to meet these goals. The editors of *Profile*, the magazine for Exxon employees and retirees, prepare editorial content to reflect those issues and concerns.

Although publications share a common purpose, the best means for achieving an organization's goals can differ from one another. In selecting the best publication format, Anheuser-Busch in St. Louis elected to change *Focus on St. Louis* from a monthly two-color, 12-page magazine to a biweekly newsletter. Editor Irene Hannon says one of her most important tasks is to provide St. Louis plant employees with timely information on company events. "A magazine just did not seem the right way to accomplish these goals," she recalls. "The magazine format lends itself more toward features, and we wanted to stress news—timely information."

Focus, now an eight-page, two-color newsletter, has a shorter production schedule and a format that allows for last-minute changes. Hannon's objectives encompass the principal areas of importance in structuring an organizational publications program:

1. Keep St. Louis employees informed about Company news, activities and policies as they relate to the St. Louis plant.
2. Build a sense of teamwork by creating an awareness on the part of employees that whether they are hourly or salaried, men or women, they share common interests and problems.
3. Provide information on departments and specific jobs to promote an understanding of every individual's importance as part of the team.
4. Humanize the organization by featuring "people" stories, stressing the individuals within the various groups that comprise the company.
5. Recognize employees for outstanding accomplishments on and off the job.
6. Build employee pride in the company and increase enthusiasm by always stressing quality and by making each employee feel that he or she is an important part of the company.

Articles in *Focus* address these objectives. In a feature on the Anheuser-Busch St. Louis Chip Cellars, where beer is aged and carbonated, *Focus* stressed the importance of teamwork. The process involves 250 people at seven different areas at the same complex, who are responsible for aging beer to consistent quality standards. A closing quote by the general foreman sums up the theme: "Without the contributions of all the employees, we couldn't get the job done. It is a team effort all the way."

A story about Anheuser-Busch merchandising personnel described the long development cycle for the point-of-sale (POS) promotional signs and print pieces most employees take for granted as part of grocery store and restaurant decor. Reading about the tremendous complexity in developing POS materials that conform to frequently conflicting state laws, for example, informs St. Louis employees about their company. It also can help make them proud to be associated with other people who successfully perform complex tasks for the company.

ArcoSpark is a major part of Atlantic Richfield's program to bring company news to more than 70,000 employees and retirees throughout the world. The weekly paper replaced a quarterly magazine and various divisional publications in 1973, because, "in an age of quick communication," the company wanted to communicate with its people "in a timely, topical and credible manner." Because issues affecting companies in energy-related fields receive frequent coverage in the mass print and broadcast media, Atlantic Richfield stresses the importance of informing employees about the company's stand on key topics. This intention, along with other generally recognized communication objectives, is cited in the company's statement of purpose for its internal print communications program: "It continues to be Atlantic Richfield's belief that informed employees are better workers, more loyal spokesmen for their employers in their communities, happier human beings, and better able to contribute to the profitability of the corporation." This statement is supplemented by specific program objectives that include the importance of recognizing employees' informational needs and contributions, and the need to present company communications creatively and attractively.

ArcoSpark articles cover news and issues in the straightforward, matter-of-fact style that epitomizes the maturation of the company publication from its origin as a "house organ" emphasizing chit-chat. An Arco employee was murdered and thousands of dollars were stolen in a California service station holdup. *ArcoSpark* published an article about the incident to show the need for the company's national crime deterent program, initiated in 1978. The consolidation of several company operations in a new city and the attendant relocation problems are often facts of corporate life. This does not make them any easier for the employees involved, however, and a company can do a great deal to ease the transition. A company division's research and development operations' consolidation was the subject of an *ArcoSpark* feature that emphasized company assistance offered to make the relocation less painful. Group presentations, individual counseling and a weekend visiting the new research center site helped some who were in a quandary about accepting a transfer decide to make the move.

Such articles are included in the *ArcoSpark* to show that the company recognizes the importance of meeting people's needs. Employees today are demanding this sort of recognition from their employers, and programs such as Arco's relocation program show that organizations can make the changes demanded by business conditions in ways that minimize the disruptions to employees and their families.

Stanford University's Alumni Association makes excellent use of the magazine format. Magazines produced by organizations vary greatly in size and cost, but the format is one of the most universally used, either as the single organizational publication or as part of a large publications program.

Della van Heyst, editor of *The Stanford Magazine*, says that it is not intended to be timely (a Stanford newspaper has that objective) but strives to capture the intellectual excitement of an educational institution, portray student life and focus on the visual appeal of the campus. The semiannual magazine combines full-color and black-and-white spreads and averages 80 pages an issue. It is printed on heavy stock that offers good photo reproduction and is durable. "Our surveys show 35% of our readers have saved all the issues since 1973," van Heyst says. "The money and effort that go into the magazine's design, photography, writing and production are all dictated by our principal goal—to project a quality image and capture the essence of our institution: excellence."

The Stanford Magazine's introductory issue in 1973 featured an interview with Ralph Heintz, inventor of the nonpolluting Heintz Straticharge engine and holder of more than 200 patents. Heintz, a 1920 Stanford graduate, has given the engine's patents to the university, which may bring Stanford several million dollars. In another issue, a Stanford art historian related the fascinating story of the planning and construction of the original university buildings in the late nineteenth century by Governor and Mrs. Leland Stanford, who founded the school as a memorial to their son.

The editor of any publication sets the pace on content and on writing and editing skills. The newcomer in the editorial office has the same responsibilities in this regard as the veteran. He or she must develop copy that is appropriate to the organization, the audience or audiences and the publication, and also must have the skill to combine words and illustrations meaningfully. Some persons learn and polish these skills in schools; others hone their abilities on the job. In either case, genuine interest in good writing and editing is vital and never-ending. Study good publications and compare your work with them. Keep aware of the trends in writing and editing.

JOAN KAMPE is director of editorial services at McKesson Corporation, a multidivision corporation based in San Francisco, California.

LYN CHRISTENSON is at Burson-Marstella in Santa Clara, California.

Example: *Coal News* in Great Britain

Coal News is a tabloid family newspaper sold for 5 pence every month to 250,000 mine workers and other employees in Britain's coal industry. There is a three-way split of the sales money among the publishers, the salesman at each workplace and a local good cause chosen by the miners. By changing 6 of the 16 pages in each issue, the paper tells readers what is happening down their own colliery and in their own community.

Coal News is published by the boss, the National Coal Board, but it is not a boss's paper. Of course it reports what the NCB is saying and doing, but it also presents the views of miners and their families and reactions of the trade unions.

The industry at work fills half the paper's editorial content. Human-interest topics fill the other half: sport, letters, cartoons (drawn by mining artists) and a monthly competition page—such as the Coal Queen of Britain contest, which the newspaper promotes; miners who work for charity, become mayors, weigh 17 stone (238 pounds), or win £300,000 on the football pools; and so on. A quarter of the space is taken by advertisements, which help communication and offset running costs. There has always been a page-one leader comment (editorial) speaking up for the coal industry and mining people.

One of the real tests of credible communication in any organization comes when the editor contacts the industrial relations manager at a crunch point in the yearly wage negotiations and says, "We're going to press tomorrow—let's report the latest negotiations." Does the chief negotiator cry out: "Get lost!" or does he say, "Our employees need to know what is going on, so let's tell them." Certainly union leaders aren't reluctant to give their views.

Coal News fully reports industrial relations topics and the readers expect it. An example is the 1979–1980 miners' wage negotiations. Coalfield editions started reporting early in the year what local miners' leaders were expecting to get. The July issue covered the National Union of Mineworkers conference debate under the headline: "Call for £140 on Face, £80 on Surface." The October front page gave details of the union's five-point claim, with the NCB's reply presented the following month.

When the union decided to hold a coalfield ballot on the negotiated settlement, the *Coal News* team worked around the clock to bring out an immediate four-page special issue, which was given away to everyone in the industry. It included a detailed table of pay raises for all grades so that everyone knew what he would get. The Coal Board chairman and the miners' president were, of course, quoted. In December, the ballot result was reported on the front page—a majority vote for the offer and against industrial action. The next month, the payout arrangements were explained.

Safety in the mines is another priority topic, and *Coal News* reported the industry's special year-long campaign called "Think Safety." The four major accident causes—haulage and transport, surface locations, machinery, and rock falls underground—were examined in detail. Miners and managers were interviewed so that action could be taken to prevent "carbon copies" of accidents recurring.

Many other events were being reported: an agreement with the power station board to use two-thirds of total coal output; action to find new markets for coking coal lost by the steel industry slump; opening new mines and closing exhausted ones; a production drive to get the most from sophisticated coalface machines; a family Mining Festival at Blackpool resort for 25,000 people (another *Coal News* promotion); the courageous story of little Fiona Bell, once disabled but determined to skip and dance her way back to a normal life....

Let's not dodge the $64,000 question—how to assess the results of another year of communicating. There is no simple answer. The paper is bought by two of every three miners, just about saturation point in this family industry where father and son often work at the same mine. They wouldn't buy the paper if they didn't like it. Selling the paper helps keep the editorial team on its toes and ensures that it remains a lively tabloid. Readers write letters, which are printed, and talk to our writers, who report their views. There is no other effective way of keeping in regular contact with employers throughout the country on such a wide range of issues.

Norman Woodhouse
Managing Editor of *Coal News*
National Coal Board

· 10 ·

Publications: Putting the Package Together

William E. Korbus

Organizational communication usually deals with one or more of four basic publication forms: newsletter, newspaper, magapaper and magazine. Your organization's particular needs may dictate which form to use. If, for example, you have many short articles, the newsletter form is probably most appropriate. If you have both short and feature-length articles, which can be supplemented with visual material, you may find the newspaper or magapaper more useful. Magazines offer the most flexibility because they provide an opportunity to use a number of short pieces, with or without images, or long feature-length material.

This discussion is primarily from the viewpoint of magazine design because magazine design can be adapted to other media. In other words, if you can design a magazine, you can design the others by making some modifications. All the principles that follow apply to all forms of design—posters, direct mail pieces, newsletters, tabloids, books and so forth. The same holds true for the layout principles: the example may be magazine, but it could easily be newsletter or tabloid.

Format

One of the first decisions to make in the design of a publication is what format to use. This includes number of columns per page, horizontal and

145

vertical grid patterns, type style for body copy, and headlines and column form (justified or ragged).

The number of columns per page has a great deal to do with how the publication is perceived. A two-column format has a symmetrical, formal look (Fig. 10.1) that is well suited to an institution concerned about a stable image, such as a hospital, a church, or an educational, insurance or financial institution. A three-column format allows for a more asymmetrical or informal treatment (Fig. 10.2). This does not preclude the possibility of a bank using a three-column format and still giving a stable, secure look. A three-column format can be balanced symmetrically.

A three- or four-column format allows greater design flexibility than a two-column format. Multicolumn formats (Fig. 10.3) allow a choice between symmetrical and asymmetrical design and also go together more quickly and easily than a two-column because the choices are greater. Images can be cropped to one column and have a vertical appearance; they can be cropped to three columns and have a horizontal feeling; a square configuration can be achieved that appears neutral on the page. In other words, when creating a modular system—the modules being words, images, headlines, negative space—there are many choices, which allow for a varied layout.

The communicator has to choose an appropriate column structure. Will the columns be justified (even), projecting a sense of order and formality?

Figure 10.1. The illustration extends from left to right margin jumping the gutter, while the headline and body copy create a base for the layout. *Design by William Korbus.*

Figure 10.2. Balancing the body on a solid base of photographs, but leaving the left-hand column virtually blank, creates a dynamism in this layout. *Design by Judith Martens.*

Or will they be flush left/ragged right, projecting an informal quality, eliminating word breaks and allowing additional white space to make its way into the layout?

The variables just examined are not all the possibilities needing attention. You may want to use rules between columns, box entire pages containing feature material, or use "mood" headlines.

The next decision to be made is whether or not to use a grid pattern to maintain a standardized design. Somewhat of a grid is established by the column structure. For example, the page will have a two-, three-, or four-column structure that divides the area into vertical modules. If those vertical modules are then divided top to bottom at regular intervals, a complete grid is formed. All images can begin 1 inch from the top of the page, headlines can appear 2 inches from the top, and no body copy will be any higher than 3 inches from the top. These 1-inch intervals can extend to the bottom of the column and be used for cropping photos, subheads, and the like. Alan Hurlburt's *The Grid* offers an extensive examination of this particular design technique. I've been content with using only the column structure, and in some cases a specified "sink" at the top of the page, but not extending the restraints further into a vertical as well as horizontal grid pattern.

Figure 10.3. This two-page spread from a folder demonstrates the use of a six-column (the three photos in the left-hand column are each 6 picas wide with 1 pica separations), a four-column (all the columns on the right-hand page are 9½ picas wide with a 1-pica alley) and a two-column format (left-hand column is 20 picas wide) all within two pages. In spite of the variations, the design is very exciting, and solid because of its underlying structure. *Design by Dick Derhodge.*

While you may be thinking that this kind of rigid structure would cause pages to be monotonous and uninteresting, you actually will have created a sound skeleton on which to arrange the design elements of type and/or image. Instead of monotony, there is a great deal of order and an opportunity to carry the reader systematically through the material.

Just as a column structure projects a sense of dignity or informality, a similar image comes about through the type chosen for body copy. A sans-serif typeface projects an image of contemporary, no-nonsense efficiency. A serif typeface gives the impression of a traditional, conservative, formal organization. Square-serif typefaces, depending on their weight, can have the attributes of either sans-serif or serif typefaces; they tend more toward sans serif, however.

The typeface you use for the text (or "body") should be easy to read. Don't use a script or italic as the dominant style for body copy because the legibility is low compared to the traditional Roman posture. Italics are better used for captions or cutlines, in a size slightly smaller than that of the

Figure 10.4. Two one-page flyers that use the three-column format in interesting ways. Note the partial type columns and the way the Woodhouse photo extends out of the center column to fill the negative space in column one. Also note the flush left/ragged right structure that emphasizes the left-hand, vertical edge of each column. *Designs by John Grant.*

body copy. Italics are preferable to boldface because italics call less attention to themselves and detract less from the important elements on the page. Reverse type, which prints white letters on black or a color, is difficult to read and should be used sparingly.

Similar considerations should be given to the typeface you use for headlines. Don't be afraid to mix a sans-serif head with a serif body, or vice versa. The style of your publication can contain all serif heads and sans-serif body copy and cause no style or legibility problems.

Design Principles

The basic design principles are balance, contrast, harmony, proportion, theme and movement. Movement can be further divided into rhythmic or direct movement.

Balance is either symmetrical (formal) or asymmetrical (informal). People's faces, for example, are symmetrically balanced on an axis passing vertically from the chin through the center of the nose to the top of the head. On a layout, the left and right sides of a page can be balanced in much the same way, by placing elements of equal size, weight, tone or texture equidistant from the center of the design (Fig. 10.5). The design also can be

Figure 10.5. A vertical axis through the center of the middle column would divide the layout into symmetrical left- and right-hand parts. *Design by Judith Martens.*

Figure 10.6. The large, heavy image in the lower left corner is balanced by the headline extending across the layout and the unequal columns of body copy. *Design by William Korbus.*

balanced top to bottom along a horizontal axis through the center of the layout and thus be symmetrical both horizontally and vertically.

An asymmetrical layout is also balanced, but in an uneven way (Fig. 10.6). Almost everyone has played on a teeter-totter at one time or another and realized that if the person on one end weighs less than the person on the other end, the heavier person will have to sit closer to the center to be balanced on the teeter-totter. The same is true in doing an asymmetrical layout; that is, elements of a "heavier" nature (larger, colored, irregularly shaped) should be placed closer to the balance point than elements that are "lighter" (smaller, monochromatic, regularly shaped).

Contrast may be achieved with one colored element versus a series of monochromatic elements (Fig. 10.7). Contrast may also result from a layout involving large shapes versus a single smaller shape. Or contrast may result from a textured element played against a series of smooth elements. Whatever the case, contrast is the spice that adds interest to a layout.

While contrast promotes sparkle on the page, *harmony* gives the layout a feeling of unity. Contrast may be evidenced by variations in type sizes; keeping all sizes in the same type family produces harmony. This harmony gives a cohesive quality to the layout (Fig. 10.8).

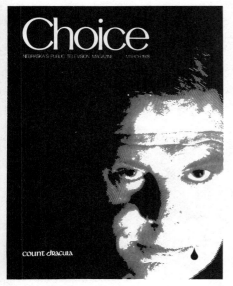

Figure 10.7. The cover is black and white except for the single drop of red blood in the lower right corner. *Design by William Korbus.*

Figure 10.8. Harmony exists between the illustration and the headline type because both have the same stippled style and are shadowed on the left. *Design by William Korbus.*

Proportion exists in design as an external dimension (the vertical proportion of a single page or the horizontal proportion of a two-page spread), as well as between elements in the layout, such as body copy to image area, or headline to body copy (Fig. 10.9). For example, an 8 × 10 page has a proportion of 4:5 in external dimension. On that page, a photograph covering half the area with body copy covering the remainder would be a 1:1 proportion. Proportions that are easily identified, such as 1:1 square, or other equally balanced relationships, are not very interesting. Proportions such as 1:3, 2:3 or 3:5 increase the interest level because there are relationships that are not easily identified by the eye. By using proportions that are a bit unusual, the communicator can add attractiveness to the material.

Theme is still another design element (Fig. 10.10). For an article on dance, the photographs might be of the stage, of dancers or of dance preparation. In the same way, the headline type style should attempt to express the fluid, graceful quality of the dance. A script or novelty typeface would be a good choice. In the layout, the images and type should reflect the "dance" theme, drawing the entire design into a cohesive whole.

Movement exists in one of two ways. Movement may be rhythmic,

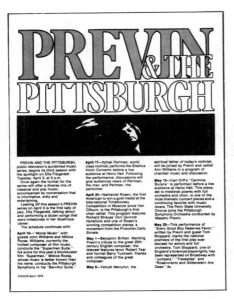

Figure 10.9. The 1:1 ratio of headline and image to text is a sample of an equal proportion of art to type. The headline is included as art because of its tonal, decorative qualities. *Design by Doug Stanley.*

Figure 10.10. Since the article is about dance, it is appropriate to use a "romantic" type style and treatment along with an illustration-like photo conversion to capture this theme. *Design by Martin Almanza.*

developed through a series of similar units moving, evolving and growing into a particular direction: a line of type, a series of photos or another repetitive element carrying the eye in a prescribed direction (Fig. 10.11). Or movement may take on a more direct quality: an arrow pointing or a photo in which movement points in a direction to carry the viewer (Fig. 10.12). All these design elements are variables used to carry the reader through the layout, through the story, and through the publication in a manner that has been carefully determined.

Layout

The basic layout principles are grouping, gridding and alignment. Grouping is the technique of keeping all elements closely associated in the layout. The designer does not allow one element to become fragmented and float off irrationally in the design. If you use good grouping techniques, you will have the sense that the layout is growing from the center, much as a Fourth

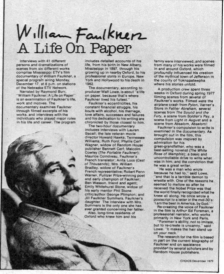

Figure 10.11. The animated staccato of the photos in column three demonstrates rhythmic movement. *Design by William Korbus.*

Figure 10.12. The silhouette half-tone of Faulkner facing and looking right from the first column "directs" the reader into the article. *Design by Martin Almanza.*

of July skyrocket explodes in the sky or a flower unfolds from the center outward.

When using the gridding principle, think of the page as being divided into squares or rectangles of a specific length and width, like building blocks. These blocks or modules are then filled by various elements (e.g., photographs, illustrations, headlines and body type). The columns of type, for instance, might be one module wide and a number of modules deep; a photograph might extend across two or three columns or modules and be any number of modules deep.

The alignment principle stresses the need to have one design module align with another so that the entire layout will relate through a series of imaginary vertical and horizontal axes. The headline may be aligned with the top of the body copy, body copy with a photograph, and so on, weaving the entire layout into a single unit (Fig. 10.13).

"White space," or negative space, contains no information elements, such as type, photography, illustration or copy. It is blank. For the new designer, it should be confined to the margin or along the outer edge where it will not become "trapped white space." White space trapped within the layout calls attention to itself, distracts the reader, and detracts from the message elements being presented to the audience.

Figure 10.13. Three different newsletters present different faces for their respective audiences. The nameplates have strong, simple identities, and the use of images (either photos or illustrations, different sizes, with and without type surprinted or reversed, scale changes within image frame, borders and no borders) helps reinforce this individuality. The body type varies from Roman to Egyptian, justified or flush left/ragged right, 9/10 to 10/11, 13½ pica columns with rules to 14-pica columns without rules. In these examples, the articles are rectangular just like building blocks, and create an organized structural appearance—much more than do the Ls, dog-legs and other nonrectangular shapes sometimes seen in newsletters. These publications come from the same design department. Within each newsletter's diversity there is the repeated use of the TVO logo and three-column format, giving the series cohesiveness and identifying it with its parent organization. It is very nicely coordinated material. *Designs by Danny Leung, Maxine Cowan, Judith Hancock.*

Typography

Typography is one of the elements communicators may manipulate according to the design and layout principles. Headline typography in particular allows you to explore a number of design and layout possibilities. You can use headline type as art, as in "Upstairs Downstairs Moves to the Roaring 20's" (Fig. 10.15) and "Stories Without Words" (Fig. 10.10), or you can use headline type in a more formal arrangement: centered, from left to right, and creating a central vertical axis that focuses the reader on that particular layout (Fig. 10.16). You might arrange the headline flush left or flush right in order to get a better grouping arrangement in the layout (Fig. 10.17), or

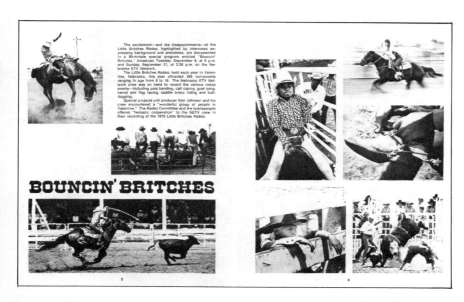

Figure 10.15. The zero is a frame for part of the headline. *Design by Mike Buettner.*

Figure 10.16. The alphabetical motif stretches across the entire page and the headline is centered to provide an axis between the two columns. *Design by Judith Martens.*

Figure 10.17. This flush-left headline aligns with the flush-left introduction and text. *Design by Martin Almanza.*

choose a more random headline style that gives an asymmetrical or informal feeling to the page (Fig. 10.18).

A headline should conform to the same restraints used for any other design element. The headline should stay within a particular margin and should be aligned and grouped so that it adds a cohesive quality to the layout. In Figure 10.18, the second line is aligned, set flush left, with the left side of the first line. The third, fourth and fifth lines are set flush right to the photograph and aligned with the top of the photo. The headline alone would have a random, unorganized quality. Combined with the photo, subhead and caption, it is an integral part of an interrelated group of design elements. All the individual units form a cohesive whole because of grouping and alignment principles.

Another decision relating to headline style is whether to use the same type family, size and weight throughout the magazine, creating a more conservative, harmonious style. An alternative is to attempt a "mood" headline system for each article, lending a more dramatic quality to the publication. If the first article in a banking publication features car financing, the designer might choose a sans-serif italic typeface that projects a feeling of movement, combining it with a car image that is moving off the

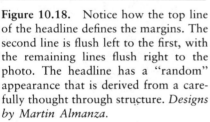

Figure 10.18. Notice how the top line of the headline defines the margins. The second line is flush left to the first, with the remaining lines flush right to the photo. The headline has a "random" appearance that is derived from a carefully thought through structure. *Designs by Martin Almanza.*

Figure 10.19. The silhouette halftone provides vitality to a page that would be less dynamic had a square-cut halftone been used. *Design by Tim Timken.*

page. On the other hand, for an article on stock and bond investment, the designer may feel more comfortable using a typeface that promotes a sense of tradition, formality and sturdiness. Either approach is acceptable, but decide on a single approach for that entire issue. Don't vacillate between mood and constant styles within the same publication.

Equally important is the type family selected. Roman type styles, whether old-style, transitional or modern, have dignified, traditional, conservative qualities. A sans-serif, square-serif Egyptian or modified serif such as Optima or Serif Gothic would be more appropriate in an informal contemporary publication. The size of the type used and the amount of "leading" (space) between lines is also a consideration. In general, use one or two points of leading when using 9-, 10-, 11-, 12-point type.

Before deciding on body copy, take the time to discuss with your typographer or printer the type styles available. Have several samples set in different faces and line widths, using varying amounts of leading, to see how comfortable the type is for the reader, how well it fits the mood and projected image of the publication, and the texture it creates on the page.

Visual Images

Many communicators whose primary function is writing do not realize the amount of communication that can take place through the use of good photos and illustrations. Just as words are symbols conveying ideas, visual images also communicate. In some situations these images communicate more effectively than words.

Images can be used to carry information to either support or supplement an article. Either use is appropriate, and the designer should recognize how the image is being used when making the choice for the layout. A photo or illustration also may be used purely for its attention-getting value, or to elicit a predetermined response.

When choosing photographs for a layout, look for photojournalistic qualities—strong photos that contribute to the article yet could stand by themselves. Captions can and should be brief. Do not use bad photographs just because they are available and do not use beautiful photographs if they are inappropriate to what is being communicated. Be discriminating in choosing photographs for a layout so the photos can do the job they are intended to do: carry supporting information or supplementary material or attract attention.

When using photographs, be aware that there are two kinds of scale or proportion: internal and external. The external size of a series of photographs may be identical, while the internal scale may vary greatly from close-ups to medium shots to panoramas. The traditional manner of dealing with photographs is through an external scale hierarchy using the most important photo as the largest with secondary photos slightly smaller and tertiary photos smaller still. A hierarchy also can be created by varying the internal scale even though the external scale of the photos is similar.

The use of color in a photo is another consideration. Full-color, duotone and tint block are three of the alternatives available. Full-color photos printed as process-color are as close to representing reality in print as we can approximate. A duotone results from adding a second color to a black-and-white photo. Two halftones are required. Printing a duotone of black and brown gives a sepia tone, which can lend a historic feel to the image. A tint block is often used as an accent in a black-and-white photo. It may color the sky or the primary element or act as a background to the primary element, thus focusing the reader's attention on the important aspects of the photo.

Photographs can be edited in a number of ways. The most common method is through cropping and sizing to fit a particular layout, eliminating extraneous material by designating only a portion of the photo to be reproduced. Editing can also be done through the caption, using words to focus on the important element in the picture. Various photomechanical means might also be used to direct attention to the important items in a photograph, such as converting the original photograph into a silhouette halftone (Fig. 10.19) or vignetting the important content. Photographs may be altered before halftones are made by retouching and airbrushing them. These techniques require skilled professionals; if retouching or airbrushing is necessary, go to a specialist.

Particularly useful reproduction methods are the use of photo-conversion screens when making film negatives or the use of positive photostats for print (Fig. 10.20). Photographs used in these ways are viable alternatives to illustrations. Most editors rely on photo halftones and often overlook the dramatic possibilities of silhouette halftones or partial silhouettes to focus on the important aspect of the photo. Using a photo conversion in the form of a line shot (Fig. 10.21), straight-line, wavy-line or "bullseye" screen to attract the reader is still another method. Vignettes, mortices and geometric shapes are other visual alternatives when using photos. Posterized photographs (Fig. 10.22) are achieved by varying the exposure and screens when making a photo negative. These options are all frequently overlooked, so communicators lose the advantage of exciting visual possibilities in their designs.

Type can be either printed over (surprinted, Fig. 10.23) or reversed out of a photo (Fig. 10.24). This combining of elements—type with photography—can simplify a layout and make it more attractive. Use these tech-

Figure 10.20. This mezzotint simplifies the images and drops out the background to provide an area for dramatic presentation of body copy. *Design by Martin Almanza.*

Figure 10.21. High contrast line conversions present a recognizable abstraction of reality. *Design by Laura Hart.*

Figure 10.22. Posterizations are a relatively simple, inexpensive means of presenting continuous tone material with greater impact. *Designs by Judith Martens.*

Figure 10.23. Surprinting type on a photo allows for combining elements and thus simplifying the layout. *Design by Mike Buettner.*

Figure 10.24. A reverse head integrates type and image for quick identification. *Design by Mike Buettner.*

niques in dealing with the image portion of the publication to create an exciting contrast of visual elements that readers will find attractive (Fig. 10.25).

Photos alone can be used as a basis for illustration (Fig. 10.26). A photo can be placed on a light table and a piece of layout paper, tracing paper, or paper towel laid over it. Use the photo as the primary image source and trace the image to create an illustration.

Illustration is an area often neglected by the organizational communicator when an illustrator is not on the staff or otherwise easily available. This is unfortunate because a great many sources of illustration are available. Sometimes hiring a nationally recognized professional is the best choice for dealing with a difficult illustration problem. A professional illustrator can be located through an agent or representative in any of the major markets in the country. Call an agent in New York, Los Angeles or any large city and ask for a portfolio of samples of different illustrators' works. After you have chosen the illustrator whose style seems most appropriate for your publication, establish criteria for the specific kind of work needed. Research material may be sent to the illustrator to help complete the assignment. The cost will depend on the complexity of the illustration and the time involved to produce it.

Figure 10.25. By combining the textures of silhouette halftones, copyright-free illustration, square-cut halftones and line conversions, an interesting and energetic layout is achieved with copyright-free illustrations. *Design by Martin Almanza.*

Figure 10.26. This wax pencil illustration was done by using tracing paper over a photograph on a lightboard. *Design by William Korbus.*

Perhaps the work of a local illustrator in a local publication or advertisement has attracted your attention. Contact the person directly and find out about availability, cost and time requirements for particular illustration needs. A great deal of talent exists in the educational institutions in our cities. It's not difficult to contact a school art department and ask to see the work of a promising student or instructor. It's an opportunity for you to obtain good illustrations and give little-known illustrators the chance to be published and earn a few dollars.

Be wary of the person within the office who has "always wanted to draw." Allowing this person an opportunity to submit material for publication may prove fruitful. If the material is of poor quality, however, it can be an unpleasant experience for both the would-be illustrator and you. This situation is a problem more often than not.

Clip-art is another source of illustration material. Many printers subscribe to clip-art services so they can offer these illustration options to their clients. Most clip-art is not useful for organizational publications, but a bit of it may be appropriate. A good-quality illustration from a clip-art service can be obtained for very few dollars.

Figure 10.27. Copyright-free illustrations were used for the figures in this award-winning cover. The inset photo of the house was an etch-tone conversion to match the style of the rest of the design. *Design by Martin Almanza.*

Most communicators do not realize that copyright-free illustrations are available (Fig. 10.27). A number of books have been published containing illustrations that are available for public use without any fee. Dover publications has *1800 Woodcuts by Thomas Bewick and His School, Graphic Trade Symbols by German Designers* and *Art Deco Designs and Motifs*. Morgan and Morgan has other copyright-free publications, such as *James Connor's Sons and Electrotype Specimens* (1888). A&W publishes *The Illustrator's Handbook*. The copyright-free images can be used individually or combined in montages to create interesting results.

Paper and Ink

Papers most likely to be of interest to business and organizational communicators are bond, book and cover, which all come in a number of sizes, weights and costs. In addition to quality, paper is priced by the pound, so the weight of the paper selected is very important in budgeting a project.

Find a reputable paper company, make an appointment with one of the sales representatives, and discuss any problems or questions you have. Paper salespeople know the current costs and availability, the companies that have the kind of stock you need, and the alternative stocks that may be better to use. A good salesperson can become a valuable asset to you by anticipating the kinds of paper that might be interesting for future use. Printers can also be helpful when you are selecting paper.

Color stock, or paper, can be useful and attractive if used properly. Look at the publications of competitors and think about the possibility of choosing a color stock that will make your publication stand out from the rest. This is the real reason for choosing color—to attract your audience. Also keep in mind that color stock used in conjunction with colored ink still must be effective, attractive and have contrasts so the message will be well displayed. If the stock color is close to the ink color, the effect will be very subtle. If delicacy is not what you want, colors too closely matched may make the material appear drab, unappealing and weak.

The communicator should be aware of the special ink choices that are available. The Pantone Matching System (PMS), a must in specifying ink colors, is available through all printers. A good investment for the organizational communicator is to have a PMS ink-sample chart, with inks printed on both dull and glossy-finish stock.

Two inks with special characteristics are metallic inks and opaque inks. When used properly, metallic inks are attractive and rich and add a great deal of "flash" to printed materials. Opaque inks are very effective on dark stock, or overprinted with halftones to give unusual effects. Consider using metallic and/or opaque inks for their eye-catching qualities.

Resources: Magazines and Annuals

A number of design periodicals can help the communicator stay abreast of current design trends and established and promising designers. Their use also can strengthen your ability to recognize good design, illustration and photography.

- *American Photographer* deals with photography and photographers. It does not focus on the latest in equipment, darkroom techniques or trick photography, as do many other photo magazines. It publishes sound, straightforward reporting of the photography field.
- *Art Direction* magazine has a very strong New York influence and regularly contains columns dealing with ethical questions regarding design/client relationships; news regarding designer moves and promotions, and articles on trends in art direction, design and illustrations.
- *Communication Arts* (CA) monitors trends in publication design, packaging, layout, illustration, photography—almost any facet of visual communication done in the world today—with an emphasis on American design. It contains a great deal of color material, does profiles on influential designers, covers design trends both past and present, and once a year publishes the *Art Annual* of photography and illustration. At the end of each year a communication annual is compiled, examining television, radio, books, magazines, letterheads, posters and advertisments.
- *Folio*, "the magazine for magazine management," is useful in dealing with areas such as budgeting, circulation, sales and production features. *Folio* also includes design articles and sponsors workshops dealing with all facets of magazine production.
- *Print* magazine does not contain as much color reproduction as *Communication Arts*, but often examines additional areas of design, such as graphic shows, visual symbol systems and annual reports.
- *U & lc* (upper and lower case), a tabloid published by International Typeface Corporation, is designed by Herb Lubalin, a top-flight American art director and designer. *U & lc* is extremely attractive and wins national and international awards every year for its excellent design.

In addition to the periodicals, several design annuals are particularly useful. *The Annual of Advertising, Editorial and Television Art and Design*, published by the Art Directors Club of New York, contains material from all over the world. *Creativity Annual*, published by the editors and publishers of *Art Direction* magazine, also contains international material. Both publications are fine references for monitoring contemporary design trends, examining particular design styles, and perhaps even finding someone to solve a specific one-time design, illustration or photography problem.

Step by Step

Now that the basic steps and techniques in producing a publication have been introduced, let's follow the process from inception to distribution.

1. The idea takes two forms: verbal and visual.
2. The copy is written and photos or illustrations are generated.
3. Paper of proper texture and tone is chosen and ink color selected.
4. The copy is edited and spec'd for typesetting.
5. Photos are chosen from the contact sheet, enlarged and cropped. Illustrations are completed by the illustrator, chosen from a clip-art service, or selected from a copyright-free source.
6. Black-and-white line art is reproduced as veloxes or photostats.
7. Copy and veloxes are pasted up in camera-ready form and sent to the printer.
8. Continuous-tone photos are prepared as halftone negatives and stripped into the layout as specified.
9. Proofs are produced for and reviewed by the designer/editor.
10. Printing plates are made.
11. Paper is fed to the press and printed.
12. The printed job is folded, collated, bound and trimmed.
13. The finished job is delivered to the communicator for distribution.

The printing methods you are likely to encounter are basically three: letterpress, offset and gravure. The largest proportion of work will be run offset. Letterpress printing is declining, and gravure printing requires long runs to make the job economical. It is best to discuss your project with your printer, who will be able to assess the needs in relation to the presses, paper and personnel available, thus producing the highest quality, most economical product.

WILLIAM E. KORBUS is a nationally recognized designer who teaches visual design in the College of Communication at the University of Texas at Austin.

• 11 •

Bulletin Boards, Exhibits, Hotlines

- 3M uses more than 850 bulletin boards to help communicate with more than 50,000 employees in the company's labs, plants, office buildings and sales and manufacturing facilities across the country.
- Triton College boosts registrations through the use of an innovative exhibit strategically placed in Chicago's North Riverside shopping center.
- Southern Company Services in Atlanta updates its newslines as often as four or five times daily in efforts to keep employees informed—up to the minute.

Bulletin boards, exhibits and hotlines are three distinct means of communicating within organizations. All three can be used creatively and, provided they are properly organized and supervised, all three media can be highly effective.

Bulletin Boards

As the information era ushers in teleconferencing via satellites, desktop video terminals, and other advanced media, it is interesting to note that an age-old tool for communication is being revived. Professional communicators are taking a new look at bulletin boards, one of the oldest and most traditional media for internal communication.

* The late Walter Anderson, ABC, contributed this chapter for the first edition of *Inside Organizational Communication.*

167

The new interest, however, is transforming the medium itself. There is a big difference between a bulletin *board* and a bulletin board *program*—one that coordinates the medium with an organization's total internal and external communication plan. Sophisticated bulletin board programs are given the same type of professional attention that organizations have given publications, information meetings, video programs, and other communication tools. That attention is being focused on the quality of information posted on bulletin boards, the presentation of the information, the frequency with which it is updated, and the coordination of bulletin board programs throughout the organization.

Bulletin boards have the advantage of being relatively inexpensive, flexible, easy to maintain and timely. A continuous stream of current news and features can provide an exciting supplement to the organization's more formal communication programs. Bulletin boards also do not have the problems of credibility that sometimes plague other controlled communications. Readers tend to view them as locations for straightforward notices of vital information.

Figure 11.1. To be effective, bulletin board items need to be clearly identified and kept current. Southern Company Services uses bold graphics to catch readers' eyes. News summaries and cartoons are changed daily; other news items and features are replaced every other day.

Because the concept goes far beyond "bulletins," there is a trend under way to rename the program in order to overcome the image of the "cluttered boards" that were previously ignored by the professional communicator and left to occasional attention by the cleaning crew. Alternative names being used for bulletin boards are information boards, employee news centers, corporate information centers, newsboards, employee communication boards, news notes, and employee information stations.

Perhaps the most important aspects of bulletin boards are their high visibility and easy accessibility. Bulletin boards should be set up in high-traffic areas to attract maximum attention, and the material should be kept current and interesting. No other medium permits an organization to announce news in printed form so quickly. A flash bulletin can be prepared and posted within minutes, even in a system of multiple boards.

News is generally posted on a regular basis, daily or weekly, but many organizations post news several times a day, depending on the need. Furthermore, boards can be organized so that news can be directed to specific audiences. General company news should be posted on all bulletin boards, and local news, only at the location of the activity.

An important advantage of bulletin boards is their economy. After the initial investment, regular maintenance is generally modest. The only expense is the cost of producing and posting the news and feature material, plus a modest amount for housekeeping to keep the boards clean and in good physical condition.

Physical Appearance of Boards

Bulletin boards may be as simple as corkboards with aluminum trim or as elaborate as illuminated showcases made of wood and acrylic. Since the boards reflect the personality of the sponsoring organization, it is important to select a model that visually communicates that the program is a permanent, modern, reliable and credible source of information. Use of the company logo or the name of the program on the boards reinforces the official nature of the information posted.

Standardizing the look of all bulletin boards within the organization helps to build credibility and to distinguish them from those boards not included in the program. Bulletin boards may be either open or glass-encased to prevent unauthorized posting and removals. Some organizations prefer locking glass doors for control purposes. Sliding covers, even though they may not be locked in place, are a deterrent to unwanted or unapproved postings.

Bulletin board sizes range from 43″ × 48″ (which includes "take-one" racks for brochures, booklets, or other handouts) to 36″ × 108″ (for a program that includes permanent personnel-related postings as well as the timely information postings).

Northwestern Mutual Life, based in Milwaukee, has adopted an unusual format, four triangular kiosks, for its "communication center." Three of the kiosks contain distribution racks for the company publications, daily news, upcoming events, newspaper clippings, job openings, training program notices, club news, meeting notices, sports activities and employee want ads, all of which have to be posted by the communication department. The fourth kiosk contains television equipment for playing in-house video programs or broadcasting events that pertain to the company.

The Herman Miller Company, in Zeeland, Michigan, also has free-standing kiosks as public notice centers. The four-sided kiosks, made in-house with Herman Miller products, provide 16 square feet of surface. Each kiosk has shelves for literature and a drop box for depositing requests for literature.

Corkboard is the traditional material used for the backboard. However, a more professional look is achieved by using upson board covered in a felt that matches office decor or the organization's color. Another alternative to corkboard is a new product from Scotch; the patented Post-it Tiles are a rugged posting material with a "touch down, lift off" adhesive surface that eliminates the need for thumbtacks or pins.

In designing boards for new office facilities, communicators should work with the architects to plan the design and placement so they fit into the overall office environment.

Location of Boards

When considering locations for bulletin boards, a communicator should study the overall traffic patterns. Although highly congested areas are best avoided, it is imperative that the location chosen is accessible to all employees within the work area. Office elevator lobbies are excellent spots for the boards. In plant sites, break rooms or lounges may be appropriate. The more favored locations are near restrooms, in well-traveled hallways, cafeterias, vending machine areas, recreation areas and near selected departments, such as personnel, medical service, credit unions and reception areas.

Areas to be avoided are those near doorways and stairwells, where employees might fall or be injured; near the paths of moving machinery; in narrow hallways; near time clocks or emergency exits or within work areas where people reading the board would be disruptive to others.

At least one board should be located on every floor of every major facility occupied by the organization. At plant sites, warehouses and facilities such as factories, the number of boards per floor should be determined by accessibility to each work group. J. C. Penney has thousands of bulletin boards at its stores and offices around the country. In its New

York office, the company has 150 boards to reach employees located on 50 floors in several different buildings.

Adequate lighting is essential to ensure ease in reading information posted on bulletin boards. If boards do not have internal lighting, they should be located near adequate external lighting.

Boards should be placed at comfortable reading levels. Place them so people of average height with bifocals can read the top posting in comfort.

Bulletin Board Content

The content of a bulletin board program should represent a good, credible cross-section of interests within the organization. Among the categories of information used in bulletin board programs, the most important is company or employee news. When news is happening, the boards should be updated quickly. Properly used, the program can effectively "scoop" or correct the grapevine, or react to press reports.

Every program needs a special feature to attract attention—a "drawing card." Among the more successful are cartoons, employee want ads, puzzles, contests, feedback articles and prizes.

Categories of information included in bulletin board programs are endless. Here are some of the more popular topics used by several different organizations:

- *Corporate (or organizational) news:* News releases, reorganizations, financial news, research projects, construction progress, new facilities, management decisions, new product lines, new contacts, plant news, hirings or layoffs, corporate positions on public issues, honors and awards, current problems, newspaper clippings.
- *Employee news:* New employees, promotions, transfers, terminations, appointments, accomplishments, marriages, births, speeches, service awards, employee sports, honor roll.
- *Personnel and administrative*: New employee benefits, safety information, educational bulletins, wage and salary changes, holidays, job openings, meetings, policy or procedure changes, suggestion program notices, training programs.
- *Industry news:* News clippings, information about the competition, journal excerpts, government regulations, industry developments.

Feature photographs or other graphic material add another dimension to the boards and enhance visual appeal. Eastman Kodak and Sperry Corporation post color transparencies on back-lighted boards and include supporting copy to explain the subjects of long-standing interest, such as company products or benefits.

Many organizations post news releases so employees can learn news about the company before local media cover it. Alexander and Alexander affixes a special "Newsflash" label on news releases to draw attention to important news. The "Newsflash" label also attracts the attention of the mailroom when important announcements are to be posted quickly.

Many organizations post press clippings about the company that have appeared in newspapers or other publications to show how the outside media view organizations, J. I. Case posts weekly management updates and articles about the company's competition to remind employees that they are competing in the business world.

Format of Materials

The manner in which bulletin board items are displayed is just as important as the editorial material itself. A bulletin board is a visual medium, so it should be attractive and graphically interesting. Good layouts, special paper stock, good typography, color, and graphics can catch the reader's eye and evoke curiosity.

Layouts. The general principles of good publication design can be applied to the display of information on bulletin boards. The layout should be simple. Blocks of copy running diagonally can't be read; the traditional horizontal format is preferred. Some organizations use a variety of formats to increase eye appeal and readership. Other organizations standardize the format of all material for simplicity and a symmetrical appearance. Both approaches can be effective.

Special Paper Stock. Colored paper stock that can be photocopied is available from most paper suppliers. It can add variety and interest to a program.

Typography. Many organizations use professionally typeset material in order to improve readability. If in-house typesetting is unavailable, electric type or Varitype units should be used. An Orator wheel or ball may be used for short copy. Large blocks of copy in Orator type are not as readable as those set in Letter Gothic.

Display Type. Headlines increase readability and help readers identify the subject matter. Some editors use standing heads to cover various categories of information: news, people, safety, notices, want ads, service awards, etc. These headlines may be typeset and printed on construction paper, hand lettered or made with rub-on type or pressure-sensitive color vinyl letters. The bulletin board then is sectionalized with related information posted under each heading.

Some organizations have standing heads preprinted in color for bulletin board notices. This method is particularly economical when dealing with a large number of bulletin boards. Messages can be reproduced on the forms either by photocopying or offset printing.

Permanent titles for each general subject also can be made from three-dimensional letters, which are available in different sizes, typefaces and colors.

Color. Color can be used effectively on bulletin boards, but it should not compete with information for attention. Introduce color on the boards with background feltboard, colored paper, color photography, pre-printed headlines, individual headlines, color printing, and even colored poster paper mounted behind postings to give a framed effect.

Use of Graphics. Because of timeliness and reproduction limitations, the use of graphics is often restricted in bulletin board programs, even though graphic elements add another dimension and should be used as often as possible. Attractive graphics can boost readership and interest in the program.

Art services, such as clip-art, can provide reproducible line art for a wide variety of subjects. Photostat equipment can be used to "compose" creative graphics or to enlarge or reduce postings. Some advanced copy machines can reproduce photographs with surprisingly good quality. Photos of new employees, company activities, or employees being recognized for special achievements always add interest to bulletin boards. Other graphic elements may be introduced in the program through the use of printed posters or posters supplied by industry and community groups and associations.

Keeping the Program Timely

Bulletin boards have an inbred sense of immediacy, their most important advantage over other print media. Quick work in posting and removing information will keep a program well read and interesting.

Postings should be made as frequently as can be managed. Daily changes of some of the material is ideal. While that may be impossible for many organizations, the turnover rate for most items should be weekly or twice weekly. Readers will look at the boards often if they think there might be something new and if they can come to rely on the program to keep them informed.

Even when boards are changed daily, the information may need to be updated more frequently if the news merits it. One company boasts of the ability to prepare, type, and reproduce emergency bulletins within one-half to one hour. Actual posting is completed within another hour. Such attention to timeliness pays off in the use of the program and its credibility. To add a sense of urgency and timeliness to postings, consider using headings such as "Bulletin," "Update" or "Flash!"

There is wide disagreement among communicators about the length of time a single item should remain posted. The average maximum limit, however, is about a week. Anything more will discourage readership. If it is necessary to post an item a second week, a new format, design or headline should be composed. An old notice gives the impression that no change has occurred and the reader may pass the board without reading it, even though the board may have several other new postings.

Bulletin Board Guidelines and Procedures

Guidelines should be developed for bulletin board programs. They should define the character of the service and resolve many of the day-to-day decisions that may arise, such as the purpose and locations of bulletin boards, the kinds of materials to be posted, and the graphics of posted materials. It is essential to obtain management approval and support and to establish the lines of authority for the operation of bulletin boards.

Areas of Responsibility. Preferably, responsibility should rest with one person—the editor—who may receive general direction from the supervisor or manager responsibile for internal communication. The editor should have authority to determine the editorial and graphic content of the program and should coordinate all aspects of the program.

The responsibilities of correspondents should be well defined. Usually correspondents are instructed to refer to the editor any questions requiring editorial judgment. If correspondents are located in plants or offices remote to the headquarter facilities, they may be delegated the authority (within clear-cut limits) to make editorial decisions concerning "local only" postings.

Reviews and Clearances. Boards should be timely so the review process should be simple. For most items, the highest level of review should be the information source or the bulletin board editor. Few items should ever require clearances beyond the immediate supervisor or manager of internal communication. For that reason, a high degree of professionalism and sensitivity to management or legal concerns is required of the bulletin board editor. The editor must use sound judgment in determining when additional clearances are required from management, lawyers, or other specialists within the organization.

Production and Distribution. A detailed list of the steps required to produce and distribute all items for posting should be available for easy reference. The outline should cover instructions for scheduling, formatting, headlining, copying or printing, collating, mailing, shipping, telecopying to off-site video terminals or teleprinters, etc.

Guidelines for Maintenance. Correspondents should be given specific directions for posting and removing bulletin board materials. Some editors include on each posting the date the item is to be removed. Others include such instructions in a cover memo to correspondents. Some editors prepare a layout grid, detailing what goes up where as well as when, with each package of materials. This ensures uniformity in the program, even though the boards may be located in various cities or states.

Checks and Controls. Editors should make an effort personally to "spot check" boards that are located outside the headquarter facilities to ensure that the boards are being kept current and neat and are operating within general guidelines given to correspondents. These checks also help determine when boards need maintenance or repair.

Some editors rely on individual or group meetings with new coordinators to communicate posting and maintenance procedures. Other editors prepare and distribute extensive handbooks, with do's and don'ts spelled out, or use layout grids and annual workshops to control the overall quality of the program.

Measuring Effectiveness

No serious communication program is complete without a means to measure its effectiveness. Questions related to bulletin boards should be included in periodic communication audits. They should estimate the number of persons who use the program regularly, the credibility of the information posted, the subjects most popular with readers, the problems that readers have with the program, and suggestions for improvements.

The effectiveness of the program can be measured informally by observing the traffic around the boards, recording the number of requests for posted items or additional information, noting the number and the speed at which "take-ones" disappear, measuring the quantity and quality of the unsolicited comments made about the program, and keeping open communication lines with correspondents to benefit from what they've learned from reader feedback. Some companies have contests and offer prizes to solicit feedback from readers. They might give a short quiz to verify employee knowledge of material posted on the boards during the contest period.

Communicators who have initiated a new or improved bulletin board program, and who may be measuring its effectiveness for the first time, may be surprised to learn that the program, while being the most economical, is also the most used and credible medium within the total communication package.

Exhibits and Displays

Exhibits and displays are another form of communication in many organizations today, frequently accompanying information centers. They permit an organization to communicate more extensively on a particular subject.

They can draw attention to a major subject or event, such as the introduction of a new product, construction progress on a new facility, or the commemoration of an anniversary or other event.

Many organizations produce elaborate exhibits and displays for trade shows, conventions or meetings. Setting these exhibits up in-house gives the organization extra mileage for the large investments usually required to construct and transport them. Hospitals, for example, can put displays in waiting rooms to help educate both the internal and external publics about specific hospital activities or problems.

Luther Hospital of Eau Claire, Wisconsin, sponsors a traveling display that promotes health campaigns. The waiting room is one of many stops for the exhibit, which makes the rounds at local supermarkets, schools, rollerskating rinks, area shopping malls, etc. Its "Shape Shop" program features a weight control clinic for children. Effectiveness is measured through the number of calls received, attendance at clinic classes and the number of brochures taken.

Puget Sound Power and Light Company of Bellevue, Washington, developed a traveling display to help employees and customers become wiser energy consumers. The elaborate display has been used in company facilities, and at county fairs, home shows and various other locations. Called "The Energy Store," the display acts as a show at which customers can find free information about energy conservation and supplemental energy choices. "Future Challenge," a tic-tac-toe computer game, provides a hands-on attraction to the exhibit. A special meter display helps customers realize how much energy different lights and appliances use, and by comparison, understand just how much more electric heat costs at 70° than at 65°. The effectiveness of the program is measured by the number of brochures taken, the number of people playing the computer energy game and the number of names registered for a free thermostat giveaway.

Exhibits and displays depend heavily on graphic elements, such as photographs, transparencies, posters, products or historical memorabilia. "They take the traditional bulletin board concept a step further to meet the more demanding, contemporary communication objectives," says an Eastman Kodak communicator.

Kodak has produced a series of dramatic displays to broaden employees' knowledge of company operations. The project was developed for Kodak's Colorado division because employees there are isolated from the mainstream and diversity of company operations. The project uses a series of photo displays of a wide variety of company-related activities. Each year, corporate communications at Rochester sends nine photo displays, each consisting of 12 to 15 photo enlargements and captions and a descriptive copy block of about 100 words. The print sizes vary and most are in color. All display material is mounted on 1/4-inch stock with Velcro backing that holds firmly to the fabric-covered display panels.

Each new display is posted on the first of the six panels and previous displays are moved to the right. Thus, each one has a life of six months and the overall display regularly has a new element. Removed displays are returned to company headquarters for secondary uses. Topics featured in the displays have included quality assurance, new products, distribution, papermaking, film manufacture, energy conservation, Kodak and the printing industry and Kodak regional operations.

Georgia Power Company, Atlanta, produces a quarterly photo exhibit on the progress of its major projects under construction around the state. The display consists of color enlargements of photos taken at the construction sites. The photos help employees in the corporate office keep track of progress at facilities that most employees may never visit, even though many of them may do work related to the projects.

Reliance Insurance Company maintains four "bay window" display cases for rotating exhibits that feature company activities and special events. In recent years, displays have included educational exhibits on the art of puppetry, deep-sea diving, unusual employee collections, art work on loan from local art schools and wild-fowl decoys. The "bay window" cases, which extend about six inches from the wall, allow for more elaborate displays than are possible on traditional bulletin boards.

Barnes Hospital has a "History Hall" display of photos, copy, portraits and other memorabilia tracing the history of the hospital. The Ball Corporation's entrance hall display serves as a museum and includes hundreds of the early Ball glass jars used in food preservation and contemporary products. The Amax Corporation arranged a group of products, ranging from a section of a metal pipeline to a car, in which various Amax products are used. The display is in a room used for receptions and meetings, so visitors can become familiar with the company's products and history while participating in social or business functions.

Organizations that sponsor art and craft shows or photo contests may display entries during or after the event, singling out those that are up for special awards. Or, when an organization has had a special event such as a company anniversary, picnic or service award dinner, photographs taken at the meeting may be displayed in the company lobby or cafeteria.

Exhibits and displays add an extra dimension to more standard channels of communication. They can reach diverse audiences, thus serving as effective public relations tools.

Telephone Information Programs (Hotlines)

Fast-moving events in large organizations often demand a system for rapid internal communication such as a telephone information program—a "hotline." The essence of hotlines is speed, simplicity and honest reporting with a minimum of interpretation or editorializing. Without moving more than a few steps, an employee can often obtain information about the company's position in a current labor situation or the price of the company's stock—or a variety of current facts about the organization.

Hotlines have the additional advantage of providing live information—that is, information delivered verbally by a human being rather than in print through an impersonal publication or other medium. Even when the caller's voice is tape-recorded for reply at a later date, or the hotline provides a taped message, there is a personal touch that makes communication more human.

There are several basic kinds of hotlines. The most popular seems to be the straight news format, in which a caller may dial a number and hear a reporter announce the latest news, usually at a specific time. The news may be reported by a "live" announcer or it may be recorded and updated periodically so that the caller always gets the latest news. This is especially useful during crises, such as a strike, plant breakdown, storm or energy failure. In some organizations, personnel not located at the company facility, such as traveling salespersons, employees at home, on vacation, ill, or off for the day, or employees' families, may keep up with recent events. Many hotlines operate 24 hours a day.

Some organizations conduct one telephone information program at company headquarters and another at division locations, with different news for each. Pennsylvania General operates a program called "Newsline" for its main office and three division locations. General Electric conducts a program that can be dialed from several locations in different states. The company also provides a live report to customers and stock holders.

The programs are usually given identifying titles such as "Newsline," "Hotline," "Call-line," "Actionline," "Dial-a-News," or simply a telephone extension number—"3562."

While the basic content of most news programs consists of significant news about the sponsoring organization, a number include what might be called social news: announcements of social functions, banquets, club meetings, picnics, sporting events, blood drives and community activities.

A second kind of telephone information service permits the employee to call in for an immediate reply to a question. The answer is provided by the person who answers, or the inquiry is recorded and the question answered at a later date. Some companies collect common calls and broadcast answers to them over a public address system the next day. These question-and-answer programs are known variously as "R.S.V.P.," "Call-line" and "Direct-line." (Some have write-in options, by which individuals can submit questions on special forms for later response.)

Questions are usually anonymously referred to a qualified person within the organization for reply. The answers are then forwarded by mail to the caller, whose name is known only to the program moderator. This anonymity encourages greater candor in the questions and assures that employees' comments, criticisms or complaints won't be held against them. AT&T, for example, initiated a "Let's Talk" program to answer nationwide questions about the company's divestiture. Employees and customers were invited to call toll-free numbers to receive personal answers to their questions.

Surveys indicate that employees like hotlines, whether they are of the straight news variety or the question-and-answer type. Communicators report that when question-and-answer hotlines are started, there is a deluge of questions, but after a while, when the novelty dies down and most questions are answered satisfactorily, the number of questions declines. One organization compiled the 100 most often asked questions in a booklet for distribution to callers who ask the same questions and to all new employees. Employees quickly learn that the company is serious about communicating quickly and honestly, and they come to rely on the newslines as a quick, reliable and serious form of communication. Even supervisors, who sometimes look upon telephone information programs as usurping their responsibilities as communicators (or as threats to their authority), learn to accept and even use the program as often reliable sources of information.

Several organizations conduct specialized hotlines to handle subjects of specific interest to the audience. C&P Telephone Companies, which conducts a regular "Newsline" program, also has an Equal Employment Opportunity Hotline to answer employee questions about the EEO and affirmative action programs, and another hotline to help employees resolve customer problems. Both Hartford Insurance and National Grape Corporation/Welch Foods maintain hotlines to help employees and their immediate family members who have personal and family problems. Through the programs, a qualified worker attempts to resolve the problem directly or refers the caller to a social agency that specializes in counseling for particular personnel or psychiatric problems. Sun Petroleum encouraged employees to call the company president directly, and in one day he received a call every six minutes. Wisconsin Electric produced a series of "Buzz the Brass" programs; on publicized dates, different members of executive management were available to answer questions from employees throughout the organization.

Cost

The cost of telephone information programs depends on the scope of the system. Beyond the initial investment for telephone answering machines, there may be no extra cost because the program is usually incorporated into the existing telephone system and requires only a special number and some extensions. If one takes into consideration the time it takes for someone to broadcast news or handle inquiries, however, the cost can be substantial.

The investment is worthwhile if it provides employees with quick and accurate information that might not be obtainable from other sources.

Measuring Effectiveness

Telephone answering services can be measured simply by electronically counting the number of calls received. A high volume would indicate that people are using the system and that they feel it is needed. General Electric, Philadelphia, receives more than 110,000 hotline calls a year. B.F. Goodrich averages 350 calls a day but has handled as many as 640 calls in a 24-hour period. A telephone newsline at Ohio Bell handles 200 to 1,000 calls a day. If popularity dies down temporarily, it may be revived by in-house publicity in other media. General Telephone's program is constantly promoted. Wilson Foods Corporation in Oklahoma City periodically publicizes its program in the employee magazine and on in-house posters. It has distributed a wallet card listing the hotline number so that employees have the number wherever they are.

Communicators who have established telephone information services stress that the success of the program depends on management endorsement and support. Employees are quick to realize that management is not serious if the program does not meet its objectives or their needs. The communicator must get top management to enlist the support of all who will be involved, especially the key people who will provide answers to questions. Replies must be substantial, candid and honest, and callers must be assured that their calls will be kept confidential, except to the moderator.

W. F. (DUB) TAFT, ABC, is in charge of communication services at Southern Company Services, Inc., in Atlanta, Georgia. He is accredited by the International Association of Business Communicators.

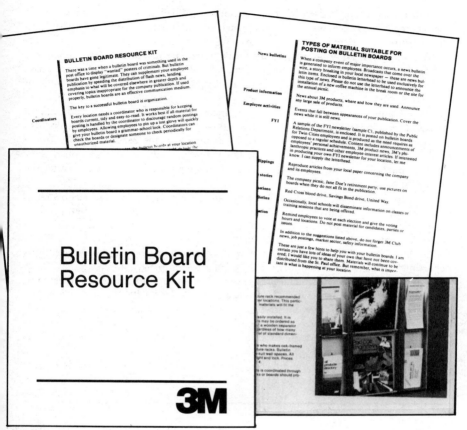

Figure 11.2. To maintain consistency in the bulletin board program, many organizations—like 3M—supply bulletin board editors with resource kits containing guidelines, policies on material suitable for posting, posting sheets and art, and a list of resources.

Example: 3M Bulletin Board Program

Bulletin boards are widely used at 3M because they provide a quick and convenient way to communicate with all employees. There are about 450 information center boards in the plants, labs and office buildings in the Twin Cities area of Minnesota, administered by the employee communication section of the public relations department. In addition, the company has more than 400 boards in its sales and manufacturing facilities across the country.

Information is posted every Monday morning. When a company event of major importance occurs, a news bulletin is posted on the board as soon as possible to inform employees before they learn the news from outside sources.

Volunteers in every building in the St. Paul area are responsible for keeping the bulletin boards up to date, attractive and readable. Once a year, volunteers are given a $15 gift certificate to thank them for the time they have spent handling the bulletin boards.

Free want-ad service is provided as an incentive for employees to read bulletin boards. The volume of want ads has grown to well over 400 a week. Volunteers also are responsible for keeping want-ad cards available in the reading racks. Survey results consistently show that 60% of the want ads submitted accomplish their intended purpose in a short period of time, usually within two or three days after the ad appears.

Key to the effectiveness of the 3M program is the variety of materials posted. In addition to news bulletins and want ads, postings cover employee activities, product information, newspaper clippings, educational bulletins, voter information, club news, jobs available, safety notices, campaign promotions for Red Cross blood drives and United Way and *FYI*, a newsletter produced by the public relations department. Picture stories add graphic impact to the program.

To help control the editorial and graphic content of bulletin boards located in sales and manufacturing facilities, 3M has a resource kit for field coordinators. The kit contains guidelines for an effective program, photos of suggested designs, posters and samples of the postings produced by the corporate office. 3M's editor is available to assist coordinators, and all materials produced by the corporate office are distributed to editors in the field.

Most of 3M's boards are covered with Post-It material, which holds notices securely without the use of tape or pins.

Dub Taft

Figure 11.3. Kiosks, and other free standing displays, offer flexibility and visibility for an organization. Triton College took its display to a shopping center to generate additional adult enrollments.

Example: Triton College Display

Shopping centers are places where people go to close a deal on a house, buy a new frock, make travel arrangements, eat lunch, see a lawyer and even go ice skating.

In Chicago's North Riverside shopping center, an attention-getting kiosk, strategically located in a heavy traffic area, is merchandising college classes with many of the same marketing techniques used by retail trade. The merchant is Triton College, the product is education, and the creative agency that took it all to market is Chipman Design, a Chicago-based firm specializing in retail store planning and design.

A marketing study concluded that Triton, a regional college, and North Riverside Mall, a regional shopping center, served basically the same market. Triton, with its broad range of educational offerings and flexible schedules, was pulling from the same broad cross section of people who shopped at the mall. Those findings led to a decision to set up shop in the mall and to employ some of the same marketing techniques that retailers use.

Thus, the objective of the project was to consummate the unlikely marriage of retail marketing techniques with higher education—in effect, selling education credit hours in a retail setting far removed from the ivied halls.

A free-standing structure was created to capture the attention of passers-by and still harmonize with the look of the shopping center. The kiosk promotes Triton College, and, for those who are sold on the spot, registration can be completed through a computer hookup with the registrar.

Graphics was the primary element in the design approach, emphasizing the Triton name and logo with a series of subordinate visual images adding an aesthetic and informative element.

Since space was limited, the kiosk had to be handled with great economy: a 6- × 7-foot graphic panel with illustrations of educational activities at Triton was mounted on a recessed wall. Three-dimensional silhouettes, campus maps and neighborhood graphics reinforced those programs that bring higher education directly into the communities through the college's satellite schools.

A video display screen provided a continuing flow of up-to-date information about the college and its programming.

Wall surfaces of acrylic brochure pockets, an "Update" panel and special display panels keep Triton's visibility high at the mall setting, while providing solid information on the courses the college offers.

Triton's program won an "award of excellence" for display and bulletin board use in IABC's 1983 Gold Quill Awards program. The program was featured in IABC's 1983 *Excellence in Communication.*

Figure 11.4. Southern Company Services' Scott Horne records the company's daily "Southern Today" program. He scans the newswires for the most up-to-date information for his reports. On busy news days, reports may be updated five to six times during the day.

Example: Southern Company Services' Telephone Newsline

"This is 'Southern Today' for Friday, June the third. On Wall Street yesterday, Southern Company stock closed at...."

Thus begins a typical morning edition of "Southern Today," Southern Company Services' telephone newsline program for more than 3,000 employees in Atlanta and Birmingham. Getting timely news and information to the employees is a primary objective of the program. On many days, the message is updated three times; whenever news is happening fast, the message may be changed five or six times.

Subject matter included in the program ranges from the latest development in a rate-case hearing to announcements on meetings, executive promotions and cost controls. Southern Company Services provides technical and professional services to five other firms within the Southern electric system, so many of the news items are selected from major events as they occur at each of those companies. Union contracts, energy sales, bond offerings, plant operating status, state legislation, regulatory actions and construction updates are among the subjects included in the program. "Southern Today" also keeps employees informed about national issues affecting electric utilities—for example, acid rain, nuclear power safety, nuclear waste disposal, new regulations and tax legislation.

News is gathered from a variety of sources: editors at other system companies, industry associations, local newspapers, Dow Jones News Wire, UPI and AP newswires, *USA Today* and a number of contacts within and outside the organization. When appropriate, an executive may be contacted for comment on a local, regional or national event. These actualities are used if they are succinct; otherwise, the responses are summarized in the report.

An important drawing card is the timely monitoring of the company's stock price. Daily closing on the New York Stock Exchange leads the late afternoon and early morning reports.

Each message is recorded on two Code-A-Phones in Atlanta and three in Birmingham. The Code-A-Phones have features that allow the messages to be changed from remote locations.

One staff member researches, writes and produces the program daily. Scripts must be written in crisp broadcast style and the message delivered in a professional broadcast manner. The length of most reports is limited to less than two minutes.

Effectiveness of the program is measured by the number of calls and through biennial surveys. On average, more than 400 calls are recorded daily, and well over 1,000 calls may be received on "hot" news days. The most recent employee survey rated "Southern Today" as one of the company's most believable and effective programs.

Many telephone newsline programs drop off in popularity after the first year of operation. "Southern Today," because of its commitment to timeliness and frequent updates, has been able to maintain a high level of employee interest in the program even after six years. And, on those days when an urgent message needs to be communicated immediately, the program proves its value again and again.

Dub Taft
ABC

· 12 ·

Audiovisuals

Stewart L. Burge, ABC

There are few absolute truths in the field of organizational communication. The nature of the work—part art, part science—is such that statements of seemingly irrefutable fact rarely can be supported with hard evidence.

There is at least one exception: organizational audiences today are radically different from audiences just a few years ago. The groups and individuals with whom organizations must deal today are more sophisticated than ever before. They are better educated, more selective, and more critical. Their expectations are high, and competition for their time and attention continues to grow at an unprecedented rate.

These factors must be taken into consideration by communicators who either occasionally or routinely turn to audiovisual media to help tell their story. We are trying to appeal to a generation of employees, stock holders, customers and opinion leaders who have either grown up or matured with television, and this significant influence has to be recognized and factored into our own communication planning. We must be aware that our task is to communicate effectively with individuals who are accustomed to visually based messages, to simplification, to having complete subjects (no matter how complex) being reduced to concise hour or half-hour packages.

Some critics insist that this "electronic spoon-feeding" has caused a serious decline in the willingness of people to actively seek out information of interest or benefit. Be that as it may, this simplified packaging of news, information and entertainment is thoroughly familiar to audiences. They are comfortable with it and, from most indications, they like what they're getting. Clearly, it makes sense for communicators to take advantage of the explicit, condensed and highly creative approach to message delivery fostered by commercial television.

When the situation lends itself to the use of a nonprint medium, audiovisual (A/V) productions can add an exciting dimension to organizational communication. Sensory involvement of audiences exposed to skillful A/V messages can lead to levels of understanding and persuasion unattainable through any other medium.

One caveat is in order, however. Because of this level of audience sophistication, organizational A/V productions must be *good* if they are to be effective. The simple fact is that no matter how friendly the audience and no matter how much they agree with what you say, they will, at least subconsciously, compare your work with the slick big-dollar productions they're accustomed to seeing in the movies and on TV.

How can XYZ Corporation possibly hope to compete with the likes of ABC Television or Paramount Pictures? While head-to-head production competition may not be feasible, organizational communicators do have reasonable access to a host of modern electronic and computer technologies in the form of extremely high quality A/V hardware.

Properly utilized, this equipment offers almost limitless production wizardry, whether in video, multi-image, film or any other format. On the other hand, it's possible for this very technology to become an obstacle to the communication process. For many well-intended but inexperienced producers, mastery of the equipment's potential for razzle-dazzle becomes an end in itself. The sad result of this hardware euphoria is that amid the flurry of animation, zooms and dissolves, the basic message can be overwhelmed or hopelessly lost.

Somewhere in the misty realm that lies between production technique and message delivery there is a point at which optimum audience impact is achieved. To reach that point requires a blend of careful planning, sound aesthetic judgment and refined technical skills.

Production Planning

The communicator's first responsibility is to make sure the message to be conveyed gets matched up with the best medium for the job. If new employees aren't getting accurate and timely information about their benefits, it may be that the benefits handbook needs to be revised or a slide/sound program should be developed. Or it may be that the vice president of employee fringes needs to do a better job of briefing new hires.

Whatever the answer, it's the communicator's job to find out all there is to know about the situation. This is usually best done during a face-to-face discussion with whoever is initiating the project. If the boss wants a videotape and you believe a multi-image presentation will be more effective, you owe it to the boss—and yourself—to state your position and support your advice with facts.

What's the Purpose?

In order to select the right medium and then assure that the message accomplishes its mission, it is essential to identify the basic purpose of the communication. The purpose should be stated concisely in terms of the desired result. Do you want to motivate? Inform? Educate? Persuade? Solve problems? Exactly how do you want members of the audience to feel or behave after seeing the presentation?

When you arrive at an appropriate statement of purpose, it's a good idea to put this in writing so that you can refer to it periodically during the rest of the production process to make sure the approach and treatment coincide with the basic reasons for producing the program. Plan and execute your presentation so that the purpose is constantly supported. No matter how much you know or how clever you are as an A/V producer, if your audience is confused about what you're driving at, your presentation has failed.

Who Will See It?

Take a close look at the audience you intend to reach. Who are they? How old are they? What's their educational level? What are their backgrounds? How much do they already know about the subject? What's their relationship to you? How are they employed? What are their prejudices? The more you know about the audience or audiences, the better your chances of having the program fulfill its purpose. Even if the subject matter is basically the same, two different audiences may well dictate two different versions of an A/V production.

Who Does What to Whom?

To avoid headaches and possible embarrassment, make sure everyone involved is aware of who is responsible for each aspect of the production. This is a critical consideration if you're working under contract with an independent producer.

Who sets deadlines? Who writes the script? Shoots the visuals? Edits the tape? Selects the music? Pays the bills? An hour before show time, it does little good to have someone say, "Oh, I assumed *you* were going to handle that." False assumptions can ruin the best intentions.

Selecting the Medium

The three most common audiovisual media are videotape, film and sound/slide. Each can be used independently or in combination with the others. Each has its own strengths, weaknesses and devotees.

In the business setting, most communicators turn to an A/V format in response to a stated problem or set of circumstances. Thus, in approaching an A/V project, a fairly clear-cut set of requirements normally evolves. A useful technique for handling these requirements is to divide them into "musts" and "wants." If the sales manager says she *must* have motion in order to demonstrate the functioning of a product, it is obvious that a single-projector slide show will not suffice. If the CEO insists that his end-of-year message *must* be distributed to all locations in *exactly* the same way and on the same date, a live presenter with a script and slides will not work. A "want," on the other hand, is something that you should try to include, but is not essential. You may want to have a "lip-sync" narrator for your anniversary film, but you may find that a "voice-over" narration will work almost as well—and within budget.

The process of listing "musts" and "wants" is an excellent way to get agreement on what is most important in the production, and what can most easily be deleted without damaging the production's effectiveness. It has been suggested that when starting an A/V production, the communicator should forget about hardware choices, staffing requirements and budget, and instead analyze the communication goals. In most cases, hardware, format and other decisions will evolve from it.

Videotape. In the late 1960s and early 1970s many organizations jumped on the video bandwagon. Unfortunately, a significant portion of that equipment is gathering dust in closets because organizations bought hardware without looking at alternative media or paying enough attention to their needs or capabilities. There are notable exceptions, however; organizations that have successfully integrated videotape into their total communication programs have backed their hardware decisions with capable staffing and effective use of the medium.

Good video is not cheap, but many organizations have found that the costs of production and distribution are dollars well spent when measured by an "effectiveness of communication" yardstick. Some are able to justify the relatively high front-end cost of in-house video hardware and production facilities. Others find it wiser to lease or rent equipment and produce their own programming, or to call in independent A/V producers to handle projects as the need arises. There is no clear-cut answer as to which approach is correct. It depends on how video is to be used, how often, and for what purpose.

Videotape production generally can be classified according to desired usage into three broad types. *Professional* productions are those in which the quality of the tapes is comparable to that of motion pictures or commercial television. These are normally high-budget programs used to convey documentary-style information to large audiences. *Semiprofessional* productions aren't necessarily amateurish, but nevertheless are characterized by production quality that is somewhat lower than that of commercial

Figure 12.1.

TV offerings. Typically, they are produced to present specific information to a captive audience. Employee orientations, news programs aimed at employees, safety programs and executive messages to employees are among the subject areas normally handled with semiprofessional productions. *Extemporaneous* productions are generally used as training aids and make good use of videotape's most alluring aspect—instant playback and review. Public speaking, sales training and helping executives get ready to "meet the press" are a few of the valuable applications of extemporaneous programming.

When you are approaching the first two classes of video production, it is important to consider what will happen to the program when it is completed. How will it be distributed? Under what conditions will it be shown? Most video productions will be viewed on normal-size monitors, which means that your audience must be relatively small for each showing or you must arrange for multiple monitors.

Compared with print media and the more common A/V formats (slides and overhead transparencies), the current use of videotape in organizational communication is relatively limited. Future uses promise to be increasingly widespread, imaginative and effective.

Film. Although there are exceptions, 16-mm films tend to be used primarily for "image" communication. Most tend to be more artfully conceived than the other audiovisual formats. This is not to say that aesthetic interpretation is limited to film productions because video and multi-image productions are increasingly using the pleasing, nonliteral, interpretive approaches previously limited to professional film productions. But companies, associations, hospitals and other institutions are, as a rule, more comfortable with precedent than with innovation. The result is that when the need arises for an "image" A/V presentation, people often begin thinking in terms of film.

Few organizations have in-house motion picture capabilities, which means that most films are handled by independent producers, a natural consideration when budgeting and planning. Some organizations have turned to Super-8 mm film and equipment as a less expensive way to get into film production. Lessened image quality plus the time and costs involved in duplicating release prints, however, have kept Super-8 from being widely used.

Sound/slide.   Sound/slide presentations, although generally simpler and less expensive than either video or film, can be extremely effective. The basic format for a sound/slide presentation consists of a live presenter whose prepared remarks are illustrated by 35-mm (2 × 2-inch) slides. Sometimes the presenter advances the projected slides without help. More frequently, an assistant follows a marked script and advances the slides. The next step in convenience and consistency of showing involves the use of a cassette

Figure 12.2.

tape recorder that plays a prerecorded sound track while the accompanying slides are advanced manually. This permits the addition of music and sound effects to a standardized narration.

Slide programs used to be limited to these two techniques. Then along came the concept and hardware for automatically synchronizing slide programs, and a whole new A/V "family" was born. Developments in slide projectors, synchronizing recorders, programmers and dissolve controls have brought a totally new level of professionalism to slide presentations.

Thousands of organizations today use single-projector programmed slide presentations to good advantage for sales, orientation, training and marketing. These represent the low end of the A/V production budget but, when well conceived and well executed, they can be powerful communication tools. The early 1970s brought a second generation of hardware sophistication, which made possible fast cuts, variable dissolve rates and simpler multiprojector control. In the mid-1970s, electronic programming equipment revolutionized the field and ushered in the "multi" phenomenon.

Multi-image usually refers to a programmed presentation that uses 35-mm slides to supply projected visuals on two or more screen surfaces simultaneously. The screen surfaces may be separate parts of the same screen or totally separate screens. A minimum of two projectors may be used, but common projector combinations are four, six, nine and fifteen. The term *multimedia* is used now to describe a programmed show consisting of two or more A/V media, live speakers, and actors, with slides normally providing the framework for the presentation.

Electronic programmers are the key to the "multi" area of A/V. They permit producers to manipulate images, to animate, to compress time, to alter space, to provide multiple viewpoints, and to integrate slides, motion pictures, video, light displays and other special effects into automatic, repeatable presentations. Sound/slide programs run the gamut from very simple to monstrously complex, from amazingly inexpensive to extremely costly.

Budgeting

Budgeting for any kind of A/V production can be a slippery proposition. There are so many variables involved that the simple question of how much an audiovisual program will cost is not unlike asking how much a new house will cost. The answer can be $20,000, $200,000 or $2,000,000, depending on how luxurious and how big you want it to be. Production costs for an A/V show depend on dozens of interrelated items: what medium you want to use; how long the show will be; how complex it is; the equipment, time and people needed to put it together; the location for showing the production, and how much of the production you can handle yourself.

Arriving at a workable budget requires a combination of two things: production expertise and accurate specifications for the program in question. Production expertise comes with experience. If you've done a dozen videotapes, you should be able to estimate how much the thirteenth will cost. If you are new to the field, you would be wise to call in a "technical adviser" to get you started. Accurate specifications for the program should be readily available if you've completed the "must/want" list described earlier. If the list isn't detailed enough for budgeting, now's the time to fill in the missing information and pin down specific requirements.

Outside Help

No matter how much experience you have as an A/V producer, eventually there will come a time when you don't have the answer to a problem and must call on the services of an outside resource person. Whether you need help from a photographer, film editor, artist, audio engineer or talent agency, or a full-service production house, the question is the same: "Where do I find a *good* one?"

Professional organizations or your telephone directory provide a starting point. Current periodicals often publish lists of "Who's who" in various areas of A/V production. The display and classified ads they carry are additional sources of current information. Perhaps the best method of locating good suppliers, though, is through their reputations and recommendations from other users of A/V services.

Regardless of how you locate your suppliers, ask them for samples and references. If they're truly good at what they do, they will be proud of what they let you see and hear.

What Equipment?

Whether your A/V message is planned for video, motion film, sound/slide, or multi-image, it's essential to determine precisely what hardware will be used. It will probably be determined by the equipment you already have on hand or are willing to buy or rent.

Audiovisual hardware is changing fast. For the most current information on hardware, contact local audiovisual suppliers. You can find them through professional contacts or in the telephone directory, and they'll be happy to talk about their wares. Not every dealer handles every brand of A/V hardware, so it's a good idea to talk with several so that you can base your buying decisions on "comparison shopping" facts.

When you talk with a hardware supplier, describe as completely as possible what your requirements are now and what you expect them to be in the foreseeable future. Will the equipment be in constant or occasional use? Do you need a complete system now or will you be adding on next year?

Will you be producing programs or simply showing them? Does the equipment have to integrate into an existing A/V set-up? Will it be used in a permanent location or taken on the road?

Get specific information from the supplier; find out about the warranty periods and availability of service and parts, in addition to prices and features of the hardware you need. Once you've narrowed your options, ask the supplier for names of individuals or organizations that are currently using the hardware you're considering. Contact them for evaluations of the equipment *and* the supplier.

The Production Process

The person who develops a trouble-free 1−2−3 system for producing audiovisual programs will be rich and famous. The fact is that for even the simplest productions, there are a variety of elements that must be dealt with simultaneously. In the case of sophisticated multi-image or multimedia presentations, the variables multiply in a geometric progression.

The secret to coordinating all the interrelated factors of an A/V program and having them come together in an effective presentation lies largely in thorough planning. And, while there is no single surefire method for planning, there are a number of accepted production practices that should be understood and used.

Outline

Start with an outline that tracks each of the main points of the story line and sketches each important supporting point. There's no need to get specific in the outlines. Just note the broad ideas that support your program's basic purpose in the sequence they will be presented. A single typewritten page should be enough for the average outline.

Scriptwriting

This is the point at which many novice A/V producers begin to go astray, because A/V scripting is a special sort of writing requiring a special sort of thinking. Most communicators write in good, effective journalistic style. When they shift to A/V scriptwriting, they tend to turn out programs best described as "talking books." Their newswriting style is polished and their syntax flawless, but they overlook the fact that they are writing for listeners and viewers, not readers.

If you write an article, you employ certain specific "signs" to guide the reader. Paragraphs, exclamation points and quotation marks are a few of the signals that let the reader know precisely what you are saying and how you are saying it. In an A/V script, neither you nor your audience enjoys the luxury of seeing an italicized phrase or the end of a paragraph, nor can you break into the script for the aural equivalent of a footnote. Your audience has no time to return to a preceding sentence to clarify a point they may have missed. An A/V script is a linear medium: once the information it contains is gone, there's no going back.

The scriptwriter not only bears the burden of writing factually and interestingly, but also must develop a clear, concise and logical flow of both visual and audible information. The entire script must be developed in a smooth, easy-to-follow sequence. Sentences have to be straightforward and easy to understand.

There are a number of simple ways to check scripts for understandability. Read the script aloud, record it on tape, then play it back and listen critically; or read it aloud to someone who will tell you "it stinks" if it really does. Go back and simplify the passages that don't quite live up to your expectations. Recast the ideas in words that are as straightforward as possible.

The Shooting Script.   Some experts recommend the development of a storyboard early in the production process, even before drafting a script. Others say that the story line normally is guided by the specific information to be conveyed, so visualization must *follow* scripting. There are times when words dictate imagery, and times when visual images prescribe the words to be used. The goal is to weave the separate elements together in such a way that the total effect is greater than the sum of the individual parts.

The shooting script is used to guide production of a program and tie together the audio and visual elements. The most common format for a shooting script consists of black rectangles (representing the screen format) down the left side of an 8½ × 11 page. Indicate in each rectangle, using words or sketches, each different visual called for. Production notes such as "long shot" or "extreme close-up" should be indicated where necessary. Each shot should be numbered sequentially.

The right side of the page is used for the audio: narration, sound effects, music, and so on. Narrative copy should be typed in upper and lower case and double spaced. Production notes regarding music and sound effects cues should be included at appropriate spots within the narrative.

Revisions.   Script revisions are unavoidable, irritating and time-consuming, but they can improve the program's flow and pacing. Don't be insulted or intimidated by script revisions. If you feel strongly about the wisdom of a change, defend your original position and ask the "critic" to prove his or her point.

The Visuals You Need

The sense of sight is powerful. It gives most of us our personal view of reality. It's little wonder, then, that visuals are the "guts" of an A/V presentation. They are what people react to, what they evaluate, and what they remember. Make every effort to ensure that the technical and creative quality of the visuals in a presentation are the best available.

If you will be shooting your own visuals and are not experienced in the field, get some good books on the subject, study them, and gain some experience before jumping into a project with a deadline hanging over your head. If you are using an outside photographer, cinematographer or videographer, make sure that the person is well qualified. Check samples of previous work and references.

Subject matter is limitless. Sorting through the possibilities and selecting the "right" visuals is the challenge. The task of determining *what* visuals to use and *how* to use them should be approached with this simple question in mind: "What do I want my audience to understand or feel?" Aside from obvious technical skills, effective visual interpretation requires sound aesthetic judgment, a thorough understanding of the program and its audience, and experience.

Generally, visuals may be classified according to where they originate and whether they are "live" or illustrated. Visuals obtained on location suggest the photojournalistic style and emphasize the candid, natural presentation of people, things and events. Location shooting conveys a "real life" feeling to the production, even though the sequences are usually well planned and rehearsed. They work best, of course, when they don't appear to have been "staged." Visuals shot in a studio make no attempt to capture the loose, natural feel of location photography. Studio sequences may involve people (a monologue or interview situation) or things (new products or a demonstration of how a machine works).

The other broad classification of visuals involves reality versus graphic representation of reality. For example, you may want to show live footage of a heart bypass operation, then switch to an artist's cutaway drawing to show the portions of the heart involved in the procedure. Or you may do an entire production with cartoon figures, or summarize sales and earnings data with charts and graphs.

Titles and graphics deserve special mention because they appear in almost every A/V production and are frequently misused. The key to successful titles and graphics is simplicity. Crowding, excessive ornamentation, poor spacing and complex design can kill their effectiveness. Used intelligently, titles and graphics can fortify the message, clarify visual data and simplify complex ideas.

Individual graphics should contain no more information than can be easily absorbed in 5 to 10 seconds. All lines, letters and numbers should contrast well with the background and have distinct separation of the various tones. Colors should be bright and complementary. Letters and symbols should be simple, with a minimum number of small openings and curlicues. Proven typefaces for A/V work include Helvetica, Univers, Optima and other readable sans-serif faces.

Structure and Program Content

In order to take advantage of the powerful communicative potential of visual images, the A/V producer must depend on a strong point of view to provide a backbone for the production. In the selection of visuals, a unified point of view helps clarify, define and delineate the purpose of the program. So, knowing what you are looking for permits you to adapt the subject matter to your needs at the very time of its recording on film or tape, thereby sharpening and controlling both the materials and their treatment.

Dramatization is probably the simplest and most obvious means of approaching A/V material. Close attention must be paid to proportion and balance, however, to avoid having the dramatic impact overpower the content or having it force viewers to draw conclusions different from those intended.

Dramatization can be handled in many different ways. You might, for example, want to base a videotape program on a simple interview that, though unexciting, contains important information. To avoid a monotonous "talking head" presentation, the program might open with the interviewee in a dramatic situation related to the program's theme. Such an opening offers significantly higher audience appeal and helps lay the groundwork for the interview. Once the interview begins, "cutaway" shots can be used to dramatize the points being raised. At the end, the interviewee can again be shown in a dramatic location shot indicating what action should be taken based on the material developed during the interview.

No matter which visual devices are selected, they must be used to construct a clear, logical path for the viewer to follow. The structure of this path may center on emotional progression, problem solving, geographical arrangement, progression through space, chronology, physical groupings, or combinations of these.

In addition to structuring the visuals to provide a smooth progression, the A/V producer is faced with building and reaching a thematic climax without resorting to devices that alter the truth or distort facts. As the project moves from shooting script to actual production, specific story units, or sequences, should be created. These are the A/V building blocks with which scenes are built. The scenes, in turn, are the production high points (i.e., its major premises). As such they must be bridged with transitional material to lead the viewer smoothly and easily from beginning to end. Transitions can be highly effective or deadly dull. They should be treated as important parts of a production.

The degree of communication expressed through an A/V program depends heavily on the selection and arrangement of its visual elements. Each shot must be included for its informational and emotional connotations and relationships. By paying careful attention to this role, remarkable communication results can be achieved.

Do You Hear What I Hear?

Too often, it seems, the audio side of the A/V equation is ignored during production planning. It is tacked on almost as an afterthought. That's a shame, because a good sound track can be a potent force in influencing an audience and driving home your message. Sound—voice, music, sound effects, silence—is an integral part of an audiovisual program. It plays a vital role in providing information about the mood, the characters, the places and the theme of the production.

Voice. Selecting the appropriate voice and then using it to best advantage are mostly matters of good judgment on the part of the producer. In choosing an off-camera narrator, it's wise to listen to a variety of "demo" tapes, available from the potential narrators themselves, or from talent agencies or recording studios. Listen for the style, tone and range of the narrator's voice. For on-camera talent, of course, make sure the person's appearance and presence are appropriate as well. Suitable voices frequently can be found at local radio stations and commercial recording studios, or at college drama and broadcasting departments.

When the time comes to assemble the audio track, everyone involved— narrator, producer, audio engineer—should have a full, detailed script from which to work. The studio engineer will assume responsibility for the technical quality of the recording, leaving you free to concentrate on directing the narrator.

During the recording session, listen critically to the delivery, pacing, pauses, conversational tone and other aspects not actually written into the script. Because the issue here is one of subjective interpretation, this is no time to be shy. These are your words and your ideas being recorded. No one knows them better than you. Don't hesitate to offer guidance and constructive criticism.

Music, Sound Effects and Silence. Music and sound effects are to an audio track what lighting and composition are to a photograph. They are important for conveying the desired mood and "tone." Because each A/V production is unique, your use of music and sound effects will vary according to what you intend to convey. For some productions, a simple musical opening and closing will work. For others, musical bridges may be invaluable as transitions between sequences, or a musical "bed" running through the presentation may be advisable.

Music used in an A/V production should not compete with other elements for the audience's attention. It should augment, reinforce and complement. It can help establish, change or intensify the mood of a production. The question of where to obtain music for A/V productions inevitably arises in "how-to" discussions. The answer usually falls into two categories: from orginal sources or from recorded sources.

If your budget allows, an original score composed, performed and recorded specifically for your presentation is ideal. It is surprising how many producers never explore this option, thinking that recording original music in a studio is prohibitively expensive. Frequently, one or two instruments played by competent musicians and enhanced by a good audio engineer can result in a sound track ideally suited for an A/V presentation.

By using original music you are assured of a sound track tailored to your needs and free of copyright problems. Some producers continue to skate on thin legal ice by "borrowing" music from commercial records and tapes without permission. The copyright law requires producers to obtain written authorization to use copyrighted material *prior* to use. The rules apply to in-house, not-for-profit, nontheatrical subjects as well as to "on-air" use for large audiences.

As an alternative to custom-made musical scores, prerecorded library music offers good quality at reasonable prices. Commercial music libraries deal in "generic" music produced, recorded and sold to anyone with cash in hand, so you may hear the music you select for your program used in someone else's program. Still, music libraries offer a huge selection of music and sound effects records. Library music rates currently vary from about $40 to $100 per needle drop, depending upon how the sound will be used.

Two other facts argue in favor of using prerecorded library music: the music is intended to be used in A/V-type situations and is written and recorded to fill that function, and it is recorded with a suitably reduced dynamic range to accommodate the audio limitations of standard audiovisual playback equipment.

Sound effects can be obtained simply by recording "wild" sound on your shooting locations with a good-quality tape recorder. Except for lip-sync sequences for a motion picture, this procedure normally yields acceptable quality and can add valuable "presence" to your program at practically no cost. An alternative is to use commercially recorded sound effects available from music libraries.

The fourth potential element of A/V sound is actually a lack thereof. Silence in a sound track may be thought of as the equivalent of white space in a publication. While technically it is "nothing," experienced producers often make good use of silence to punctuate, emphasize or define the accompanying "real" elements.

Once it is understood that sound is not a tacked-on "extra," most A/V producers begin using it with great care. Although a good sound track cannot salvage an otherwise second-rate production, it has the potential of making a good A/V program significantly better by reinforcing the mood and adding richness and color to the message.

Putting the Track Together. Once all the necessary elements are selected and recorded, it's time to put them together in a single, cohesive mix. Mixing is usually handled by a trained audio technician in a studio where multitrack recording equipment is available. By using individual recording channels for each audio component, a skilled engineer can weave the elements together into a smooth, balanced sound track. Nonetheless, it is the producer's responsibility to oversee the final mix-down and bring the benefit of his or her knowledge of the production to bear on the finished product.

The Challenge

The challenge to the A/V producer, whether novice or experienced, is to "get inside" the technical and artistic characteristics of all the elements involved in a production, then to select and use those that best carry the message and support the program's basic purpose. Audiovisual communication stands as the new frontier for organizational communication. Whether it serves as a dynamic motivational tool or a stumbling block to the communication process depends on the diligence of the individuals responsible for its use.

STEWART L. BURGE, ABC, is director-public affairs for GTE Network Systems in Phoenix, Arizona. He is accredited by the International Association of Business Communicators and has served on IABC's Executive Board.

Example: The Aerospace Network

Prior to 1971, employee communication at Boeing Aerospace Company in Seattle followed traditional lines—a companywide newspaper, the *Boeing News*, supplemented by specialized publications, surveys and occasional audiovisual programs. In mid-1971, as a result of economic pressure, Boeing's defense and space arm experimented with an electronic solution—an in-plant public-address system news program—to a widespread morale problem. The newscast experiment, 12 years and numerous communication awards later, operates as an integral part of the internal communication effort.

Born of Hard Times

The Aerospace newscast came to life during the "Boeing Bust," the period in the late 1960s and early 1970s marked by massive layoffs at Seattle's major employer, triggered by the cancellation of the U.S. supersonic transport program and the winding down of the manned space program. Over a few months, Boeing's work force plummeted from more than 110,000 to about 30,000. Morale was best summed up by the now-famous local freeway billboard that read, "Will the last person in Seattle please turn out the lights?"

After hitting bottom in mid-1971, the remaining employees turned business around by winning small contracts in nontraditional Boeing areas such as hydrofoil boatbuilding, energy and agribusiness. Within months the business base improved. But with a devastated communicators' force and a one-person newspaper staff working on a biweekly schedule, how could the improving news be spread quickly among the work force? Then Aerospace employee communication manager Jim Douglas proposed an experiment—a two- to three-minute news program, broadcast during business hours, using the plant's paging system.

The Price Was Right

The idea was approved by management. It had considerable appeal, not the least of which was cost. The paging system, already installed for security and safety reasons, reached nearly all of the company's Seattle locations. Because it was not an actual broadcast station, the "studio" required was nothing more than a tape recorder connected to a paging outlet by a telephone device that cost 50¢ a month. One staff member could prepare and broadcast the program in less than two hours. It was just the sort of communication boost needed by a technology company down on its luck.

Getting the Word Out

Once the system was established, there was little problem finding news. Information was supplied by company personnel and industrial relations groups. Among the biggest contributors were division managers, who competed among themselves for morale-boosting exposure for their organizations. They all wanted the immediate recognition the daily audio newscast could provide.

The Electronic Advantage

In a working environment still smarting from the threats of constant layoff, rumors flourished, resulting in considerable lost time. The company switchboard was often jammed with employees calling outside to find out what was going on. The problem was compounded by a constant communication worry of the defense contractor— releasing news concerning its government customers. Government contractors often have no control over the timing of news releases. There were frequent fast news breaks and employees complained they often had to wait for days to find out what had happened that day at work. The short response time of the newscast worked to eliminate those complaints. Unlike a telephone dial-in system, the network's "live" nature could carry a message to thousands of employees within minutes, freeing telephones for company business.

New Directions

Since its early days as a two- to three-times-a-week program, the network has grown into a daily channel for a variety of employee-related information, some of it aimed at specific audiences. On occasion, the system is used to relay emergency traffic or weather information to homeward-bound employees. Through the use of short public service messages, the network has supported campaigns to eliminate unnecessary paperwork and encourage energy conservation.

In recent years, a special effort has been made to include more of the employee audience in the communication process. Coverage of employee activity has been increased and telephone recording equipment has been added to allow the use of the actual "voices" of the employee newsmakers whenever possible. Listeners now hear more from people like themselves, not just from the company spokesman or management.

They Do Listen

The Aerospace newscast has shown up in surveys as a major source for employees' company news. In a 1983 interview survey, first- and mid-level managers overwhelmingly indicated that the program provides employees with valuable news about their jobs and the company's future. On a daily basis, the newscast's impact is measured by response to news items. A historic example was a story concerning the company's efforts on the Trans-Alaska pipeline. Within hours of a broadcast about a need for 100 engineers with specific skills to move to the Far North, more than 500 qualified applicants responded.

John Kvasnosky
Supervisor, Employee Communication
Boeing Aerospace Company

· 13 ·

Face-to-Face Communication

Jerry Tarver, Ph.D.

Most of us do so much talking and listening that we tend to take face-to-face communication for granted. We don't get around to studying our speaking behaviors. Let's begin by recognizing that we engage in three primary kinds of face-to-face communication, as illustrated in these three hypothetical situations.

Interpersonal Communication. Monday. Today I want you to join me for lunch simply because I enjoy your company or because for some reason it is important for us to get along well. The only real objective for lunching together is to maintain or improve our relationship.

Our interaction will be pretty much one-on-one—you and I, I and you. We'll sit by ourselves but if others drift to our table we can interact with them without losing our contact with each other. (Look at the big table in the corner—11 people, but most of the talk is in groups of two or three.)

We may talk business, but we don't have to stay on one subject very long. A lot of sentences don't get finished; a lot of ideas get dropped. We'll probably behave just as we would if we were talking in the hall or having a chat in the office. We may say some things that are quite personal. I may admit a secret worry or brag about something of which I'm proud. You might let out some hostility or confide your feelings about a friend.

If everything goes well, each of us will let the other know (with or without words) that "it was a nice lunch."

Group Communication. Tuesday. Is it okay with you if we schedule that committee meeting during lunch today? We've got six people, and the noon hour seems to be the only time we can get together.

The tone of our talk at the table is a little more formal than it was yesterday. People who seem to be heading our way realize we're having a

205

meeting and they find another place to sit. You and I can still exchange comments, but today we are aware of the impact of what we say on all the others in the group. When we speak now, we are in a "one with a few" situation.

We are more organized today. We have a leader; a recorder has been appointed to take notes. Handouts have been prepared, and an agenda lists the topics we hope to cover. We have lost some of our freedom to make personal comments. Expressions of our private fears or deepest feelings might attract a stern glance from our leader if they don't bear on the subject at hand.

I understood the committee was appointed to solve a problem our organization is facing, but another person thinks we should simply gather relevant data and report back to the organization. It's up to our leader to see that the group comes to a common understanding of our tasks. Then we will measure our results by the amount and quality of the data we collect or by the viability of our proposed solution. (At lunch yesterday, I don't recall either of us using the terms "viability" or "data collection.") Obviously, we are more purposeful today than we were yesterday.

Public Communication. Wednesday. I am pleased to be in the audience today for the speech you are delivering to the club after lunch. The occasion becomes much more formal than it was on Monday or Tuesday. There is some kidding around but, obviously, the procedures being followed are quite rigid. You rate an introduction to the group, even though many of us already know you. You sit in a designated place before the talk, and you are expected to stand at the microphone when you speak. There is a smattering of conversation in the audience and it quickly dies away. You have the attention of everyone in the room.

I find the ideas in your talk well organized. The points you make emerge more sharply than when you were speaking in the committee yesterday. Then, you were willing to go along with the committee's decisions; today, I see you as an advocate of the point of view expressed in your speech. You seem to want to influence my thinking.

In broad outline, the chart that follows indicates the distinctions among the three kinds of communication examined:

	Interpersonal Communication	Group Communication	Public Communication
Interaction	one-to-one	one-to-few	one-to-many
Purpose	enhance relationship	learn or solve problems	influence an audience
Setting	casual	informal	formal

Next we need to discuss how we can best function in each situation.

Public Speaking

You should speak only on subjects you know and care about. If you don't have the interest or the time to prepare, don't agree to speak. If you are writing a talk for someone else, be sure you are allowed enough time to do the job and can write for the other person. Keep the topic simple and limited because most speeches these days should not last more than 15 or 20 minutes.

Preparation of the Speech

Don't prepare speeches merely to take up an audience's time; plan to do something for them. Perhaps you want to *inform*, perhaps to *stimulate* or stir up feelings. Some occasions call for you to change beliefs—to give a speech to *convince*; others, to cause *action*.

Consider the variety of ways a single topic—safety—might be handled. A speech to inform might explain the operation of a new item of safety equipment. A speech to stimulate might be given when presenting a safety award. A speech to convince might be given to community groups in an effort to persuade them to believe your organization operates with no danger to them. A speech to cause action might be delivered to a meeting of top management to get a favorable vote on the budget for your safety campaign. Every speech should be designed to bring about a change in an audience and the speaker should know at the outset what change is desired.

To know what effect you want to have, study your audience with care. Collect facts about age, sex, education and ethnic background. Find out how many people will be in your audience. One writer prepared an address about energy at the height of an energy crisis and was told at the last minute that the college audience he was writing for would have in it a large number of students from Iran. Obviously, knowing that fact would have been a great help to him in preparing his speech.

Learn about the speaking situation. Consider the time of day, the exact length of the speech, and whether to allot time for questions and answers. Ask about other speakers on the program, the physical arrangements for the meeting, the type of microphone. During the Vietnam War I prepared a talk on "Humor in Communication" without finding out I was to follow a speech by the wife of a well-known prisoner of war. Don't let that sort of thing happen to you.

Do the best you can to learn the attitudes of your audience. Will they be friendly, hostile, open-minded, or uninterested? If they are negative, avoid the speech to get action and settle for a talk to inform. If the audience is

Figure 13.1.   A speech should do something for an audience other than just take up its time.

favorably inclined, you may have a good opportunity to call for action.

Knowing about your audience can help you select the right material and language for your talk. Good speeches fit the specific audience and usually cannot be used for another occasion without rewriting. Knowing your audience can also cushion you against surprises and give you a psychological advantage.

Ordinarily you should not rely on any one person to give you information about an audience. While you may get some data from the individual who chairs the program, you might want to ask questions of any members of the group you know personally, speakers who have addressed the group, or their speech writers. Oral comments are better than material written on an audience analysis sheet, because the spoken word can provide you with more shades of meaning than you will get from a written report.

Structure of the Speech

Good speeches should always follow a logical pattern. The listener cannot stop and "replay" a speech if an idea fails to stand out clearly, so careful organization is important.

The *opening* precedes the solid content of the speech and probably should take from 30 seconds to two minutes. If you start with an acknowledgment of the introduction, it should be brief and simple. Don't overreact to praise in an introduction and don't embarrass the person who introduced you by attempting to correct mistakes. A plain statement such as

"Thanks for your words of welcome, Alice," will help the audience begin to tune you in.

The goals of the opening of a speech should be to capture the audience's attention and interest, to get them into a good mood, and to prepare them mentally for the substance of your talk.

Here are five techniques for openings. Although they are frequently used, they won't be trite or boring if you apply a little imagination. Select as many from the list as you think the occasion requires to accomplish your three goals for the beginning of a talk.

Honest Compliment. When you can sincerely say something nice about an audience, do it. Comment directly on the audience's accomplishments or characteristics, or make indirect references to your host city or even something as routine as a local athletic team. Above all, remember that the compliment must be genuine.

Here's how Joseph P. Flannery, head of Uniroyal, used a compliment as part of his speech opening to the Akron Rubber Group:*

> Thank you and good afternoon. Anyone who has ever listened to a speech knows that the opening is always the same. The speaker begins with a few pleasant comments about the city in which he's speaking and the organization that invited him. The trouble with the standard opening is that after you've heard it several dozen times, you begin to doubt the speaker's sincerity. That's unfortunate for me because I really do enjoying visiting Akron. When I was president of Uniroyal's chemical division, I frequently visited our customers in Akron. I miss coming out here and meeting you people as often as I did.

Common Ground. Mention an interest you and your audience share. We often begin a conversation with strangers by asking, "Do you know this friend of mine who works in your field?" A common interest almost always helps start the flow of communication.

Ralph Earle, II, began an address at Brown University with this technique:

> It is an honor and pleasure to be here to deliver one of the Ogden lectures. I am truly grateful for the invitation—in part, because many of the previous lecturers were my colleagues and are my friends; in part because I have a special feeling for Brown, from which one of my children graduated and with which I am affiliated on a part-time basis.

A Story. Telling a story can arouse curiosity and get listeners involved in your speech. A president of a major corporation once began an important speech by relating an incident involving an argument he had engaged in at a cocktail party. He got the audience's attention and moved smoothly into his subject.

---

* This example and the ones that follow are from *Vital Speeches of the Day* (July 1, 1983), a publication that contains valuable model speeches.

Julia Thomas, president of Bobrow/Thomas and Associates, began a speech on ethics by capturing the audience's attention with a story from the news:

> You may recall an accident that was reported in the paper about two days ago. It involved a DC-10, and it was a charter flight on its way from Malaga to New York. The pilot aborted the flight when they had attained about 30 feet of altitude. He felt something was radically wrong, but he wasn't sure. On impact approximately 50 people were killed, many due to smoke inhalation, others because the chutes in the rear ceased to function. When interviewed, the pilot, an employee of Spantex Airlines, said the following: "I don't know if I killed 50 people or saved 200." Now that's an honest man. He cared.

Humor.   Be cautious in opening with humor because it's hard to know what will make an audience laugh. There is no agony quite like standing alone in the awful silence following a joke that failed. Be especially careful not to offend anyone. Often, the safe approach is to poke fun at yourself or some group to which you obviously belong. Consider using a "one-liner" rather than an elaborate anecdote. Good jokes travel fast, and the speaker can't ask, "Have you heard the one about...?" If you use humor, remember that you don't need to have people rolling in the aisles. A few smiles and chuckles will be enough to show you've accomplished the goals of attracting attention and establishing a pleasant mood.

Labor leader Herman Rebhan chose a little low-risk humor as part of the opening of a talk to members of a management symposium in France:

> I like the remark of the Chinese leader Chou En Lai when General de Gaulle asked him what he thought of the French Revolution. "I don't know," replied Chou, "it's a bit early to say."

Reference to Your Subject.   Start by mentioning the topic of your talk only if your audience has a strong positive attitude toward your subject. "I'm here to tell you how to save $500" is a better opening statement than "I am sure all of you are interested in knowing why we are adding 10% to your next bill."

Discussing a timely and critical subject, Chemical Bank's Donald C. Platten opened a talk to a business group with:

> Good afternoon. I'm delighted to be here today and to discuss with you a way out of one of the most serious problems facing managers and regulators in the financial services arena today, the question of what is or should be banking.

The *theme* of your speech should be explicitly set forth after you have your audience's attention and your listeners are in a friendly mood. Even if you have already made a reference to your subject, it's usually wise to say in a sentence or two exactly what you intend to cover in your talk. You might elaborate by adding a concise preview of the major ideas, or "points," you will develop.

In a speech on "misology"—the hatred of ideas—Professor Donald Walhout used the preview method to explain his theme:

> When I was growing up, I used to hear sermons which almost invariably had three points, which were almost invariably alliterated. Recalling that practice, though this is not a sermon, let us look briefly at some customary causes, some dreadful dangers, and some calculated cures for misology.

The *body* of the speech, which follows the theme, consists of the main points and supporting evidence. Clear and logical main points will make your analysis of the subject meaningful and make it easy for the audience to follow your ideas.

You can present your points or ideas in chronological order, as in this example:

1. Gather your material. (*discuss*)
2. Build the product. (*discuss*)
3. Market your creation. (*discuss*)

You can organize ideas in a spatial relationship:

1. Let's consider the inner city. (*discuss*)
2. Let's examine the suburbs. (*discuss*)

You can divide a topic into its "natural" or "logical" parts, with each becoming a main point. For a speech on the topic "Who benefits from profit?" you might identify the groups that benefit and make each group the subject of a point:

1. Stockholders profit. (*discuss*)
2. Customers profit. (*discuss*)
3. Employees profit. (*discuss*)

Sometimes you can use a "problem-solution" pattern of organization. For the annual safety talk, begin with a point that emphasizes a problem and follow with a point that offers solutions.

Once you have logical points for the body of the speech, make sure they stand out clearly so the audience can follow your ideas. Here are some tips to help listeners keep up with you:

• Don't have too many points. Two to five main ideas are about all most audiences can retain. If your speech has "14 steps to success," try to reduce those steps to three or four categories. Be sure that your points are of approximately equal weight; you don't want to spend half of your speech on just one of five points.

- State your points directly in concise language. Too many speakers plunge into a discussion of an idea without identifying the idea first. Perhaps this practice results from our experience with the print media, where titles and headings identify points.
- Number or label your points. Don't worry about insulting your audience's intelligence. Remember that audiences find it difficult to keep up with the order of spoken ideas. Help them by saying "First" or "The number one step" or "Our initial concern must be."
- Use transitions. After finishing a point, indicate that you are ready to move on. "But stockholders are, of course, not our only concern" or "So much for the inner city. But we must not neglect an area with problems that are in many ways more pressing" or "Now you've gathered your material. What next?"
- Use summaries and previews. As Professor Walhout demonstrated in the example cited, a well-organized speech can begin with a preview of the points to be covered. Summaries also are useful. After completing three points in a four-point talk, you might say, "So far then, we've seen . . ." and briefly review your speech up to that point.

The conclusion to your speech should be short and positive: a restatement of your main idea, a summary of your points, a quotation that captures the theme of your talk or a brief illustration that will leave your audience with a vivid final impression. Avoid ending a speech with "thank you." If you want to express your appreciation to your audience, do so with a sentence or two that has some substance to it.

Content of the Speech

The content of a speech should provide concrete evidence to support the points you plan to develop. Each point should be backed up with examples, illustrations, statistics, quotations or comparisons. Use as much evidence as you need to make sure your audience understands your point. Where possible, material should come from your own experience. Instead of saying, "The latest figures show," say, "The figures I read last week show . . ."

Excellent use of supporting material for ideas may be seen in a 1982 speech by Roland C. Frazee of the Royal Bank of Canada. Speaking to the Economic Club of Detroit on "Canada-US Relations," Frazee's first point was, "One—we have too little awareness of the very real differences between us." Here are five consecutive paragraphs devoted to establishing that point:

"For example, while I know the idea of a state-owned oil company is not popular here, it is a common and acceptable device in most countries. Canada's Petrocan is widely supported by the general public, not only as an instrument of government policy, but as a very capably managed enterprise." (*Use of an example to make the point. Note the personal language introducing the evidence.*)

"Much is made of our undefended border, but in practical terms, it could hardly be any other way. As a Canadian diplomat once pointed out, in our case arms are futile; in yours they are superfluous." (*Vivid language in a quotation.*)

"You dominate Canada, not through malice, but merely by being big and by being close. Your culture—movies, television, books, magazines and music—is inescapable." (*Examples.*) "Your investment in Canada, direct and indirect, exceeds $70 billion. You directly own and control 54% of our oil and gas industry; 58% in chemicals; 70% in petrochemicals; 41% in mining and smelting; 42% of all manufacturing. Eighty percent of all foreign investment in Canada is American." (*Statistics.*)

"When your economy gets the sniffles, ours catches pneumonia." (*Analogy or comparison to make the point.*)

"Canada is the source of your snow—as your weathermen tell television audiences for four or five months a year, and the United States is the source of our sunshine—as travel agents tell Canadians. The result is a perennial balance-of-payments deficit, in tourism as well as in other service categories—and to finance it, our interest rates need to be higher than yours, and usually are." (*Use of an illustration or a brief story. Note that as in all the material Frazee cites, the illustration is designed to drive home his basic point on differences between the two countries.*)

Delivery of the Speech

Body language is important when you stand before an audience. Consider eye contact, posture, gestures and voice. Look at the people before you as you speak. See their responses. If they appear restless, speak louder and use more action. If they look puzzled, restate your idea or give a few more examples. Look directly at several people in the audience; don't focus all your attention on one or two.

Stand with your weight on both feet. Don't take the one-legged position of a stork, and don't lean on the speaker's stand. Don't twist or sway.

You can solve the problem of what to do with your hands in three ways: let them hang comfortably at your sides, let them rest lightly on the stand, or put them in your pockets if you have pockets of comfortable size and can use them without distorting your posture. Use your hands to gesture when you feel it naturally appropriate to emphasize, describe, or hold interest. Don't plan your gestures in advance. Unless you are an actor, "canned" gestures almost always destroy timing and make your gestures appear awkward.

Speak in your natural voice. Don't strain or try to reach a lower key than you normally use. Remember, most people don't like their own voices, but audiences soon grow accustomed to a speaker's particular sound. You will be tempted to talk too fast, so make an effort to slow down to a listenable pace. Don't be afraid to pause occasionally to look at notes or let an idea sink in.

Try to speak from an outline rather than a manuscript. Except for extremely short speeches, never memorize a talk. Your outline should be on note cards. The function of the outline is to remind you of your next idea. Glance at your outline and then express the idea in a conversational style. Key words and incomplete sentences are all you usually need.

Language of the Speech

A public speech is an "enlarged conversation," so use short words, contractions and colloquialisms. If you are writing a speech, you will have to violate some of the rules you have learned in English and journalism. For example, you cannot put a high premium on conciseness because it usually takes more words to express an idea in speech than it does in writing. Look at some examples. Those on the right are designed for the ear, not the eye.

Language for the Eye	Language for the Ear
Management audits attest to our efficiency.	I've read a study on the way we run our company that shows we're doing a first-rate job. (*More verbose, uses shorter and more personal words.*)
We must all help, for productivity is everyone's responsibility.	We must all help, because we all have a share of the responsibility for productivity. (*"For" is an "eye" word.*)
	or
	Can we afford to leave concern for productivity to company officers? Don't we have some of the responsibility? Maybe *most* of the responsibility? (*Use rhetorical questions, repeat words, permit sentence fragments.*)

Donald Walhout, Professor of Philosophy at Rockford College said...	Rockford College Philosophy Professor Donald Walhout said... (*No clause, smoother flow.*)
Being concerned about this problem I am happy to take on the job.	I'm concerned about this problem, so I'm happy to take on the job. (*Direct sentence.*)
Note the following suggestions for action.	Let's look at several things we can do. (*"Following" is an "eye" word in this context.*)

Of course, many of the rules for good writing do apply to speeches, just as to any other sort of writing. Jargon and specialized words may be useful inside the organization but they often confuse outside audiences. While some speakers realize they shouldn't refer to the "extroplasmotic extrusion process" without explaining it, they will slip in such deceptively simple terms as "our plant department," or "FY '83" without thinking. Speakers also should avoid sexist language but in the process, should avoid using awkward substitutions that distract listeners as much as sexism. In speaking, as in other kinds of good writing, vivid terms can be used to paint a visual image for a listener. When in doubt about applying a rule, read the passage in question aloud. It if *sounds* right, you have probably applied the rule correctly.

Writing a Speech for Others

Most of the public speaking skills previously discussed can be applied to writing a speech for someone else. You need to be concerned with delivery only if you are involved as your speaker's coach after the manuscript has been accepted, but the principles of audience analysis, goal setting, content and language are the same no matter who gives the speech.

One of the unique problems speech writers face is the challenge of making the speech fit the speaker. Your starting point should be to make sure you have adequate access to the speaker during the time you are writing and to determine what the speaker wants to accomplish in the speech before you start to write. Beware of the intermediary who will try to speak for the speaker. Direct contact between speaker and writer offers the best means of finding out what the speaker actually wants to say.

Getting access to your speaker may require you to cultivate a good relationship with the "gatekeepers" who guard most of the top people in organizations. Establishing a bond of trust with the boss's secretary and administrative assistant may open doors for you.

You also will want to get to know those individuals who can supply you with information for a speech. It's better to get acquainted with them *before* you have to rush in with an urgent request for data.

Be sure to give feedback to those who assist you with a speech so they will be receptive the next time you turn to them for help.

In many organizations, speech writers do not automatically have the status of editors or attorneys or CPAs. A speech writer may find it necessary to be somewhat more assertive than other professionals in acquiring the respect of fellow workers.

Give yourself time to write. We all appreciate the boost we get from an approaching deadline, but remember that speech writing involves considerable research and thinking before you sit down to hammer out the final product. Because of the variables involved, it's hard to say exactly how long it takes to write a speech. After the research has been done, many writers find an hour of writing time for each minute of the speech is not a bad rule of thumb. You probably have other duties to perform, so don't forget to spread out the writing time. Some writers have agreements that all speech-writing assignments are made six weeks in advance.

Capturing another person's style is often difficult. Read your speaker's earlier speeches. Listen to him or her talk. When it's feasible, have the speaker read an early draft aloud to catch phrases that sound out of character. By all means, try to hear the speaker give each speech you write. If you can't attend, have someone tape the speech so you can play it back to get an authentic version of the speech and the audience's reaction. The experience may be painful, but you will benefit in the long run.

You might want to use a large typeface for the manuscript your speaker will take to the podium. Leave a wide left-hand margin for the speaker to make notes. Use only the top two-thirds of the page so the audience won't be treated to a view of the top of your speaker's head as his or her eyes travel all the way to the bottom of the page. End each page with a complete sentence so the speaker's thought won't be interrupted as each sheet of paper is turned.

Group Communication

Committees and other groups would waste less time in meetings if they determined the purpose of their meetings and established reasonable procedures to follow. Why do groups meet? Two answers might be to solve a problem and to gather and exchange information. Here is a procedure to follow for problem solving:

- *State the question.* Be sure everyone knows exactly what problem is to be solved. Don't assume that everyone knows the issue confronting the group, and don't assume everyone understands the terms used to state the problem. Get necessary background information before the group. What is the history of the problem? What limitations of budget or time will affect proposed solutions? By what standards will a solution be judged to determine if it is successful?

- *List all possible solutions.* The emphasis in this step is on listing, so don't stop to discuss any proposal. Try to get as many ideas before the group as possible, and don't worry about overlapping or contradictory ideas. Have someone serve as recorder to write down each idea.

- *Discuss the advantages and disadvantages of each proposed solution.* Take up each suggestion in order and get from the group all the good and bad points of each idea. Try to avoid argument; the group should be working toward a joint solution, and there should be no winners or losers when the final decision is reached. During this stage, do what you can to spread the talk around so that no person does all the talking.

- *Choose the best solution.* A group should aim for consensus rather than compromise in making a final decision. The solution to the group's problem should be agreed upon by all. A number of solutions may be combined in a final answer, but everyone should fully agree. Try not to take votes because once a person is committed to a particular answer by voting for it, he or she may find it hard to see the value of other possibilities.

The above process should be followed as closely as possible, although you will often find that groups have a habit of wandering off the subject and getting ahead of the agenda. Do your part; prod gently to keep participants on the track. You can use this process with a group as small as three or four or as large as six to eight. Larger groups are difficult to work with and should be broken into smaller units.

A manager often finds it better to assign a group to solve a problem than to solve it alone because groups have a stronger commitment to ideas if they are involved in producing them. For example, if there is a controversy about next year's vacation schedule, resist the temptation to issue an edict. Ask the concerned parties to sit down with you and solve the problem as a group.

In some situations, a group rather than a single speaker offers the best means of transferring information to an audience. To plan a panel discussion, take the total time allotted for the presentation and divide it into two parts. During the first part, have the panelists discuss the information. Each person can give a brief formal presentation, or the panelists can engage in a conversation for the audience. During the second part, allow the audience to ask questions or make comments.

A panel discussion is a dynamic communication activity that allows, even promotes, listener involvement. Make sure the audience is aware of the procedures being used.

Only in most unusual circumstances will a panel solve a problem. The usual aim is to generate information and get people thinking. You might use a panel instead of a speech for the annual safety message or to present a new program or procedure.

Interpersonal Communication

Do you ever say, "No, no. You didn't understand what I said." A far better choice in most cases is, "I'm sorry, I didn't make myself clear." An appreciation of how "understanding" comes about should show that the responsibility for getting a message across rests more with the communicator than with the receiver.

Since there is no way to transfer a message directly from the mind of one person to the mind of another, we must rely on "symbols" to carry our meaning, and the person who sends the symbol should know that the receiver may not interpret it in the same way the sender does. Consider the following dialogue:

"Do I turn left here?"

"Right!"

Obviously, "Right" can mean either "Yes, turn left" or "No, don't turn left." The sender knew exactly what was meant, but to the poor receiver, "right" is merely a symbol that must be interpreted. All too often the interpretation is followed by a heated argument.

In interpersonal communication, it's especially important to remember the role of symbols in transmitting ideas and feelings. Be careful in your choice of symbols and tolerant if a listener fails to attach your intended meaning to your words. If you choose the wrong words, your intentions won't count for much. To illustrate, look at the problem of sexism in language. A friend told me of a salesperson who invited a husband and wife to ride with him to look at some property. As the three of them got to the car, he said, "And the little lady can sit in the back." The salesperson *intended* to be courteous and friendly. But the words were interpreted as "I regard you as an inferior person in this important transaction." The salesperson didn't have a chance of making a sale after that.

When someone fails to convey a message, it's easy for the listener to become defensive. For instance, a supervisor says, "You didn't get it right." rather than "I didn't explain it clearly," and the listener's defense mechanism is tripped. To reduce defensiveness, find the symbols that will make sense to the other person.

One important distinction between two classes of word symbols can be useful in interpersonal communication. Some symbols are "descriptive" and others are "evaluative." As a rule, descriptive statements will cause less resentment. For example, "Tom, there are six changes I need in this report," uses descriptive symbols or words. This would be better than "Tom, you made a half-dozen mistakes in this report," which is an evaluative way of expressing the idea. One way to handle the problem of evaluative statements is to cast your opinions in terms of your own perception. Say, "I don't enjoy slide talks," instead of "Slide talks are terrible."

Of course, people use symbols other than words to send messages. Body movement, tone of voice and a variety of other nonverbal symbols may often be more important than language in sending messages. Consider the case when you ask a friend, "Will you help me work on this project?" Even if the answer is yes, you may drop the request if you pick up unspoken clues suggesting the *real* answer is, "I don't want to do it." There might be a slight pause before the answer, or perhaps the voice sounds weary, or your friend may avoid eye contact in giving the reply, or facial expression may show distaste for your suggestion. The tongue said yes, but the rest of the body said no.

For good interpersonal relationships, be sensitive to these nonverbal messages: If you say to a friend, "You look upset, what's the matter?" and your friend answers, "Nothing," the reply may satisfy you or may suggest that your friend has a serious problem. The true answer is in the sound of the voice rather than the choice of words. Most persons have little trouble recognizing the importance of vocal tone in instances when the vocal emphasis is strong. We need to be alert to cases when the voice transmits a more subtle message. The first warning of a problem may well be a slight chill in the way someone says "Good morning."

Watch your own use of vocal tone in sending messages. Be alert to detect that hollow sound in your voice that tells your listener that you aren't really interested in the conversation. Don't let the annoyance or boredom of the moment slip into your voice when you answer the telephone. The party on the other end may get messages you did not intend to transmit.

You have only to observe people in your next elevator ride to remember that people tend to be cool to the message sent by strangers touching in public. A firm handshake is almost always in order, although some people occasionally pump the other person's hand too forcefully and too long. Backslapping is limited to fairly close friends (or teammates), and the person who pounds away at casual acquaintances is likely to offend. There may be differences between the rules for public touching for women and for men, but the best advice is to try to sense what your particular interpersonal partner finds acceptable.

All of us have rather strong feelings about the proper distance to be maintained when we communicate in various circumstances. If you keep a subordinate too far away from you in an office conference, you may hurt the person's feelings; if you get too close, you may frighten the person. Be aware of the other person's zone of private space and don't invade it, but if someone gets too close to you for comfort, or stands too far away, try not to let the behavior interfere with your reception of messages. As a skilled communicator, you should understand what is happening and be able to handle the situation.

Gesture, posture and eye contact are other important areas of body language. For example, the gesture of "steepling" (the fingertips of one hand are pressed against the fingertips of the other) may signal "I've got you where I want you." It may make the other person uncomfortable or wary.

Posture often can give clues regarding the positive or negative thoughts in a person's mind. An angry, frustrated child may sit slumped back deep on the sofa with stiffly crossed arms. That same child, watching an appealing TV commercial, may sit on the edge of the sofa with hands on knees as though ready to run out and buy the product. These same gestures are seen in business encounters.

Too little eye contact can suggest a person is untrustworthy; too much may make a person squirm. When talking to only one person, shift your gaze occasionally from the person's eyes to objects in the area of your conversation. Don't avoid eye contact by looking off into the distance, except for purposes of reflection, and avoid the shifty look that results from moving your eyes from side to side.

Hair, clothing and jewelry all send messages. Obviously, the circumstances in which you communicate have a great impact on the way symbols of dress and appearance are interpreted. A college professor used his pipe as a dramatic tool in lecturing. He thought the pipe made him impressive. When students evaluated the class, one of the most forceful suggestions was "Get rid of the pipe." When it comes to the way you look, impressiveness should probably take second place to appropriateness.

In analyzing nonverbal signals, look at the total pattern of behavior rather than just one symbol, and consider the range of meanings a symbol may have. For example, drumming the fingers on a desk might mean impatience, but if the person doing it is smiling and talking with animated expression, maybe the nervous energy signals excitement over your idea.

Successful communication can occur only when someone assigns the intended meaning to the signals you have sent. It's a complicated process, whether it takes place at the interpersonal level, in public communication or during the deliberations of a committee.

Face-to-face communication in all its forms continues to be important. When David Rockefeller was asked to speculate on the responsibilities of business leaders in the year 2,000, he predicted that direct human contact will always be vital in communication. Business communicators should see the challenge they face in Rockefeller's statement that the business leaders of the next century "will have a personal responsibility for advocacy, activism and outspokenness" and must represent their companies and industries "articulately and coherently."

JERRY TARVER, PH.D., is professor of speech communication and theater arts at the University of Richmond in Richmond, Virginia; director of the Effective Speech Writing Institute, and editor of *The Effective Speech Writer's Newsletter.*

◆ 14 ◆

Media Relations

Wilma Mathews, ABC

Just as many other elements of the total public relations/communication spectrum are now being handled by full-time, in-house professionals, so is media relations being brought back to where it should rightfully belong: inside the organization, close to top management.

Media relations is not advertising, nor is it publicity or a contrived barrier set up to thwart journalists' inquiries. Media relations is the application of planned procedures and tactics designed to help the organization and the media meet their respective goals.

To properly understand what media relations is and how best to perform the function, a communicator needs to understand the terms used in the field, how to draw up a media plan and then set that plan into operation, how to get information to the media and increase its chances of being used, the ethics that guide professionals on both sides (organizations and journalism), and how to measure the results of the work.

Definition of Terms

"News" in its simplest form is what one doesn't know. That's a broad definition that implies that every newspaper, magazine, television or radio broadcast should always report all the information available to them because not everyone will be familiar with the information.

Time and space dictate the impossibility of reproducing all the information received by an editor or news director so, clearly, guidelines are needed to decide which information should be used and which should be omitted.

For the media relations practitioner, this selectivity is critical. Corporate executives and elected officials each think his or her own news is the single most important item of the day. A media relations practitioner sometimes must explain the newsmaking process in order to prevent delusions of grandeur and to help make the entire media relations program run more smoothly.

One public relations handbook says news is anything that is interesting and significant to readers or viewers. A handbook on media relations establishes two criteria for news: (1) the first information about any event that interests a large number of people, and (2) not what you want to tell other people but what other people want to know about you.

A definition that best puts the *function* of news making into perspective is this: "News is whatever an editor says it is on any given day." It is imperative that top management understand that the power of news selection rests solely with the media.

Whatever definition you choose, news is a perishable commodity. Nothing is deader than yesterday's news. If the decision-making ability is with an editor, then what can a media relations practitioner do to try to get his or her news to become the editor's news? These questions correlate well with what most journalists believe to be the criteria for news:

1. Is the story local? Does it have a local "hook," something that will interest readers or viewers or listeners in this area?
2. Is this information unusual or unique?
3. Is the material timely? Is it something happening now or will it happen in the near future? Does the material relate to an issue or event currently being discussed publicly?
4. Does this information concern people?
5. Does this material create human interest? Pathos? Humor?

If you can answer "yes" to these questions, you have a chance for your news becoming the editor's news.

News generally falls into one of two categories: hard or soft. Hard news happens by itself. An explosion or fire is hard news. A labor strike is hard news. Election of new officers is hard news. Soft news, on the other hand, is news that the public doesn't need to know. It's the story of the worker employed by the company for 40 years or the dedication of a park fountain, and most media relations activities focus on trying to place soft news items—trying to interest the media in timeless material than can inform, educate or entertain their audiences.

The Media Relations Plan

Getting started in media relations means understanding your role and your objectives, and sticking to both. Few executives seem to appreciate that your role is to help reporters meet their objectives and, at the same time, to help your organization meet its objectives.

This means that when you speak to a reporter you are representing your organization and when you speak to the people in your organization you are representing the reporter.

If your organization pursues a passive media relations program, it means that it has determined not to seek public attention. Privately held companies sometimes practice passive public relations. They can do this because they are not required by law or regulation to divulge earnings or other financial data. But even an organization obligated to divulge information to the public can have a passive program. In this case, nothing is reported beyond what must be reported.

If you have an active media relations program, it's important to understand what "active" means or, more to the point, what it doesn't mean:

- Active doesn't mean a release every day or every time someone requests one.
- Active doesn't mean holding a news conference at the drop of an executive's name.
- Active doesn't mean just taking reporters to lunch.
- Active doesn't mean counting column inches and declaring yourself a success.

Active *does* mean that you plan, implement and measure a well-developed media relations program that supports your organization. The first step in this process is to know well the direction in which your organization is going. For example, if your organization is like most, it will have as a goal the intention of maintaining a well-trained, well-paid employee population with low turnover. This may appear to be an internal matter but remember, employees come from the public and they can be attracted to your organization by what they learn from public avenues of communication—newspapers, magazines, radio and television. Your role in this area can be to make sure the public is aware of what a good place your organization is to work, by issuing announcements of promotions, retirements, long-term anniversaries, suggestion award winners, employee club activities, plant and office improvements, safety awards, corporation donations, and so forth. A formal goal structure is shown in Table 14.1.

After you've completed your plan, send it to the key executives for review and comment. This action accomplishes two things. First, it shows your top management that you are attuned to the activities of the organization and intend to support it through a planned approach to media activities. Second, it allows each person the opportunity to have input to the plan. One result is that you will be able to learn how your top officers

Table 14.1
Model Goal and Objectives for Media Relations

Media Relations Goal 1: To support the company's goal of hiring and maintaining well-trained employees and a low percentage of turnover.

Objectives

A. To inform the community about the accomplishments of our long-term employees.
    Strategies
    1. Work with personnel to establish a system for notifying media relations about all personnel advancements and retirements.
    2. Create a form to be filled in by each promoted or retiring employee to get information that can be used in a press release.
    3. Upon notification of promotion, issue a release to selected business media within five days; if appropriate, issue a release to employee's hometown and alumni publications within two weeks.

B. To show the organization's efforts as a good corporate citizen.
    Strategies
    1. Compile a list of all employees involved in civic and volunteer activities.
    2. Select possible feature story ideas from that list.
    3. Interview the employees and supervisors and try to place the resulting material in area weekly newspapers or (if a visual story) with local television station.

---

perceive the media. If, for instance, you have executives who are shy or antagonistic toward the press, you can begin helping them to meet the press.

Setting Up the Operation

Physicians will not open the doors to new offices until they have equipment. Similarly, an accountant can't begin serving clients without the latest reference books and guides. However, many people begin practicing media relations without proper equipment or materials.

Besides the basic office equipment and plenty of work space, you should make sure your telephone system meets your needs. A reporter should never have to become frustrated because he or she can't reach you. You need either more than one line to your office or successive lines that automatically jump to a subordinate's or secretary's line for pick-up. The objective is to make sure reporters can reach you when they want to, not just when it's convenient for you.

Your office should be a stand-alone resource center. Among the items you should have within arm's reach are a dictionary, a thesaurus, a list of subject matter experts, media directories, your organization's annual reports for the past several years, and a history of your organization. You should also have organization charts, recruitment brochures, benefits booklets, policy manuals—whatever the organization has, including product promotion brochures, catalogs and employee publications. Update and keep on hand about 25 general information kits as well as a calendar of events.

Professional journals and books that deal with the practice of media relations also should be available.

All of these are used at some time, in some way. Reporters can ask obscure questions and you have to be ready to reply as quickly as possible.

When reporters call for interviews, or just to get some general information, they don't begin by asking to speak specifically to "Mr. Smith, the manager of safety requirements." Instead, they will ask to speak with "someone who can talk about safety requirements in the industry." Reporters don't always know the people in your organization; that's your job. Start a list of subject matter experts by thinking like a reporter and asking yourself: "Who is knowledgeable about pricing policies? Labor relations? Safety requirements? Product lines? Food services? Financial statistics?" List the subjects alphabetically and, under each category, the experts and their telephone numbers.

Ways to Get into the Media

There are numerous ways to work with the media. The more ways you are familiar with, the better chance you have of placing a soft news story with the most appropriate medium.

The most misused method of getting into the media is the press release. While each media relations practitioner is convinced that his or her news release is "different" or "better," editors feel differently. According to editors, who see hundreds of releases daily and discard almost the same number, most news releases miss the local angle and have missing information, meaningless management commentary and corporate jibberish. Editors also know that some news releases they get are poorly written, have typos and errors, and do not follow basic rules of journalism. Don't let yours fall into the "poor" category—the waste basket.

News releases are not designed to take the place of reporters. Instead, they are memoranda to editors. They should acquaint the editors with the basic facts of a potential story, just as a memo would. The editors then can decide if the proposed story warrants attention; if so, a reporter will be assigned to gather more information and rewrite the material to fit the format of the publication or station.

The trick is to get editors to read your release. Just as a memo should be short and to the point, so should a news release. Learn the difference between writing a release for the print media and writing one for the electronic media; writing for space is different from writing for time.

Talk shows should be on your list. Programmers for these shows, whether radio or television, have to fill that time slot every day or every week. They are looking for ideas, for guests, for the unusual. You, on the other hand, have an abundance of ideas and people available to suggest to the programmer.

Radio talk shows give you and your organization the opportunity to present a new program or a twist to an old one. Call-in shows offer a valuable forum for your organization and also give you the opportunity to find out what's on the public's mind. Television talk shows offer opportunities for hard news and feature topics with visual support. Nothing is duller than 30 minutes of a "talking head."

Topics for talk shows are practically limitless. They include such standards as education, health care, consumer affairs, new technology, law, religion, business, minority affairs, energy conservation, sports and personal finance.

Op-ed pieces are relatively new media relations tools. Named for their position in a newspaper, opposite the editorial page, op-ed pieces offer your organization the chance to present its opinion on a subject or philosophize about a current issue. Op-ed pieces run about 750 words. While other specifics may vary, editors agree that the pieces should have two things: timeliness and creativity. Be sure to define the issue or state the problem as you see it. Provide whatever background or history is needed, then suggest ways to change or improve the situation. The writing should be similar to that for white papers about a particular issue, though here it is much briefer.

Letters to the editor are another way to get into the newspaper but again, this method is often abused. Letters should not be written about each and every minor error, misquote or suspected bias. Letters generally should respond to specific articles in the paper. They can be used to clarify a point, to refute a charge, or simply to react to a situation.

There is no guarantee that your letter will be used, nor is there a guarantee that the letter, if used, will still be timely when it appears. Finally, there is no conclusive way to prove that the letter did any good.

A rule of thumb is that a letter to the editor to clarify an inaccuracy is welcome because journalists are as concerned with accuracy and professionalism as you are. On the other hand, a letter written in spite often appears juvenile and is treated as such.

Just as a release has "news" as its objective, so should a conference. A news conference should offer both news and a forum for the exchange of information. Unfortunately, the news conference has been badly mauled by publicity-seeking persons or groups who offer little more than an orchestrated attempt to gain free publicity.

If you aren't sure if you should have a news conference, ask yourself these questions:

- Is this a major announcement?
- Is this announcement something that will significantly affect the audience?
- Is this a complex issue that cannot be explained in a news release?
- Does the occasion involve a celebrity from whom the media would want quotes, photographs or tape?

If you have to conduct a news conference, try to gain all the time and assistance you can. The logistics of hosting a news conference are sometimes complex, and the follow-up work after a conference can be as time-consuming as the conference itself.

Not all the ways for getting into the media involve such instant returns as a news conference does. As part of your ongoing relations with the media, you should consider having backgrounders, briefings or seminars.

A backgrounder is a written piece that can be given to a writer or editor explaining the history of an issue—how it came to be an issue in the first place.

A briefing generally is face-to-face. Journalists are gathered to hear a speaker or speakers discuss an issue instead of relying solely on the written material in a backgrounder.

A seminar is used to explain very complex topics. Generally, these are held for specialty writers, such as science or financial writers, who need to have the issues explained in depth.

The interview still remains one of the most favored ways to get into the media, but, like the news release, the interview is often mishandled. An interview should not be a free-wheeling conversation; it should be a planned situation for exchanging information, a programmed question-and-answer session.

The chief executive officer is not always the best person to be interviewed on a subject because while the CEO is involved with all aspects of the business, he or she is not necessarily an *expert* on every topic. Sometimes you will have to persuade reporters that someone other than the CEO is the best source for the information they desire. Choose the interviewee carefully, remembering that your goal is to help the journalist get the best story possible and to help your organization meet its goals in that particular subject area.

Try to decide ahead of time the key points that should be stressed during an interview, and discuss these with the person to be interviewed. Use them for a rehearsal, if possible. Remind your spokesperson to keep answers realistic, short and positive, to avoid jargon, and not to be afraid to say "I don't know" to any question.

Ethics

Without ethics, or a code of behavior, the exchange between the media relations practitioner and the journalist becomes a time-wasting excursion into mistrust, speculation, innuendo and frustration.

Examples of the lack of ethics abound. Most notable, and perhaps of the greatest impact, was Watergate. The house of cards erected by so many public officials came crashing down, bringing with it a distrust of government that has lasted, in some arenas, to this day. Also lasting, however, are the lessons learned from Watergate. Those lessons, for the most part, translate into a code of behavior:

Trust: Fear and respect often are synonymous. Respect for the power of electricity causes linemen to work more safely. The same is true with the media. Because the media are powerful, they must be respected. But to fear the media is to put yourself in the subservient position, not in the position of a professional exchanging information with another professional. It is essential to trust the media unless or until an individual representative of the media does something to cause you to distrust that *one person.* Journalists are performing a job, not staging for a lynching.

Lying: "First, businessmen must realize that both reporters and the public are sophisticated enough to recognize smokescreens, if not penetrate them. Honesty *is* the best policy," wrote Joseph Sullivan in *Business and Media.* Lying in public is no different from lying in the courtroom under oath. The sentence, however, is tougher: loss of credibility, loss of respect and loss of trust. There is no such thing as a "half-lie," a "small lie" or a "white lie."

No comment: Few words create such frustration to a reporter as "No comment." The phrase really means "Won't comment" and connotes a deliberate barrier to cooperation.

A reporter is trying to do his or her job. For a reporter to hear "No comment" is the same as giving a welder a job to do and then refusing to allow him or her to have access to the pieces that need welding.

"No comment" is assumed by many to be a safeguard against putting one's foot in one's mouth. For instance, saying "No comment" seems safer than saying "I made a mistake." Many reporters and the public have assumed, because of the misuse of the phrase, that "No comment" means "I am guilty as hell but I won't admit it."

The best course is to answer the reporter's question or to say that you cannot answer for specific reasons.

Off the record: There is no such thing as "off the record." If you're in doubt on this point, use the following guideline: Never say anything to a reporter that you aren't willing to see in print or hear on the evening news. This guideline applies at all times, even in social settings. Reporters do their jobs 24 hours a day; so should you.

Many people feel that "off the record" material is needed to curry favor with a reporter. Others know from experience, however, that many reporters will use "off the record" material if it helps enhance the story, or will surmise that you might have other material that you're holding back.

Advertising: The temptation to use the media for free advertising, however great, must be resisted. The media are there to report *news*, not to take the place of your advertising budget. If you are closing your store or plant for vacation, don't expect the media to report it; instead, buy advertising space if it's important for the public to know.

Don't ever use your company's advertising strength to "blackmail" the media into thinking your way or using your news releases. The information in a news release must be determined on its own merits, not on its association with another department.

Saying "No": Don't confuse "No comment" with "No, I can't answer that question because...." There are legitimate times when information can't be disclosed. Reporters will continue to try to get that information, but you can continue to not give it. For example, many judges impose restrictions on the media in a criminal or civil case to prevent prejudicing jurors through discussion in the media. Thus, if a reporter asks about a court case, it is understandable if you reply, "I'm sorry but we're not allowed to discuss this case under terms agreed to in court." Another example is when you are asked to disclose proprietary information. Financial information, such as projected revenues, can be withheld if the giving of that information would help the competition form conclusions about your organization's strategies and tactics.

Making demands: Because top management approves annual reports, employee publications, brochures and other material before publication, it is understandable that they might feel they have a right to review copy prepared by an outside journalist. The media relations person must, if necessary, attempt to educate management about the differences between a reporter and a company staff writer.

Andy Rooney was once asked if he thought the way the management of a large corporation imposed limits on the questions to be asked damaged the company. He replied, "It made me suspect they had something to hide. And because it was difficult to get information from them, I got it from a dozen less sympathetic sources... former executives of the company, drivers, pilots and dissidents from within the company itself."

Measurement of Media Relations Results

Measurement is most often the forgotten element in the media relations program. When it is remembered, measurement often takes the form of a quick, knee-jerk reaction, such as, "How'd we do on that story about the employee who collects corn husks?"

Measurement should be as well planned as the rest of the media relations program. You should make a decision early about what you want to measure:

- The relationship you have with the media?
- The numbers of people who read or hear your message?
- The way your message is received by those people?
- How many media outlets use your message?
- Where those media outlets are located geographically?

Regardless of the size of the operation, every well-run media program should have a defined method for monitoring the results. It used to be that measuring media activity meant counting the column inches in a newspaper story and presenting that information, with a flourish, to your boss. The idea was that the more column inches you had, the more successful your program. Changes in the media and increasing sophistication in measurement techniques have changed all that.

You can monitor your own activity or you can retain an outside firm to do it. To monitor your own work, subscribe to all the publications to which you send news releases, and make sure you have people monitoring the radio and television programs on your media list. Note the date and publication or station call letters and time for each use of your material by the media. For instance, if you issue a release on Wednesday to all local publications and electronic media, with an afternoon release time, you need to first pay attention to the electronic media for all evening newscasts. Beginning the next morning, check daily publications for use, and then check the next issues of any trade publications you might have included on your list.

After a full cycle of possible use has been completed, compile all your clips and notations and prepare a package showing how the release was used. If you send to monthly publications, you need to wait for at least the next issue or possibly two.

Clips and notations should be broken out by category—print and electronic media—and should be presented chronologically. The clippings should appear in their entirety. Prepare a précis of the total coverage, summarizing whether the release was used by a majority of the outlets or not, if the material was drastically rewritten (and if so, why), and whether there is an indication of editorial comment, including any negative or positive slant to the presentation.

You also can count the column inches for each publication and relate what the same space would have cost if you had had to purchase advertising space.

For media relations programs that cover a broad geographical area, consider engaging a clipping service to monitor publications and/or electronic media. It can be expensive but the expense can be justified by the assurance that hundreds or even thousands of publications can be covered, accurately, at a fraction of what it would cost if you had to subscribe to those publications yourself.

A benefit of engaging a service is that you can monitor issues as well as use of your releases. For instance, if you wish to see how the media are dealing with a topic or issue, such as health care of the aged, you can ask your clipping agency to send you those articles. From the resulting material, you can see what is now appearing on the topic and compare that with what your organization *wants* to appear on the topic. In other words, clipping services can help you plan your next phase of operation and at the same time monitor and measure your existing program.

Electronic clipping on a large basis can be quite expensive. Investigate carefully all the electronic offerings to see how they meet your needs. Unless you have a reason to use a video or audio clip right away, it's senseless to buy that clip and have it gather dust on the shelf. An alternative is to buy the program transcript. It can be included with the print clips in your report or review. Transcripts are expensive but they have a longer "shelf life" than tapes.

Measurement can be both short-term—determining how one release was received and long-term—determining how well an issue is being handled over one, two or three years. If your organization is trying to educate and inform the public on a particular topic, it will take a long time to determine whether your efforts are paying off. This is especially true if your company is trying to get the public to see an issue in a new light. For example, if your company has been known as one that dumps chemicals and you wish it to be known as a company that promotes environmental safety and high standards, you have months and years of media relations ahead of you.

Close monitoring of every step of the way during such a campaign allows you to alter the program as needed while still heading toward your original objective. Such scrutiny allows you to determine whether your message is correct but going to the wrong medium, for example, or whether your message isn't getting across because it isn't prepared properly for the medium, or whether your mailing list is out-of-date.

Certain measurements should be done by an objective outside agency. These include measuring your relationship with the media (how editors and journalists view or rate your media activities), measuring how people are reacting to your overall campaign, and measuring subjective elements, such as the positive, neutral or negative implications of articles.

Trained opinion experts and pollsters should be retained for this type of measurement, but it's expensive. If it's necessary for you to have this information in order to meet your organization's goals, such expense is more than justified, however.

Take your time in selecting the agency, detail what your organization wishes to measure and why, and seek references from others who have used the agency. You've put a lot of work into creating a program that will tell your organization's story to the public, so you should measure the impact of that program and relate how that helps your organization meet its goals and objectives.

WILMA MATHEWS, ABC, is media relations manager for AT & T Technologies, Inc., New York, New York. She is a former member of the board of the International Association of Business Communicators and is accredited by IABC.

• Part IV •

SOME SPECIAL NEEDS AND TECHNIQUES

◆ 15 ◆

Important Single-Purpose Programs

Rae Leaper, ABC

Everything a communicator does should have a specific purpose, and the part that purpose plays in the overall plan and the specific audience addressed should always be clearly in mind. The importance of planning, the need for audience identification and skillful media selection, and the necessity of winning top management support are clearly seen in special-purpose communication.

The topics discussed in this chapter are specific. They are also extremely diverse: safety campaigns and shareholders' meetings, patient information programs and organizational moves, economic education, and communicating in a crisis. Each one gives the communicator the opportunity to reinforce his or her role as a member of the organization's management team by using communication tools and techniques to solve problems.

The chapter is divided into two sections: (1) special-purpose communication as part of ongoing communication programs, and (2) one-time events, activities and disasters.

Single-Purpose Communication in Ongoing Programs

Employee Orientation

In most organizations the responsibility for employee orientation belongs to the personnel department. However, it is important that the communication department cooperate in the production of the program, perhaps in a customer–client relationship.

237

Good employee orientation programs can help reduce turnover, training time and cost, waste, tardiness and absenteeism. They can also improve productivity and product quality, as well as employee loyalty and morale. In addition, well-informed employees are an effective medium for telling a company's story in the community.

The importance of establishing open, two-way communication in an organization gives the communicator an added and personal interest in the content and presentation of employee orientation programs.

In the Beginning, There Are Always Goals.   An effective orientation program makes an immediate, permanent impression on a new employee and may mean the difference between the person's success or failure on the job. Before planning such an important program, there should be specific goals to direct its development and against which it can be evaluated. One major consulting firm suggests the following as possible goals:

- To provide new employees with a clear picture of what the organization offers them and what it expects from them.
- To provide new employees with a basis for sound decision—on the job, in compensation and benefits, in career planning.
- To provide new employees with ongoing access to individuals who have detailed knowledge of various aspects of the organization.
- To provide new employees with an introduction to the work and those with the same or similar jobs.
- To provide new employees with an awareness of the channels available for problem solving.

Instead of a program aimed at accomplishing a logical set of goals, too many orientation programs fall into one of four designs identified by Robert W. Hollman of the University of Arizona. The Paperwork Design finds the personnel department saying a brief hello and then devoting its enthusiasm to getting all the necessary forms completed. The Social Darwinism Design throws the new employee almost immediately into the job with the idea that the "most fit" will survive. The Mickey Mouse Design turns the new employee into the department "gofer" or assigns *all* the organization's policy and procedure manuals. The Overload Design thrusts an elaborate and comprehensive body of information on a new employee in a short time.

What Goes into an Orientation Program.   Employee orientation can be divided into two distinct parts: general orientation to the organization and specific orientation to the job and department.

Although an orientation program must be tailored to the size and nature of the company, the general orientation should include an overview of the organization—what it does or makes; its basic structure; its history and position in the field; its policies and procedures on hours, vacations,

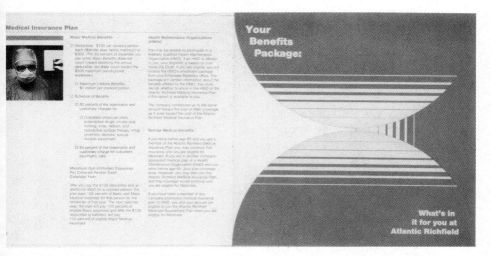

Figure 15.1. Printed materials often are the heart of employee information programs—reinforcing audiovisuals and allowing employees to review important information at their leisure.

holidays and training; salary and wage information; benefits; and a description of physical facilities.

Job and departmental orientation usually includes the department's objectives and activities and how these fit into the overall organization; specific duties, policies and procedures of the department; a tour of the area, and an introduction to others in the department.

The general orientation is usually covered by a formal program designed for all new employees; the specific orientation, by a new employee's supervisor.

The major flaw in many, and perhaps most, employee orientation programs is that they do not tell the new person what he or she needs to know to feel comfortable and to get started in the new job. The new employee is often nervous, withdrawn and anxious. Many well-intended orientation sessions only compound this anxiety by drowning the new person with a flood of confusing information on benefits, stock plans, time sheets, retirement plans, work rules and on and on. The successful program meets the immediate needs of new employees.

A vital but often overlooked element is letting the new employee know that the company expects him or her to succeed in the job.

How Long and When? Timing the formal orientation, both the length of the session and when it is given, is important but there is no universal rule. The lengths vary from a couple of hours to several days. Many organizations set an orientation session for the employee's first day on the job. Some large corporations have regularly scheduled orientation sessions and new employees attend the next one available.

Perhaps the most common practice is to structure the orientation as a half- or whole-day process, during which the person or persons conducting the session uses a variety of printed materials and audiovisual aids.

Printed materials are usually the heart of orientation programs because employees can use them for later reference when questions arise. Two obvious and effective formats are looseleaf notebooks or packets of individual leaflets or sections, which can be updated without changing the entire contents.

Don't overlook the important role of employee publications in announcing a new or revised orientation program. It's an excellent opportunity to remind all employees of important facts about the company and to demonstrate that it's an organization that gives attention and consideration to those who work for it.

Diamond Shamrock carries this a step further and distributes a special edition of *News* for new employees. The headline on the lead story says, "Special Edition welcomes you to Diamond Shamrock." The eight-page magapaper includes a letter from the chief executive officer, background

Figure 15.2. New employees need more than an introduction to the company and their work area. Diamond Shamrock welcomes its new employees with a special edition of its monthly *Diamond Shamrock News*.

information on the company and each of its major units, and articles on the company's interest in community affairs.

Many organizations make effective use of films and/or slide presentations for orientation. They can be simple (one slide projector and a tape cassette) or complex (a multiprojector slide show, a 16-mm color film or a television program). One advantage of audiovisuals is their impact. They can present what employees need to know in color, pictures, words and sound. They also can bring to the audience people who otherwise could not be there or scenes that many employees may never see, and they tell the same story each time, to each group of employees in each location.

Many companies include a tour of the facilities as part of the orientation. It helps the new person put things into perspective, provides an often much needed break and stimulates questions.

Keep in mind that new employees are not able to absorb an infinite amount of information, especially on their first day on the job. If it's communication you're after, orientation should be handled as a long-term process, not a crash program. Orientation should not stop when the film ends, the lights go on, and the handbook is issued. It takes most people months to feel really comfortable in a new company. Formal and systematic follow-up to the initial orientation is essential.

During the first year there may be times when employees become eligible to participate in certain benefit plans. These are the logical times to give in-depth information on these plans, as extensions of the orientation process.

Specific, job-related orientation is the responsibility of the supervisor, but the communication department also has a helpful role to play here. More than likely, it falls to the supervisor to make sure that questions are answered and that important information is restated when necessary. The communicator can assist by preparing guidelines for supervisors, outlining topics to be covered and describing sources of detailed information for answering specific questions. The Atlantic Richfield Company's orientation packet includes an employee checklist of items the supervisor will be discussing. The introduction points out that the list is provided so that employees can develop questions pertaining to their personal needs in advance.

Employees who have been on the job for a year or less are good sources of feedback on the effectiveness of an orientation program. Employee turnover statistics, especially if it's a new program or if significant changes have been made, also can provide an excellent means of evaluation.

Safety Campaigns

The role of communication in maintaining safety is clearly recognized. Countless studies have shown that most accidents are caused by unsafe practices, not unsafe conditions. Awareness is the key factor, and the need to think constantly about safety must be told and retold. Communicators must keep finding effective ways to do this, in cooperation with the department or departments specifically charged with the responsibility for safety.

To be effective, a safety program must have top management support—and this includes support for its communication components. In IABC's 1978 survey of the chief executive officers of 50 of the largest corporations in the United States and Canada, 48 said they believe communication can make a difference in the company's safety record.

Which Medium Should Carry the Message? An organization's publications, of course, play an important role in safety campaigns. They can be used to call attention to ongoing safety campaigns; to announce new plans; to recognize goals, achievements or anniversaries; to document with personal experiences the importance of following safe procedures, and to cajole and compliment. Editors are remarkably resourceful and they have created a wonderful variety of stories and photos to carry the message.

Communicators don't have a monopoly on creativity, though. One way to involve employees and to recognize their contributions to safety is to run contests. Pennsylvania Power & Light Company, for instance, ran a quarterly safety slogan contest as part of a larger safety communication program. The winning slogans were posted on bulletin boards, run in publications and featured on the monthly employee video program. The winners were honored at a lunch and presented with $100 savings bonds.

Communicators also have devised a seemingly endless list of media to get across the safety message: films, slide/tape presentations, meetings, demonstrations, video programs, booklets, billboards, posters, brochures, drawings, bonuses, awards, decals and stickers, calendars, letters, paycheck stuffers, special days or weeks, bumper stickers, flags and T-shirts.

Not all safety campaigns are organization-wide. It's possible to mount special short-term programs to solve particular problems. Be on the lookout for hot spots and move in with a plan. The short-term emphasis, even without a trouble spot, can help keep the overall program fresh.

There's a tendency to think of safety in terms of heavy equipment, hard hats and safety goggles. Employees who push nothing heavier than a pencil also face hazards, and communicators who work for seemingly "safe" organizations are not exempt from planning and carrying out safety awareness programs. Off-the-job safety campaigns should be developed, as well as plans for such emergencies as fires, earthquakes and tornadoes.

Safety programs and achievements also are news for the external media, but use caution or they may be interpreted as confirming the existence of an unsafe workplace.

A pleasant side effect of a safety campaign is that it can demonstrate the communication department's effectiveness in numbers and dollars.

Financial Communication

The Annual Report.   The flagship of a company's financial communication flotilla is the annual report. On it are lavished the love, money, attention, and perhaps the paranoia that go with putting the organization's best foot forward for very important audiences: shareholders, investors and security analysts.

The pages of annual reports have become showcases for the printing, paper, photography and design businesses of the world. During the recent worldwide recession, designers faced an added challenge: to create a report that is impressive and memorable, without looking lavish or expensive.

In many annual reports, the beauty of the design and production often seem to be in reverse proportion to the quality of the writing, but that's changing. The annual report is too valuable a communication tool and reaches audiences that are too important to the company to waste the opportunity to say something significant.

In the past, a few organizations found the courage to speak candidly about a bad year. Most feared there would have been a collective corporate coronary if anyone had suggested that the president say, "Last year was not a very good year." When it happened, neither the world nor the stock market collapsed. Unfortunately, the past few years have given more corporations the opportunity to speak candidly about hard times, and many have not shirked the responsibility. In the 1982 Potlatch report, the chairman used words like "painful," "rocky" and even "devastating" to describe the year. Boise Cascade's CEO described the company as "buffeted by the worst economic conditions in decades."

Corporations also are using their annual reports to show that they are run by concerned human beings who participate in civic and community activities.

Quarterly Reports.   In the United States, the Securities and Exchange Commission requires many organizations to file financial data with the SEC each quarter. Although there is no federal requirement to share this information with shareholders, more and more organizations are issuing quarterly reports. The primary intent of quarterly reports is to transmit fiscal information about the corporation, but most do not neglect appearance. To stimulate readership, many companies mail their reports with their quarterly dividend checks.

Some companies also produce quarterly publications for other audiences. Standard Oil Company of California mails *Chevron World* each quarter to shareholders, employees, the media and others. The four-color magazine includes articles on legislation that affects the industry, offshore drilling, and other subjects of interest to persons investing and working in the oil industry.

A number of organizations send special letters on a variety of topics, including legislation, regulation and finances. They keep shareholders informed of major political and legislative developments affecting their companies and suggest actions they can take.

Typecast.   Until recently, financial communication was almost exclusively the province of print media. Now communicators are showing that there are other interesting and effective ways to communicate financial news to a corporation's audiences.

Emhart Corporation has pioneered the use of television for financial reporting. Starting in 1979, the company has videotaped its annual meeting and edited the 2½ hours down to a crisp 25 minutes (including video clips of plant scenes), and has made 100 cassettes that are available to shareholders for home viewing. Emhart has produced a 22-minute version of its printed annual report. The videotape followed the flow of the printed report and presented the chairman's commentary and important financial numbers. Cassettes were offered to shareholders and the company presented the report on a one-time network of 22 cable systems in eight states. The prime audience was about 10,000 shareholders, representing more than 50% of the outstanding stock. The total potential viewing audience was 1.1 million. Employees were able to view the tapes on the company's internal television system.

Ashland Oil in Kentucky provides closed-circuit television coverage of its annual meeting to shareholders and security analysts in New York City. The action was prompted in 1979 by bad weather and a desire to save the security analysts two days of travel to Kentucky. The television coverage has been extended to Columbus, Ohio, where the company has a major facility.

Other corporations are putting new life and meaning into the required annual meetings of stockholders by taking them "on the road" to cities where the company has important facilities and substantial concentrations of shareholders.

In a note of warning, Emhart's vice president for public relations, John F. Budd, Jr., cautions that "heavy-handed, slanted corporate propaganda served up as the facts will abuse the flexibility of the medium, and perhaps bring on regulation."

The Employees' Right to Know.   Ironically, a corporation's employees have only recently been considered an important audience for financial information. Today's employees feel they have a right to know about the organization for which they work. They want to know how the company is doing and how the competition is doing, where the company is going and how it plans to get there, the future of the industry and the security of their jobs.

The communicator should recognize this right and need to know, and be ready to provide the information through a variety of media. Employee publications and management newsletters are two of the most effective ways of keeping employees up to date on the fiscal health of the organization. Audiovisual presentations, closed-circuit television and meetings are a few of the other media available.

Even if organizations weren't responding to employees' need and right to know, there now are legal requirements for reporting at least some financial information to employees. In the United States, the Employee Retirement Income Security Act of 1974 (ERISA) requires an annual disclosure of benefit-plan financial information to employees.

The key element in financial communication for employees (and all other audiences) is credibility. Employees want to know the unfavorable news as well as the favorable. They expect honesty.

Employee Annual Reports. Perhaps nowhere is the recent acknowledgment of the employees' right to know about the organization for which they work more clearly demonstrated than in the increasing popularity of employee annual reports. Great Britain was perhaps 10 years ahead of US corporations in producing annual reports specifically for employees.

In most organizations, the employee annual report has grown out of the

Figure 15.3. Economic education programs should suit the needs and times of each organization's special audiences.

practice of giving employees copies of the annual report for shareholders—which is better than no effort at communication but also an example of mismatching a medium and the intended audience. Employees have a different stake in the company from that of stockholders.

In 1979, the Clorox Company of Oakland, California, mailed corporate and employee annual reports simultaneously to a representative sample of employees. A survey conducted by a consumer research firm showed that 71% of those interviewed preferred the employee report; 81% felt that their own report gave them the feeling that Clorox has a positive attitude toward employees. The Bank of America conducted a random telephone survey following the production of its first employee annual report, which replaced an issue of the bank's monthly employee magazine. More than 90% rated the publication "good" or "very good," and 86% said they would like to receive future editions.

Not all efforts are successful, however. Many reports are more propaganda than revelation. They tend to be "preachy," poorly written, or both. Too often they emphasize how little money the company is making and at the same time herald the benefits to employees. About 50% don't even include financial data. Such reports may do more harm than good because most of today's employees see through the veneer of attempted goodwill.

The basis of the employee annual report, like the corporate annual report, is financial. However, there are significant differences in what kind of financial information employees and families are most interested in and how it should be presented. Employees want an interpretation of the figures as they affect jobs. The best reports explain where the company is headed, what its strategy is and what that's going to mean to employees.

An ideal employee annual report should contain the following:

- A freewheeling discussion by the chief executive of the firm's goals, prospects for reaching them, problems, accomplishments and failures.
- A summation of the year's major events.
- A discussion of employment in the organization, addressing the issue of job security.
- A discussion of trends both in the firm and in the industry.
- A projection of operating results.
- A graphic analysis of expenditures with accompanying narrative explanation. Emphasis should be on expenditures that often confuse employees, such as borrowing money, payments to stockholders and depreciation; the how's and why's of material costs, compensation and benefits, machinery and equipment costs, interest payments, taxes and retained earnings.
- An analysis of income, which is generally easier for most people to understand than a mere statement of income, and an explanation of profits.

- Comments on the contributions various divisions make to the entire organization's financial picture.
- An easy-to-understand explanation of financial jargon.
- If possible, a parallel between "economics" familiar to employees (e.g., budgets and wages) and the "economics" of the firm.
- A tie-in, if possible, to relevant external social, political and general economic issues.

There are many ways to present information. A report can be built around a theme or a diary of the year's significant events. Annual reports naturally lend themselves to comparisons—either a long-range (5- or 10-year) historical analysis or a comparison of this year and last. There are many kinds of information that can be compared: employment rates, company growth, diversification, benefits. For years Pitney Bowes has presented charts showing the growth of employees' pay.

One of the most popular approaches to an employee annual report is the photo story. The report is for and about employees, so what better way to illustrate it and tell the year's story than through photographs of the employees? Closely related to this is the trend to have employees speaking for themselves, rather than the company speaking to employees.

Employee annual reports come in a variety of formats, although the most common are inserts in the regular publication or a special edition of the publication. Most efforts are rather modest because companies do not want to spend as much money on these reports as they do on the annual reports to shareholders.

This does not mean that the field is without creativity and innovation. Bemis Company has presented a simple and readable report in the form of a checkbook. Thorn EMI in London created an eight-page, four-color publication and nine different two-page inserts so employees in the various divisions could compare the financial status of their divisions with that of the company as a whole.

Because of all the effort that goes into producing an annual report for employees, it's worth a little more planning and effort to gain added impact at the time of distribution. The regular employee publications, special publications for supervisors and managers and bulletin boards all should be used to stimulate interest in the forthcoming annual report. Employee meetings at the time of distribution can help make maximum use of the report.

Although print predominates, a few organizations are using other media. Daniel Freeman Memorial Hospital in Inglewood, California, used a slide presentation to supplement its printed report. The 1,500 employees viewed the slide presentation over a three-day period and hospital officials were available at the meetings to answer questions. The slide presentation became a communication technique in itself. It brought employees together for open communication and gave employees on the night shift a rare opportunity to meet officials and participate in discussions.

Burlington Industries in Greensboro, North Carolina, has been producing video employee annual reports for the past 20 years.

Economic Education Programs

In spite of the fact that decades of economic education programs have not significantly shaped or changed the attitudes of the public, stockholders or employees, there are at least two excellent reasons for initiating economic education programs. One is the almost symbiotic relationship that exists between business and government. Few, if any, major decisions of business today can be made without government approval of some type at the federal, provincial, state or local level. The second reason is the increasing number of probing questions being asked by employees, stockholders and neighbors, to which they expect honest answers.

Figure 15.4. Employees want an easy way to understand organizational finances in their annual reports. Some organizations include the annual report in a regular issue of the publication; others issue separate reviews.

Both reasons are present in the following statement of the chief executive officer of a large multiproduct corporation:

> I go to Washington frequently these days and generally get clobbered whenever I'm there. So, I turn to our employees and shareholders for support. And they're not there. They're sidelining me.... As for our employees, they're great on the job, but they seem to change identities as soon as they leave the gate. On the job, they are loyal, devoted and efficient. Off the job, they act as if they don't know their company and stay aloof or even hostile when we lock horns with the government.

A survey of United States businesses showed that only 10% to 30% have at least a fairly systematic economic education program. Of these, many are more talk than action; they boil down to occasional speeches by executives on free enterprise or pamphlets for grade school children.

Past attempts at economic education have been called "one of the most spectacular marketing disasters of recent years." Early programs grew out of the Great Depression and the tremendous changes it caused. Since that time, programs have been generally ineffective and, not infrequently, self-serving to the point of being offensive. The reason for the unenviable track record of most economic education programs is that they have been based on two erroneous assumptions: (1) people, including shareholders and employees, are economically "illiterate," and (2) people are hostile to business and the free enterprise system.

Although surveys turn up significant gaps in information and knowledge (one of the most consistent is the overestimation of the amount of profits businesses earn), there is no evidence that the public is not interested in the economic system. On the contrary, there are indications that the public today is more knowledgeable about economic trends and developments than ever before and not only supports the United States economic system, but says it is willing to make sacrifices in order to preserve it.

Fortunately, a few businesses have programs that seem to be successfully getting their economic messages across. They are designed to restore confidence in business and its leaders, to win "constituency" support for company goals and to answer the concerns and questions of these constituencies in specific ways.

Guidelines for Success. Towers, Perrin, Forster & Crosby conducted a survey of large corporations for the Financial Executives Research Foundation in 1977. Based on an analysis of 130 separate programs reported, TPF&C offered the following guidelines:

> *There is no universal program.* What works in one place is not always effective in another. Each organization needs to plan its own program to suit the needs of its audiences.

Define the subject. Economic education does not mean the same thing to everyone, and unless it is clearly defined in management's mind, only confusion can result. For some, economic education means an academic approach that is unbiased and that deals with principles and laws of economics. For others, it means an advocacy approach with political activity the desired result.

Think small. The programs that seem to work best aim specific and limited messages at specific audiences; they put general topics into the perspective of their business and employees.

Know the audience. It is important to know which questions people want answered, which existing positive attitudes can be reinforced, which negative attitudes should be addressed, and which gaps in information or knowledge need to be filled. Letters, meetings or surveys can provide answers to these questions and thereby shape the content of the programs being planned and give benchmarks for measuring progress.

Make it an ongoing program. One-shot programs are more likely to be seen as self-serving and manipulative.

Keep it part of the established communication channels. When an economic education program works well it is usually integrated in an existing communication program. Blaring introductions usually are counterproductive.

The chief executive must be involved. Programs that thrive and succeed have the active support of the CEO.

In employee programs, the first audience should be management at all levels. It is often overlooked that managers' information needs are just as intense as those of rank-and-file employees, perhaps more so. Although the differences between the interests and concerns of employees and managers are not great, they are significant.

Don't forget to listen. Employees want to know more about the business and how it affects them. They want to listen and to be listened to.

Keep it cheap. There is no evidence that expensive programs work better. Expensive, elaborate productions (films, videotape, four-color brochures) may provoke hostile questions about costs.

Keep it flexible. Most economic education materials have a "shelf life" of little more than one year because events move so rapidly. With the exception of materials of historic nature, avoid producing "permanent" materials.

Patient Information Programs

Perhaps the term "captive audience" is a bit strong, but once a person checks into hospital, he or she may feel that way. Whatever the length of the stay, there are certain things a patient needs to know.

The most popular medium for providing this information to the patient is a pamphlet or booklet. These are produced in a boundless variety of sizes, shapes, colors and designs. For most, the purpose is straight information—what the patient, family and friends need to know about the hospital, plus as warm a welcome as can be offered on the printed page.

The pamphlets or booklets attempt to answer every question a patient might ask—everything from "admitting procedures" to "menu selection"

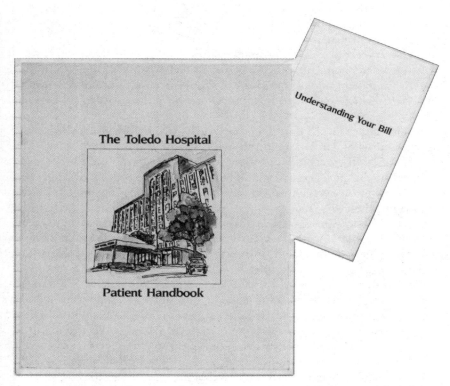

Figure 15.5. Hospital patients have many questions—give them straight inform-ation in an easy-to-read manner.

and "what to bring." The copy should be brief and to the point; the type, large and readable; the sections, clearly marked. The 27-page booklet developed by The Toledo Hospital, for instance, uses whimsical four-color drawings to illustrate the many services provided. The booklet also gives brief background information on the hospital and its place in the commu-nity, and a back pocket holds a leaflet, "Understanding Your Bill."

Hospitals also frequently develop booklets for special groups, such as children or maternity patients, and the contents and designs are modified to suit the audience. An imaginative maternity information piece has been developed by Santa Monica Hospital Medical Center in California. It's a die-cut replica of a carryall bag that can be carried by its own handle, just like a small suitcase. It opens to show a realistic four-color photo of a baby's travel kit, and into it are tucked two small brochures—an information piece and a fee schedule.

Many hospitals develop special pamphlets for the families and friends of patients. Although these contain much of the same information, their messages are different. The Baptist Medical Center in Birmingham, Alabama, for instance, produced a pamphlet that lists motels, restaurants and shopping areas near the hospital.

Other media. Many hospitals use closed-circuit television to tell patients what's happening each day and to review some of the information covered in patient booklets. Video can supplement, but not replace, printed materials, which must be at hand when the patient needs to look up something specific.

Hospitals also use tray liners, tray tents, flyers, daily newsletters and special "hotlines" to communicate with patients.

None of these communication tools can replace face-to-face communication during a hospital stay. They may save many questions, but there always will be others that need to be answered by a member of the staff. It is important, therefore, that everyone who comes into contact with patients knows the basic information on hospital procedures and policies. Using the established communication channels to keep the staff up to date on changes and to remind them of existing services makes the patient information program more effective.

For Those Out-of-Ordinary Times. Into every hospital communicator's life there is bound to fall at least one time when a special patient communication effort is needed. It can be something pleasant, like an anniversary, the dedication of a new wing or a special service. It can be something difficult, like construction or remodeling in or near the hospital. It can be something unpleasant, like a labor dispute with disrupted services.

The media used are often special or expanded versions of existing communication channels. Hospital communicators seem to rise to new heights of skill and creativity when the pressure is on. When leisurely planning a happy event, they have produced beautiful communication packages. In times of stress, they have developed timely, clear emergency communication programs, including such things as daily newspapers or news bulletins, to keep patients informed.

When the Hospital Stay Is Over. Since one of the main objectives of a hospital information program is to build goodwill with patients, their families and friends—and through them, the community—many hospitals follow up with an evaluation. Some have "exit interviews"; others distribute forms when patients leave or send letters a few days later. The information gathered can be used to improve services and communication for future patients.

Membership Drives

Most communicators probably spend more time on the receiving than the sending end of membership drives. If you find yourself in charge of a membership drive, the receiving end is not a bad place to start. There's little evidence to indicate that we are not influenced and motivated by the same things as others.

Variety, creativity, novelty, enthusiasm and originality all play an important part in membership drives. The competition is keen just to get your message noticed, let alone acted on. A membership drive is a good time to let your imagination go and dream up new ideas, slogans, themes and designs. Brainstorming can pay off handsomely, but keep in mind that whatever brilliantly creative idea you come up with must suit the audience you're trying to reach.

Some of the most successful drives count on the active participation of the current membership, but getting members fired up to go out and sign up more people is not always easy. It takes planning, work and creativity. Catchy slogans and themes are handy. It helps to have something to call the drive, something that people can talk about and become involved with. Prizes and other gimmicks also may give the drive a boost, but it usually comes down to building a sense of mission and competition.

IABC's 1982–1983 membership drive was built around the theme "IABC: It all computes." Everything produced for the campaign carried this theme and a special logo. The grand prize was an Apple II home computer, naturally. Other prizes included subscriptions to *Personal Computing* magazine, posters, apple cider and a monthly apple pie from a favorite local bakery.

Many membership drives rely entirely on direct mail, a specialty—indeed a world—all its own. If your organization is considering a major direct-mail campaign, the best recommendation is to go to an experienced consulting firm for help.

Rules to Campaign By. The American Society of Association Executives lists 12 "keys" to boosting membership:

1. *Figure out how much a member is really worth to you and how much it costs the organization for each member.* Until you know that, you don't know how much you can spend to attract each new member. ASAE predicts that you'll probably find that members are worth more than you expect and that you therefore can invest more in campaigns to sign up new members.
2. *Set goals.* Sound planning is as important to a drive as it is to any other communication effort. You cannot know how to reach your objectives until you know what they are, and you cannot evaluate a drive if you have not set realistic goals.
3. *Use a selling theme.* Develop a strong selling message around a single idea—the most compelling reason for prospects to join. Be careful with your creativity. Whatever theme you develop also must say something about your organization. Once developed, use the theme with everything—visually and verbally.

4. *Simplify.*   Find the essence of your message and your appeal—why should someone join your organization?—then put it across simply and directly. Keep your graphics and your writing on target. Don't make people hunt for the message. They won't.

5. *Sell the benefits.*   Identify and promote the one benefit that will be most helpful to new members. Don't jump to conclusions—it may not be the service that is most used by current members. Remember, the prospective member will be asking, "What's in it for me?" Provide that important answer.

6. *Don't bore people.*   You're competing for the prospective member's time and attention. Don't waste it. Get to the point as interestingly as you can. Don't assume that a long list of services is necessarily a shortcut. A list can be as dull and as meaningless as long blocks of copy. Look for ways to visualize your organization and its services and then let art and photos tell as much of the story as possible.

7. *Use a letter with your membership package.*   People are more likely to read a brochure and act on it if there's a letter with it. Next to face-to-face visits or telephone calls, a letter (even if it's printed) is the most personal form of communication. Use it to "talk" about the benefits of joining. Make it interesting and specific.

8. *Develop a graphic identify.*   For most people, what comes out of the envelop when your membership message arrives is what they'll know about the organization. Start with the logo and make sure that everything carries the visual message and impression you want.

9. *Try new media.*   Don't limit your drive to a brochure and letter. Use displays, your publications, ads, posters, "take-one" boxes, telephone calls, postage meter messages....

10. *Make it easy to join.*   Don't make your membership an aptitude test for the gifted. Make it easy for the prospective member to jot down the key information and send it back. Take care of small details, such as making sure that the paper isn't too glossy to write on.

11. *Use your members.*   If the organization is providing good services for members, they should be your best sales people. A "member-get-a-member" campaign can be the most successful and cost effective.

12. *Keep at it.*   A single membership drive, even a successful one, is not enough. Don't feel that a membership offer rejected means "no" forever. Make several contacts.

A Penny Saved.   If you paraphrase the adage "A penny saved is a penny earned," you could say "A member retained is a member you don't have to go out and look for." Don't spend so much time looking for new members that you neglect the ones you have. Many new members drop out after the first year. Find out why through sampling and surveys, and then carefully plan ways to hold members in the future.

Special-Purpose Communication of One-Time Events and Activities

Mergers, Acquisitions, Major Reorganizations

Few business events require more communication skill and planning than mergers, acquisitions and major reorganizations. What is needed in each case is a communication effort that is complete, honest and impeccably timed. Frequently it must be carried out under soul-trying conditions of secrecy, mistrust, hostility and government regulations and restrictions.

The timing of information is crucial and generally difficult. If publicly owned companies are involved, in the United States all communication must be done within rigid constraints set by the Securities and Exchange Commission.

Ideally, information about a merger or acquisition should go to employees of both organizations at the same time, and at the same time it is released to the public. The communicators in both companies must coordinate their efforts and move quickly and efficiently. This first announcement to employees should outline the basic facts, give the reasons for the merger or acquisition, and explain how it is likely to affect the companies. The best way to communicate the essential information rapidly and accurately depends on several factors, including the type and size of the organizations, the number of locations involved and the existing communication channels. One of the worst things that can happen is for the employees of one or both companies to learn about a merger from the media.

The communication effort cannot hope to succeed without the support and cooperation of top management. Management, of course, has a great interest in seeing that the merger, acquisition or reorganization takes place as smoothly as possible. Without a good communication program, thousands of hours can be lost while employees and others speculate about what is or might be happening. Any delay or gap in communication will be filled immediately by rumors and the grapevine.

During these delicate, unsettling business maneuvers, it is impossible to answer all questions to everyone's satisfaction, but a well-planned communication effort can anticipate and develop answers to as many questions as possible. These answers must be as honest and as complete as possible. Avoid platitudes and false assurances. The truth will come out eventually and it's better to have it come in the beginning from management.

But That's Only the Beginning. The need to communicate definitely does not end when the union is consummated. Unfortunately, just when communication is needed, companies often go silent, leaving their employees, communities and other publics wondering what the new, unfamiliar entity is all about. Without communication, a new and coherent identity cannot emerge.

The employees of the company that has been acquired usually are the ones most anxious and eager for information. Will they lose their jobs? Will they be asked to relocate? What kind of policy changes may be in store? Employees in the company that did the acquiring also have concerns and doubts.

Often management does not have the answers to all these questions as the new organization takes shape. Although silence may. be the easiest solution, it is also the most dangerous. It's better to admit honestly that "we don't have all the answers yet" than it is to say nothing. Postmerger silence gives the impression that secret plots or insoluble problems exist.

Communication has an important role to play in the long-range efforts to mold two organizations into one. A variety of media can be called into play—publications, newsletters, special booklets, bulletin boards, closed circuit television, "hotline" telephone systems, meetings and feedback programs.

When Nabisco and Standard Brands merged and became Nabisco Brands, the 61,000 employees were introduced to the new organization with a handsome 48-pa,'e, four-color magazine. The history of each organization was traced in words and photos, the scene was set for the merger, and the goals of the new company were briefly stated. Two existing publications, *Inside SBI* and *Nabisco Magazine* were merged into a slick new four-color magazine, *NB Eye*. The lead article of the first issue told the story of developing the company's new trademark.

An Organization Moves

A move to a new location, whether it is across town or across the country, can be traumatic for organizations and the individuals who work for them. Throughout any relocation, one thing will remain constant—the need for accurate, timely information. Employees will have a seemingly endless supply of questions, concerns and doubts. On the other hand, the organization will have a continuous stream of news that needs to be communicated. The communicator's task is to plan, establish and maintain a timely two-way flow of information.

Start Early. You cannot start planning the communication program on a relocation too soon. Whether it's a decision to build a new building, move to a different building, or relocate to a different part of the country, getting off on the right foot is important. Special care should be given to the timing and content of the first announcement.

A move means dislocation as well as relocation, so everyone will be concerned. Once the word is out, surveys of employees can be used to help determine which aspects of the move are causing the most concern. Tune in to the grapevine and be aware of any misinformation that's flourishing. Help management find ways to involve employees in the planning process.

Figure 15.6. A company move requires a special-purpose communication effort to address specific needs. AT&T Long Lines developed *Oakton in a Nutshell* to effectively answer questions on transportation, the new building, services and the community to make the move easier for all employees.

People are less threatened by things they have a part in, and feel more committed to those they help plan.

The well-planned communication effort must anticipate and answer questions. Where's the cafeteria? Is there parking? Where's my desk or office? Where's the department that used to be just down the hall? Are there restaurants in the area?

The families of employees have an important stake in any relocation, particularly a move to a different part of town or to a new city. Much of a well-planned move to a new area involves orienting families to the new community and helping them find homes. As more and more families have two working members, attention also should be given to helping spouses find new jobs.

A major relocation inevitably means that some employees will decide not to make the move. This is a difficult issue that must be treated with honesty and with sensitivity. The counseling and other assistance offered to employees should be clearly communicated.

The media that can be effectively used to communicate information on a company move are limited only by the communicator's imagination and budget. The employee publication is a logical place for major articles before and after a relocation. Many have capitalized on the hassle of the move with amusing photo stories. It's an excellent way to involve numerous people and encourage camaraderie.

Many organizations produce special newsletters to keep the lines of communication open during a move. Before its move to a new headquarters building in downtown Regina, Saskatchewan, for instance, Sask Tel launched *Update, Head Office.* The simple, four-page publication showed floor plans, kept employees up to date on the construction schedule, described the area and pointed out the building's special features.

Letters, brochures, booklets, information centers, hotlines, meetings and audiovisual presentations also can be effective. AT&T Long Lines produced a prize-winning 48-page, four-color special magazine to introduce its new Eastern Region headquarters building. Imaginative design, whimsical drawings and terse copy created a readable and useful guide for employees moving into the new building.

A premove tour of the new location also can be an effective part of the communication plan. When Sentry Insurance relocated 1,600 employees from four locations into one building, it started taking busloads of employees to the new building two months before the scheduled move. Each employee was given the chance to visit the spot where he or she would work.

Once the move is over, an open house becomes an important communication tool. It gives the employees, their families and community members a chance to take a good look at the facilities. Open houses are usually accompanied by other communication media—brochures, maps, guided tours, lectures, films, slide presentations, letters of invitation and media coverage.

If the move is to a new area, it is important to tell both the old and the new community what the relocation means and why it is being made. To the new community it means new jobs, new people, added income, a market for houses and more people using the services. For the old community it means houses for sale, loss of income and a lower tax base. All this is news and will probably attract local media attention. The communicator will have to plan carefully and use a variety of techniques to get the story across honestly and as positively as possible.

A major relocation also is news within the industry, and the appropriate trade publications need to be kept informed.

Name Change

A key ingredient of a successful name change and the accompanying corporate identity is a carefully planned, detailed and complete communication program.

In fact, unless there are reasons of security or competition, the communication effort can begin even before the decision to make the change has been made. When Mutual Service Insurance of St. Paul, Minnesota, was contemplating changing its name, the company publication carried a news story that discussed the need to consider a change, pointed out that firms specializing in corporate identity were being screened, and gave a proposed timetable of events. The story indicated that "employees, agents, key department heads, top management, policyholders—everyone will have the opportunity to express opinions."

A project as all-encompassing as a name change calls on the planning, coordinating, managing and creative abilities of the communicator to think of everyone, everything and every way to get the word out and to generate the cooperation that will be needed at all levels of the organization.

One of the first steps is the development of a complete, detailed guide for the use of the new name, logo and colors. Include such things as specific rules for where the name should be positioned on stationery and business cards, the exact ink color of the logo (if there is one), how the name may be abbreviated (if it may be), and so on.

Getting the Word Out. A personal letter from the chief executive officer to all employees is a popular and effective way to announce a name change and new corporate identity. The letter should include a concise and positive reason for the change and briefly answer the questions perceived to be most common and important.

The initial letter can be followed up by such things as articles in the company publications, employee meetings and bulletin board notices. Many organizations prepare name-change bulletins, which are issued frequently and regularly to cover aspects of the process.

Letters, brochures or announcement folders can be sent to shareholders, financial audiences, customers and other key audiences. News releases, press conferences, advertising and sales promotion campaigns all become part of the total plan to establish the organization's new name and identity. Special attention should be paid to one of the most important communication tools—the telephone. People who are used to hearing "Good morning, Amalgamated Buggy Whip," may be startled to hear "Good morning, High Tech Corp." A transition message might be, "Good morning, our new name is . . . ."

Communicating in a Crisis

The crucial test of the effectiveness of the entire communication program comes with crisis—when it's too late to build trust, credibility and lines of communication. Whether the crisis is a strike, natural disaster, scandal or major industrial accident, communication will be more effective if the important audiences are already favorably disposed or at least neutral toward the organization.

Although you cannot predict a crisis, you can anticipate and be prepared. Having a definite, practical plan on paper will help prevent panic just when fast, decisive action is needed most. When disaster strikes, it is the communicator who will be on the firing line.

These basic steps can help you plan for communication in a crisis:

1. Obtain commitment from top management to honest, open, timely communication during an emergency. Even organizations normally committed to ongoing and candid communication have been known to develop stage-fright in a time of stress. Silence implies guilt and breeds suspicion. Information given openly, honestly and promptly is infinitely better than that which is pried out or uncovered or told only after the fact.

2. List every crisis that could conceivably happen to your organization. This is a good project for a staff meeting. Start with the obvious disasters, then keep going. Life is full of surprises. After a while, you'll see that they fall naturally into categories, which will make the list easier to manage.

3. Determine the policy that should guide the handling of each major category of potential crisis. Clarify the policies and make sure they're available in concise written form that is readily retrievable.

4. Construct a basic plan for dealing with emergencies. If the major categories of potential crises require different handling, make sure these variations are covered. The plan or plans should be as thorough as possible. Try to foresee all the problems that could possibly develop. Try a "what if—then" approach. What if the plant is hit by a natural disaster? Then we'll have to.... What if it knocks out all telephones and power? Then we'll have to.... What if there are serious injuries? Then we'll have to.... Don't hesitate to include seemingly small details. The more you prepare in advance, the easier things will go in an emergency.

5. Write down *your* emergency plan and be sure the persons who will need it have copies. One emergency to be prepared for is a crisis that happens when you're away.

6. Identify the key spokesperson or spokespersons for each potential crisis. In most cases, it is better to have a single source, especially for the external media. The best source may vary with the situation, and it may be necessary to include a person or persons with technical expertise.

7. Make sure you can reach the identified spokespersons at all times. Have home telephone numbers of key management people. Know how to reach them if they're away. Make a list of reliable substitutes. If there

are key people you'll need to rely on for background information or technical data, add them to the "Find Fast List."

8. Vice versa—make sure that the key people know how and where to reach you if there's an emergency.

9. Brief and coach your spokespersons so that they will have some idea what to expect. Whether it's the glare of television cameras or the heat of an employee meeting, prepare the spokesperson as much as possible in advance, when life is calm. Look for opportunities for the spokespersons to handle difficult situations.

10. Anticipate that there may be situations when you and the spokespersons will not have the answers. The best action is to admit it; never guess or speculate.

11. Develop written background information in advance for highly technical areas. Develop a simple glossary of terms that clearly and briefly explains key points of your organization's business.

12. Develop a plan to monitor all media in order to counter false or misleading information.

13. Be prepared to set up a news headquarters. It should be adequately staffed and equipped with power outlets, telephones and typewriters.

14. Evaluate and update the plan every six months because situations and personnel change.

Other Specialized Media

There are other ways to reach specialized audiences. Bill Dunk of William Dunk & Partners and staff members of CorpCom Productions compiled the following list of many specialized media being used successfully by small and large organizations:

Letters to employees. From the plant or office manager these can be particularly effective if they are not overworked. To most employees, the local manager is the most authoritative, most "real" person in the whole organization. Messages from him or her provide a personal touch that other media don't have and can reach members of the employee's family, who can have an important impact on the views of the employee.

Billboards. Along highways or in airport terminals, they greet visitors with *Welcome to Middletown, Home of Ace Plastic Corporation* or some similar message that can communicate the corporate identify effectively. They make a point for the organization or they supply welcome information to the traveler.

Corporate art exhibits. Hung in plants or public places, art works can communicate important messages to skeptical publics. They can convey the idea that corporations are not entirely profit-minded and that they can take the lead in advancing an appreciation of the arts. Through its corporate art collection, Chesebrough-Ponds communicates an understanding of contemporary fashion and trends vital to a consumer company. The company also supports children's art programs.

Benefit books.   These should give employees an explanation of benefit plans in words that can be understood by the average employee. Many companies pour in too many details, and as a result, hamper communication. A major corporation should be able to tell its benefits story to employees in a handbook of 50 pages or fewer.

Benefits films and slide presentations.   Audiovisuals should augment booklets on benefits. They are excellent instruction tools, if kept brief.

Personalized benefit computer printouts.   These have the advantage of telling employees about their personal benefits in dollars and cents. Some organizations print a weekly message on paystubs, sometimes announcing benefit changes.

Recruiting booklets.   The most effective recruiting materials tell applicants what the organization can do for them. They describe what it's like to work for the company, what jobs are available, salary levels, opportunities for advancement and greater responsibility and opportunities for further study.

Orientation media.   The first few days and weeks employees are on the job are the most impressionable time of their stay with the organization. They are alert at this stage to sponge up information about the company, its management, its products, its policies and its objectives (see Chapter 5). Effective orientation presentations, either print or audiovisual, take advantage of this high learning potential. One caution: Be alert to the information capacity of employees and don't overload.

Postcards to employees.   One service company in Great Britain effectively uses a monthly postcard to employees instead of a newspaper or magazine. Cards provide tips on how employees can render better service to customers.

Pay-envelope stuffers.   When paychecks are conveyed in envelopes, messages can be enclosed in or on them. It should be positive. Many companies deliver paychecks to salaried employees in envelopes and to wage employees "bareback"—without an envelope. This procedure itself communicates the message that the company puts wage employees in a different class from salaried employees.

Paycheck stub messages.   These can explain changes in deductions or include a wish for a happy vacation, birthday or holiday. (Couldn't the computer be programmed to say "Happy Birthday!" on the paycheck just before each person's birthday?)

Company histories and anniversary books.   Too often, company books are monuments to the past. Good company histories and anniversary books show company progress and propel the reader into prospects for the future. They can show how the passage of time has brought maturity, foresight and strength to deal with changes and progress, thus keeping the company in tune with the future. They show what the company has learned from past concepts that it can use profitably for the future.

Literature for students and teachers. Educational information is always in demand. An electrical equipment manufacturer, for example, can supply information about electricity. Elementary and high schools in particular seek special information in the form of illustrated books and booklets, motion pictures, videotapes and slide presentation.

Students are at a highly impressionable age; for the rest of their lives, they will remember the information about your organization that came into their classrooms. Offer authentic, useful information with a minimum of plugs for your company. If you get into the educational information field, be prepared for an avalanche of requests. Books about the industry are another way to reach educators, the press, authors, students, elected officials and other audiences important to the organization.

Sample kits. Materials for students and teachers can be made available for a small charge, usually 50¢ to $5. One rubber company, for example, offers a kit containing a variety of rubber samples and a booklet explaining how natural and synthetic rubber are produced. It describes simple experiments that can be performed with the samples. Thousands have been sold.

Dividend stuffers. These get a free ride with dividend checks—and arrive at a pleasant moment for shareholders. A brief message about the company can help reassure shareholders that their investment was a wise one. The chief executive officer can take this opportunity to discuss legislation affecting the company and the industry, and to invite shareholders to make their feelings known to their elected representatives in government. Combustion Engineering has put questionnaires, address update slips and other data in its stuffers.

Continuing education books. Programs offered by the company and nearby educational institutions can be reviewed. They should spell out company policy on tuition refunds.

Company scholarship books. They should be attractive and explain completely and explicitly any programs the company supports for employees' children, including eligibility and the selection of candidates for scholarships.

Essay, photo and art contests. People get involved and participate, whether the contests are essays or coloring by children, or essays, photos, painting or sculpture by adults. Whatever the vehicle, communication about the contest can build prestige for the organization.

Ad reprints. Sent to key audiences or posted on bulletin boards, these provide an opportunity to tell various audiences the strategy behind the ad program and to explain the behind-the-scenes story of how they were produced.

Calendars. Often things of beauty, calendars are on view not just for a day or a week, but all month long, 12 months a year. If they are strategically planned and tastefully done, they can project a potent and lasting message.

Quizzes and puzzles. These can help build interest in organizational publications. Whether a message about the company is worked into a quiz or puzzle is less important than the fact that the quiz or puzzle is there, drawing readers into the publication and providing entertainment.

Company fact books. These provide security analysts with the facts they want to know about the company. The most important role of the fact book, however, particularly in a multi-industry company, is to encourage additional security analysts to become interested in and follow the progress of the company. The fact book should disclose the basics of your business so that analysts will become familiar enough with the company to recommend its stock for purchase. It should provide genuinely useful information not available elsewhere, in an attractively designed format so as to project your company as up to date and progressive.

Portfolio managers' booklets. These should provide a macroeconomic perspective of the company, showing how it is affected by business trends and new economic developments. These booklets should discuss corporate goals and objectives, position the company against its competition and provide other responsive information. They should be easy to scan and read. In short, they should win the trust of portfolio managers by being specifically responsive to their information needs.

Rep books. For registered representatives, the account executives of brokerage firms, these are often used to interest potential shareholders. They should sell your corporation to the reps and give them the ammunition to sell your corporation and its securities to their clients. The rep book should highlight the company's competitive strengths and, if appropriate, indicate why now is a good time to buy the company's stock. Most important, it should impart a clear message quickly—one that can be passed on from the rep to a customer in less than two minutes on the telephone.

Corporate ethics book. Many corporations are issuing such books stating their positions on corporate relationships with the public. They contain corporate policy statements, public relations and employee communication policies, and the company's position on equal opportunity, consumer relations, the environment, energy, and so forth.

Research and development brochure. This can be a good indicator of the future success of the company. A booklet that tells the R&D story can make good points for any company.

Key-issue white papers. Organizations prepare white papers to tell the backgrounds of key issues—from their perspective. To be believable and effective, white papers should be candid, presenting the black along with the white.

Contribution booklets. These outline policy on corporate giving to schools and charitable organizations. They are designed to promote understanding in the minds of all parties concerned. Most important, these booklets bring credit to the company and help dispel the notion that the corporation is unfeeling and unresponsive to people's needs.

Tour booklets. Designed for visitors, they will remind them of what they saw and heard while touring your facilities. They often include additional information about the organization. Tour booklets are likely to be seen by friends and relatives, thus multiplying your audience.

Other special media might include customer-service books, merger-partner books, coloring books, comic books, questionnaires, corporate advocacy brochures and ads, jingles, games, pins, banners, pens and pencils and T-shirts.

Summary

Whether a special-purpose communication is part of an ongoing program or

Figure 15.7.

a special one-time event, the basic ideas that have been stated and restated in each section of this chapter are essential:

1. Every communication effort must be carefully planned. Have clearly stated goals and objectives and the basic strategies for reaching them.
2. Every communication program or project must have the support of top management.
3. The communication program and the communicator are integral parts of management.
4. Credibility must be established and maintained through honest, open, timely two-way communication throughout the organization.
5. Communication plans should carefully identify all the audiences, and use the most effective medium or media to reach each of them.

RAE LEAPER, ABC, is senior editor in the corporate communication department of Chevron Corporation, in San Francisco. She served as chairman of the International Association of Business Communicators in 1978–1979 and is accredited by the association.

◆ 16 ◆

Financial Communication

William P. Dunk

Scottish Investment trusts. Red herrings. Rule 415 and shelf registrations. In-house transfer systems. Valuation analyses. Takeover defenses. These are just a few of the esoteric issues with which many financial communication professionals have to grapple.

This chapter is not about the esoteric, however. It is about basic financial communications that have demonstrable impact in both domestic and international capital markets: the annual report, corporate advertising and the analyst meeting.

In each of the sections that follow, experts are cited and checklists are provided for readers who want to soar beyond the ordinary in their financial communication efforts.

Annual Reports: New Age of Simplicity

A large report in the early 1960s was 32 pages. It had a short president's letter, which bragged about the past and glowed about the future. It had a few pictures and a very short financial section. Time and the Securities and Exchange Commission have changed all that, at least in the United States.

Today, annual reports of 40 to 80 pages are common. The prose is copious and often tedious. The color photographs and the artwork are expensive. The financial section alone often is as extensive as complete annual reports were in the 1960s. For many readers, the reports are strikingly similar—long, elegant and quite hard to read.

But there are exceptions. Some reports are shorter and make do with austere black and white photography. A recent article in *Fortune* heaped praise on the report of Chairman Warren Buffett of Berkshire Hathaway, who has *no* photographs in his report. It simply does a candid job of explaining his stewardship at Berkshire.

The great reports today are simpler than most. They emphasize clear, straightforward writing. Chuck Wheat, whose annual report for Armco, Inc., has been praised by its shareholders and a host of company chairmen, says:

> My friends in finance, law and the more woozy realms of corporate communications tell me I look at shareholder reports from a pinched point of view. That's because I say annuals and quarterlies have but one primary purpose: *To say what you want to say to one shareholder at a time.* All the rest is peripheral. I agree that shareholder reports can be useful to security analysts, friendly politicians, various monitors of corporate conduct, and employees—particularly if you have a goodly number of employee shareholders. But don't write for them or you'll get too much tinkering with your script.
>
> Write for Aunt Nellie. She's often male, rich and very sophisticated, but she has a personal stake—rather than merely a professional interest—in your company and its stock. Let those secondary audiences eavesdrop on your chat with Aunt Nellie. They all love gossip. If they think you aren't talking to them, they're more likely to believe what you say.
>
> Remember your primary purpose. Your report's job is not to serve the SEC (Securities Exchange Commission) or the FTC (Federal Trade Commission) or Wall Street or Main Street or Jane Fonda or the Ayatollah Khomeini. Its task is to say what you want to say to give investors and browsers a memorable reason for buying your company's stock.
>
> Memorable and believable. You get that from straight talk. Slick layout and jazzy design may win awards. But when was the last time you heard Aunt Nellie say, "Whee—that annual report was so gorgeous I ran right out and bought the stock."
>
> Rely on your writing.
>
> Tell Aunt Nellie what your company is doing. Not just how you are doing, and why—but what. Sum things up. Leave in her memory at least one simple statement, burning like a flame she can warm to. Slap that statement out there right on the cover of your report. Use really big type.
>
> Make your statement a sentence. Beware of slogans. You are talking to someone, not yodeling at them in an ad. To me, there's something basically squalid about sloganeering. Talk, don't preach.
>
> Think about shortening your annual report. Cull the clutter. Use the required Management's Discussion & Analysis section to tell Aunt Nellie how your company is doing. Don't do a separate "review" piece. Use only the required one, turning it into plain English and straight talk. Stick in graphs when they seem useful. Explain things. Throw the boilerplate away.
>
> Now you can use the Chairman's letter to chat—not about the year, but about the company and what it is and what you're doing with it. Boil things

down to the essentials you want. In the letter, tell Aunt Nellie she can find out all about the year by turning to the MD&A. She might actually do it!

As for the Chairman's letter, use it to build a proper setting for the flame-like statement you're putting on your cover.

Finally, if you feel really frisky you can dig into the notes to the financial statements and turn them into straight talk, too. Aunt Nellie will thank you. So will a surprising number of analysts.

Think about making better use of your quarterly reports, too. Usually you have far more freedom in quarterlies because most corporate functionaries forget about them. So apply the same thinking process to quarterlies as you do the annual. Tell Aunt Nellie things you want her to know.

I started a little column in our quarterlies, quoting letters from shareholders. Some loved us. Some hated us. Some cried out for answers in the column. We get about 2,000 cards and letters every quarter, and I can sense some of my Aunt Nellies having the time of their lives sharpening their quips.

. . . Our shareholders tell us they appreciate how we care about them and their views. Confidence that you care about them gives shareholders some comfort when your earnings skid.

But most of all in both quarterlies and annuals, do your best to give your company a voice that is human, friendly and credible. That takes straight talk. . . . Just use the active voice, plenty of personal pronouns, a few contractions, and here and there an idiomatic figure of speech. Most of all, when in doubt put a period. Then start your next sentence.

The real test is getting straight talk past the usual gaggle of company clearers—law and finance and whoever whispers in the ear of your CEO. In the clutch, lawyers fear straight talk is risky. Beancounters find some nuance they claim is inaccurate. The whisperers worry that straight talk makes your chairman sound unstatesmanlike.

"Statesmanlike" is a euphemism for pompous. So your hardest task is likely to be getting straight talk into print without the clutter of jargon, long synonyms for sharp, bright words, cliché treacle, and run-on sentences full of subordinate clauses.

The ability to talk simply depends on having a management with a passionate devotion to candor. Joe Floren has written 20 annual reports for Tektronix, a company that business reporters applaud for both wit and candor. He says, "Our founder and board chairman once objected to my having described Tektronix information systems as 'threadbare and ramshackle.' His objection was not, as you might expect, that we were admitting a flaw to shareholders—merely that I had chosen words that didn't fit. So I changed the objectionable wording to 'obsolescent and erratic' (a stronger self-criticism), and he nodded approval."

Simplicity. Candor. And solid plans for the future. Mark Appleman, editor of *The Corporate Shareholder* and an astute observer of investment community psychology, says that professional investors read the president's letter to see how good a grip management has on where it's headed and how it's going to get there. He often quotes Mason Haire, a consulting professor of management at Stanford's Graduate School of Business, who collaborated with Dean Bowman of Ohio State University on an exhaustive study of annual reports. In reporting the findings at a meeting of financial analysts and investment managers in Chicago, Haire said:

> I urge you to read annual reports. Not the numbers in the report but the prose. I always skip the numbers because I know they can fool me with them. I glance at the notes to the financial statements—there are often some interesting clues there—but I read the president's letter in great detail.
>
> . . . The things the CEO selects to put in and leave out can be very revealing.
>
> Companies with dim prospects give themselves away by being long on excuses and short on plans and value added. Although they complain about government, labor conditions, the economy, foreign competition, interest rates or whatever, they fail to spell out a realistic plan for overcoming the difficulties. As a result, management comes through as passive or reactive—not a very good sign for the future.
>
> In contrast, companies with bright prospects come through as active, coping, flexible and adaptive, because in addition to pinpointing problems, they discuss strategies for getting on with it.

Tips for Annual Report Success

Here are a few questions to ask if you want to prepare better annual reports:

- Have we paid attention to the back of the book? The financials are long and important. Have we included the charts, variance analysis and explanatory financial material that will make the annual reports worth reading?
- Have we cut out repetitive material? Have we cut the division reviews down to size?
- Have we told the reader what the company will do next year and the year after?
- Have we talked about industry trends? Does the report show that the company understands its markets?

Corporate Advertising: Need for Mega-Messages

In 1979, a natural resources company for which we had placed large amounts of annual report advertising asked us to find out what it was getting for its money. In response to its advertising, business magazine readers were requesting 15,000 reports a year from the company. The question was, were they serious investors or were they paper collectors? We found an amazing number were investors in our clients' company.

Students of corporate advertising have discovered many ways to make corporate advertising more effective. Discovery one has been that corporate ads should try to reach elite audiences: the rules of consumer mass advertising don't work here. Discovery two has been that the key to such advertising is to have a *big message*.

Fortunately, there are big things to talk about. A number of contemporary books suggest that our business environment is undergoing cataclysmic change as we move from an industrial to an information services society. The task of corporate advertising should be to show that major companies understand what the change means to them and how they must adapt to the tide of the future.

One of the most successful corporate advertising campaigns in the past 20 years was crafted by the LTV Corporation in Dallas. A gun-slinging, high-flying conglomerate in the 1960s, LTV in the 1980s had to portray its new self as a well-managed, responsible company that is soberly and sensibly looking at the things that will affect its future. John W. Johnson, advertising vice president, talks about LTV's objectives and campaigns:

> LTV was an $8 billion company, once again coming on the scene as an important factor in the business community. Again, we were going to be active in the merger and acquisition business, but not as a high flyer this time. All of our acquisitions would have to be in related fields and make good business sense. Our image in the business community and Washington would be just as important as the image on Wall Street. We needed to achieve a relatively high profile again, but as a responsible, thoughtful company—a leader in our various industries.
>
> In taking advantage of the beginning of the new decade, we developed a Wave Two program aimed at probing the future of the industries in which we operate, as seen through the eyes of outside experts. Our strategy was to position ourselves in terms of the outlook for our industries in the new decade, and then position ourselves *vis-à-vis* those industries. Both campaigns would be united through one strategic focus—LTV would be the corporation that is "Looking Ahead." That became our slogan, our new banner—our copy platform.

Through dignified, thoughtful advertising about national issues and about the industries in which it participates, LTV hoped to achieve broad, positive awareness about itself and its future. Subsequent research confirmed that it accomplished that task.

Tips for Corporate Advertising

It's easy to waste time and money in corporate advertising. Here are a few thoughts from advertising managers on how to avoid some pitfalls.

- Prepare for the long haul. Corporate advertising begins to really pay off after the third year. If you can't sustain a budget for five years, don't bother.
- Have a big and consistent message. LTV does it by saying "Look, we want to talk to you about very big issues."
- Back up the promise of your ads in other ways. Sperry, which says it's the company that understands how important it is "to listen," has conducted hundreds of listening seminars for employees and potential customers.
- Review your media budget with a fine-tooth comb. Corporate ad budgets are small, so you have to make the dollars work harder. Spend smart.
- Do your audience research with some care. Most ad research provides a few useless numbers; in-depth work with your target audiences will tell you more.

Analyst Meetings: Can We Talk?

I recently attended a meeting with investors that was a failure. Why? Because they didn't ask questions. An uncomfortable hush fell over the room during the question-and-answer period and the chairman nervously twiddled his thumbs.

The purpose of analyst meetings is just that—to meet and to have a talk. Dialogue, exchange, feedback. When you have conversations, you build relationships. Companies often spend so much time preparing their presentations they forget that the real objective is to build relationships.

Marvin Chatinover, editor of the *Investor Relations Newsletter*, thinks the question-and-answer period is the acid test of any meeting. He looks for a "favorable reception to the presentation and penetrating questions (i.e., they got the message) and satisfaction with company response (i.e., you have credibility)."

Koppers' Roger Beidler spends a lot of time making sure that key investment community influentials attend corporate investor presentations. He says:

> The mix is different for different cities. And in any one city, the local society or investment banker may or may not turn out a good crowd. We can't leave this to chance so at Koppers we maintain a computerized internal list which we're constantly updating. And we access the outside list houses, such as Technimetrics, to make sure we're missing nothing. The question here is *quality* of turnout, not quantity of turnout.
>
> I want to emphasize mix. We work to turn out sell- and buy-side analysts. But you have to go beyond analysts—to portfolio managers, registered representatives, even the financial press. You want to know that you've put together

a blend that will definitely affect the financial network which is peculiar to the region of the country or part of the world where you're meeting.

I can't emphasize enough what part consistency plays in the effort. We're in New York four times a year—usually within a few weeks after the close of a quarter. On the same day, we make three separate presentations there to 100–175 carefully selected people. We go to Boston twice a year. And we reach every other important location in the country every eight to sixteen months.

The key to it is our very intense selection process. We phone present owners, then buy-side analysts, then our registered rep list. We cover the segments. We know we're getting the results we want when a good selection of high priority analysts and portfolio managers keep turning out for meetings quarter after quarter, year after year.

In the process of developing an audience for a presentation, a company has a chance to stimulate questions from attenders and probe for concerns that should be addressed at a meeting. Chatinover describes what can be done on the phone before the meeting:

If the meeting is to be with a small group of industry specialists, contact some by phone to ascertain their particular interests and concerns about the company. You can, if the meeting is scheduled far enough in advance—at least two to three months ahead—do the same thing with a larger group via a random process, or contact directly analysts with whom you have had previous contact and/or those known to be opinion leaders among their peers. Use such intelligence in planning the presentation. Remember, you must address the customer's basic concerns if you want to sell the product.

Tips for Analyst Meetings

So many meetings are mediocre that the smart company can rise above the pack in a hurry. Analyst meetings, or "road shows," consume large amounts of management time and energy. Here are some tips to make them worthwhile:

- Get the right people to the meeting and address their concerns. This means lots of advance telephone and survey work.
- If the whole meeting is an hour, limit the company presentation to 20–25 minutes.
- Provide a written outline of the talk to all attenders, keyed, if possible, to the slides.
- Have two or three informed members of management talk with attenders during cocktails and after the meeting. That's when many ask their real questions.

- Follow up by telephone immediately with as many attenders as possible. Find out how the presentation was received and what the attender thinks of your company now.

WILLIAM P. DUNK, a communication strategy and investor relations consultant, is managing partner of William Dunk Partners, Inc., in New York.

◆ 17 ◆

Handling Organizational and Professional Problems

Frederic Halperin, ABC

You're putting your monthly magazine to press when the boss calls:

- The company's space-age widget (the feature lead for this issue) has been recalled.
- The company is on the brink of bankruptcy.
- The chief executive officer has been fired and the new one (formerly the comptroller) thinks no news is good news.
- Your budget's been cut in half.

Or you're in charge of communication at a nonprofit organization and the chairman calls:

- One of your agencies has been accused of squandering funds.
- "Unexpected" expenses have forced an overall reduction of budget.
- The executive director has quit.
- You've got to increase your output at 60% of your prior budget.

You've got a "special problem." What do you do?

First, recognize that most special problems are usually not the real problem at all. Rather, they're symptoms of a larger problem: lack of written policy, objectives and an action plan that reflect management's needs. There is a several-step process you can use to solve these special problems until you can tackle the larger issue.

This chapter introduces a problem-solving process, then deals with some specific problems many communicators face. The intent is to pose some questions and offer insights that can help you move past the barriers. That way, you can get back to your primary function—advising management and helping to plan and implement communication programs that move the organization toward its major goals.

The Problem-Solving Process

Describe the problem in detail as you see it. Be sure to cover every aspect—the who, what, where, why, when and how of it. This will probably require some research on your part. Next, share your analysis with some of your peers and ask for comments and suggestions. If possible, ask your boss to provide some insight. Then, rewrite your description of the problem if necessary, taking into consideration the comments and suggestions you've received. Once you've redefined the problem, you can take steps to solve it.

There are a number of ways you can develop alternative solutions. Past experience always helps. Have you or others had the same or a similar problem that you solved in the past? Many times you can reapply the solution with good results. Are there other ways to solve it? Try the traditional approach of listing likely solutions along with the potential advantages and disadvantages of each. Then narrow the field to the most likely candidates.

Try brainstorming. Assemble a small group (five or six people) of concerned professionals and let your imaginations fly. No judging, no commenting on one another's suggestions. Each person says everything and anything that comes to mind, and one person lists the ideas. The objective is *quantity*, not quality. The idea is to maintain a high energy level in the group; everyone should be shouting ideas as quickly as they arrive. After 10 or 15 minutes of brainstorming, evaluate the ideas, add to them, reshape them and build on them. Narrow the list to the best half dozen, then analyze the advantages and disadvantages of each to decide which one or two seem the best.

No matter how you have chosen your one to two proposed solutions, the next step is to write up your recommendation and a plan for implementation. The plan should state not only what must be accomplished but also the deadline for each step of implementation and the name of the person responsible for that part of the plan.

Have your plan approved before you implement it. If at all possible, obtain management commitment to the plan—not just a signature, but an assumption of responsibility for at least part of the solution. If you can get management to accept ownership of the plan, you can rest assured the job will get done.

How do you get management to assume ownership? It will help if the solution seems to be in the best interests of management—that's obvious. More important is to have management participate not only in solving the problem but in developing the solution. Involve management in the whole problem-solving process. Invite affected members of management to join you in analyzing the problem, in identifying the solution, and in creating the plan. Then it's only natural for them to take responsibility for carrying out the plan.

Inheriting a Mediocre Communication Program

If you take over a less-than-effective communication program, you will be expected to do some evaluating and changing. That does not mean change for change's sake. But no one will be surprised if you study the effectiveness of the program and implement improvements where warranted. In fact, if you are considering a job where a mediocre program exists, you should be sure management understands that you will make changes.

A mediocre program is not necessarily a bad one, so don't hurry to make piecemeal changes that may or may not be viewed as positive. You are too new in your job to assess the reactions to those piecemeal changes, either from management or from others. Some members of management may have helped build that mediocre program; others might resist trading the familiar for something new. Management will be more impressed with a businesslike approach. In other words, set objectives for the program, evaluate the current program to see how well it meets those objectives, and draw up plans to correct any deficiencies. The plan should include specific actions, timetables, budgets and responsibilities.

What happens if you are required to do a quick fix, if you have no time for research and evaluation? Here's where the problem-solving process comes into play. What's the problem? Does it pertain to the communication staff? Are there enough people to do the work? Are they the proper people to do the work? Do they have the proper skills, knowledge and abilities? Are they properly motivated? Do they have the tools or facilities they need to do their jobs? Is the budget insufficient? Is that because it isn't allocated properly, or is it just too small? If there isn't sufficient budget, is that because the organization just doesn't have the funds, or is it lack of management commitment to communication? Or did your predecessor never ask for sufficient dollars or never justify a larger budget? Is the problem the quality of graphics and printing or production? Is that tied back to budget considerations, or does it have to do with lack of commitment or ability on the part of your suppliers?

Perhaps everything is well written and well produced, yet has no impact on employees, management or both. Why? Is the source of the problem management's communication philosophy? Many mediocre programs stem from a management philosophy of "we'll tell them what we want them to know." If that's the attitude, you've got a major education job ahead of you before you can move forward. Do your communication objectives tie back to organizational goals important to both your employees and your management? Have the goals been explained in such a way that people understand the impact on their jobs and on the organization? Do people know how your communication objectives are tied to those goals? Are your messages sent to a place where your audiences can receive them at a time when they are willing to receive them, and in a form that they are able to receive?

Those are some potential problems that can cause a mediocre or worse communication program. Once you have identified the problem affecting your program, define it carefully and follow the problem-solving process outlined at the beginning of this chapter.

Coping with an Uncooperative Top Management

One of the most difficult problems any communicator can confront is dealing with an uncooperative top management. Not all uncooperative managements are alike. Many can be turned around quickly, some take years to educate, and some are terminal cases—that is, you'll have to put your life on the line first. As in any problem-solving situation, your first step is to define the problem:

What does uncooperative mean? Does it mean they won't give you the time of day; they're truly not interested in communicating or not sure they need a communicator on staff? Do they see your job as putting out the "house organ" and not making any waves? Or does it mean they leave communicating up to you—that's what they hired you for? It's not so much that they don't care about communication; in fact, they used to enjoy it themselves when the place was smaller and they didn't have so much to do. It's just that they are too busy and really don't understand magapapers and video and all the stuff you need to know now.

Who, specifically, is uncooperative? Is it the chief executive officer? The president? The executive director? The vice president of administration? Personnel? Public relations? Marketing? Manufacturing? The general counsel or comptroller? The chief surgeon? Your boss? Who in top management *does* cooperate?

Are there particular times when members of top management are uncooperative? Are there times when they cooperate? Are there particular subjects about which members of top management are uncooperative? Are they helpful on others?

Are there particular circumstances under which members of top management are uncooperative? Under what circumstances do they cooperate? Under what circumstances do they provide enthusiastic and wholehearted support?

Once you've identified the problem and defined its perimeters, you can build a better working relationship with those members of top management whom you need to educate. In most cases, you have an interpersonal communication problem with a particular audience, and that kind of problem is usually curable.

Start with common ground. Perhaps it's with the subjects or circumstances you've identified as being a real turn-on for top management. Can you develop a program that supports this interest? Can you provide other support services for these officers of the organization? The idea is to create some outstanding programs based on mutually agreeable goals, to build personal credibility with top management, and to demonstrate how well-thought-out communication programs can help management achieve organization goals.

Your ultimate goal is to have a common understanding about the role of both communication and the communicator in the organization. That doesn't usually happen in a week or a month or even a year when management is uncooperative. It usually takes a series of steps—steps that create trust and credibility for you and for the value of well-planned and executed programs. Here are some other tips you may wish to consider:

- Be cooperative and enthusiastic about management's programs. If you think they're off base, offer some creative, constructive suggestions that will show that you are an important part of the management team.
- Find out about problems in the organization. Where you can, pitch in and help solve them. The people you help will be your greatest supporters.
- Don't take on more than you can handle. It's important that you succeed while you are trying to build credibility.
- Use the problem-solving process.

Once you are accepted as part of the management team, you'll find larger and more difficult problems to solve. That is one of the prices of success at problem solving. But you can use the same problem-solving process no matter what the scope of the problem. And if you become good at it, you'll find your services are always in demand.

When Top Management Changes

A new chief executive officer or other top officer can create problems for you. The new boss will have a lot of things on his or her mind, and one of them is the evaluation of current programs and the elimination or improvement of programs where warranted. Your job is to help make the transition smooth and to demonstrate your competence and the value of your programs. In other words, make the evaluation easy and make yourself useful.

If you have based your communication program on organizational objectives, have evaluated their effectiveness, and have taken steps to keep them on target, you have a good story to tell. Offer to share your objectives with the new boss. Suggest that any changes made in organizational priorities have an effect on your objectives and programs. Certainly, you'll want to take into account the new boss's concerns when reshaping your programs.

Figure out a way to demonstrate your competence to the new boss. Introduce the leader of your organization to constituencies. An interview in your publication is a natural vehicle. How about a videotaped interview? Perhaps meetings are in order. It is important that you assess the boss's strengths and weaknesses as a communicator so that you can help present his or her ideas as effectively as possible. Communication training is a possibility—many chief executive officers find speech and interview training invaluable. What opportunities are there to introduce these ideas? What opportunities are there to assist in this difficult transition period? What helpful information can you provide? Once again, the problem-solving process can be invaluable for coming up with ideas that can ensure a smooth transition and keep you and your communication program on track.

There is another aspect of your job when there is a change in top management. If it is important to communicate with the new boss, it is of equal importance to communicate with the entire organization. Changes can create havoc in an organization, especially when they are changes at the top. People at all levels become uneasy because new leadership brings uncertainty. You and communication can play a key role in minimizing uncertainty and keeping the organizational ship on course.

You should try to anticipate the questions that will be on people's minds and answer those questions so that the organization can proceed with its normal routine. Your new boss will appreciate your efforts in this, especially if your analysis of the situation is thoughtful and your proposed communication solutions are effective.

Many communicators fail to recognize this as an important, even critical, job. And you probably should involve a number of thoughtful members of management in the process. Given some careful planning, your communication programs at times of top-management transition can contribute greatly to your organization's success.

Handling the Sensitive Story

These days, there are few communicators who do not have to deal with sensitive issues periodically. Strikes, accidents, charges from government agencies or activist groups, controversial legislation, environmental and energy issues, affirmative action, revolutionary products or services, mergers and acquisitions, plant closings—these and many other issues can and will be viewed as sensitive by decision makers at many organizations.

How will you deal with them? Will you be able to cover them at all in your internal communication program? The best way to ensure that top management considers communication essential and that you understand your role in helping the organization cope is to have a communication policy and a set of objectives. These can help you create a thoughtful position for the organization and share it with employees.

Even so, every situation is different, so it's important to follow a problem-solving process in determining your recommendation. Research the situation completely. Know all sides of the sensitive issue, especially your management's position. If management doesn't have a position, help them agree on one; your research could be invaluable. If management's position cannot be defended, help them see the shortcomings the opposition will point out.

Once you know management's position, decide what to communicate to employees or to your other important publics. Is it just enough information to understand the organization's position, or is it a program that asks them to take action? The point is, you have to decide what you want people to do with the information. That will help determine the angle of the story.

Should you tell both sides of the story? If you can easily and effectively refute the other side, then a point-by-point rebuttal can be very effective. What if the argument is moot? In that case, it's probably best to recognize that there are two sides to the issue but not dwell on an explanation of the organization's position. Tell the story in a way that will appeal to employee self-interest or to your other publics' self-interests.

Sometimes, communicating sensitive issues can be detrimental to the organization. If the organization has made an error, it may be best to say nothing rather than risk beginning a dialogue that would cause more harm than good. This can be especially true when there are legal ramifications, and when admitting a problem or a past error could hurt the organization in court.

Many times, there are conflicts between the organization's legal and communication needs. You must recognize both these needs as valid. Then you must do your best to build the case for communication if you feel it is necessary. Top management will have to decide which need is more important.

An excellent example of a conflict between communication and legal needs occurred during the building of a skyscraper in a major metropolitan area. Citizen's groups formed and threatened suit as the construction began to interfere with their television reception. Employees of the company were torn. Some of them were also experiencing "ghosting" on their TV sets. Others were sympathetic to their neighbors whose reception was affected. Still others didn't want the company to stop building their new headquarters. The communicators recommended a complete internal and external communication program detailing what the company was doing to ensure that TV reception would not be adversely affected. Their point was that their employee relations and customer and community relations were too important to risk. The general counsel, on the other hand, said the suits would likely go to court, and he would have a much stronger case if the information was withheld for presentation to the judge.

Both points of view were valid, and both were based on a concern for what was best for the company. They were presented to a committee of top officers for decision. The officers decided to effect a full-scale communication program, and some citizens changed their positions. The case was later won in court.

Reviews and Censorship

A perennial thorn in the communicator's side is getting approvals. Often the problem arises because we do not have a written communication policy and a set of objectives that management embraces. Sometimes the problem is the result of our own misguided concept of communication's role in the organization.

Few organizations encourage or even tolerate investigative journalism on the payroll. That's not the reason we were hired; we are employed to help management achieve organizational goals through better communication. This means we need to understand management's point of view, and we ought to be willing, even happy, to work with management to decide on the substance of our programs.

To a large degree, you decide whether you and those who review your copy will work together constructively or in an adversary relationship. If you are forever trying to sneak sensitive stories past management, you will not be trusted and you will find most of your programs watched carefully and often censored. If you work with management and become recognized as a reliable and credible member of the team, you will find the comments of those who review your stories helpful. In fact, you will begin to get involved in planning stories you might never have heard about were you not a member of the team.

What ought to be reviewed? Most of us know which stories are sensitive, and it's in everybody's self-interest to get a second opinion on those issues. You should voluntarily discuss your story lines with those in the know and solicit their comments. It's wise to get another opinion even on stories that have a remote chance of causing problems. It is better to know about the problem in advance; if you still feel the story is necessary, build your case knowing both sides of the issue, present it to a higher level, and accept the decision.

Who ought to be the reviewer? Your immediate boss is usually a good sounding board if you trust his or her understanding of the organization. Someone who is an authority on the subject of your story ought to get a chance to share insights with you. Sometimes it's a good idea to set up a working committee that represents the various areas in your organization.

A review committee? Yes—properly selected and used, it can be your best ally for effective communication. If you ask that a committee be formed, you'll probably have a chance to suggest good representatives to serve on it, so take the initiative. Initially, you'll find the review committee is an excellent group for you to prove your competence to. Once done, they'll not only help you with their advice on sensitive stories, but they'll support you within their various departments. They'll call you with ideas for stories, get you involved with important issues at the planning stage, and help you to meet the organization's communication objectives.

It is important to share your objectives with this committee and entertain their ideas on altering your objectives. You should educate them on how you go about doing your job and what kind of steps are involved in producing a communication piece. Finally, you should come to some agreement with them or what their role is. Style is not their concern, for example. Their insight on the facts and the implications of stories is.

That's the ideal situation, but let's say your reviewer is not so understanding or doesn't care about the communication implications of an issue. For some reason beyond your control or understanding, your story or program is censored. What can you do? First, don't take it personally. Anger and frustration are not necessarily your best friends when there's disagreement. Take a walk if you can, or a breather, and think about the situation. Is the issue important enough to argue?

If it is, and if you have a good case for disagreeing with the censor, try reasoning with him or her. If that doesn't work, you have to escalate. Get the support of your boss and ask that the issue be resolved at a higher level. In some cases, your boss may resolve it without consultation. Usually, the boss will attempt to find a compromise that will satisfy both you and the censor. Sometimes the decision will have to be made by top management.

Here is one example of a censorship situation that turned out well. Customer service complaints at a large consumer company were increasing. The communicator prepared an article to show employees how they could solve the problem. At the review stage, the vice president of operations, who was responsible for customer service, rewrote the article to indicate there was no great problem—he didn't want his department to look bad. The communicator couldn't convince the vice president that the problem had to be recognized before it could be dealt with, or that the article would not ring true with employees. The communicator explained the situation to his own boss, who referred the problem to the president of the company. The article was printed in its original form. The president decided that dealing with the problem was more important than saving face for the customer service department.

None of us like censorship. We can usually avoid it by planning our programs carefully, researching our stories completely, and using review committees to our best advantage. Sometimes compromise is necessary. Sometimes we lose. Losing shouldn't be a problem for you unless you haven't done your best job preparing yourself for the fray.

The review committee can be an excellent problem-solving group. If you use it to develop solutions to your communication problems, you'll find you have a great deal of help in implementing your plans.

Your Budget Has Been Slashed

This situation rears its ugly head so often that it's questionable whether it should be treated as a special problem. Budget cuts are routine in many organizations when income and expenses fall out of line or it looks as if things might get bad.

The budget problem is a fact of life. The solution is one that can be planned for, just like life insurance. If you review past communication budgets, you ought to get a good idea of the extent of budget cuts in the past. If there's no history to rely on, talk to some other communicators in your industry and guess what your typical budget cut might be. Talk to others in your organization. That's how you get a handle on the potential problem.

What if you discover your budget may be cut by as much as 20%? Can you absorb that kind of a cut and still meet your communication objectives? Surely you can meet at least your high-priority objectives.

Review your current programs. How much can you cut by using less expensive paper? Making your publications one-color? Changing the format to one that is more cost efficient? Reducing the number of pages in publications or the length of some A/V shows? Delivering publications at work instead of mailing them home? Delaying the beginning of a new communication endeavor? Doing some of the work yourself that's normally done by suppliers?

Have you saved enough to continue your current programs, though they may be somewhat altered? If you cannot meet your budget cut through these choices, you will probably have to reduce your program. This may be your opportunity to kill that publication you feel is ineffective, but which management keeps holding on to. At least you may be able to alter it in the name of good management. What are some other alternatives? Can you cut the number of issues of some of your publications, or the number of A/V shows scheduled for this year? Combine two publications into one and take advantage of some printing and distribution economies? Eliminate a part of your program? Eliminate staff? Require departments for which you are doing programs to finance their own endeavors?

You will have to choose carefully from among these alternatives. The idea is to do as little damage as possible to your program so that you can continue to meet your high-priority communication objectives for the year. Also, remember that when budgets are being slashed and layoffs are being considered, your employees need to know more than ever what is happening and how it will affect them. In the interest of keeping the organization from panic or depression, you may need to scrap your fancy magapaper and substitute a newsletter you can write and issue within one workday.

Talk to your suppliers and get their help and recommendations. They've been through this hundreds of times and may know "the answer" that will work for you. Get your advisory board involved. Consider your objectives. Consider current communication needs. Consider the future. And make your decision logically, using the problem-solving process. Don't wait until you receive formal notice that a cut is required. Make your contingency plan now so that when it happens, you have a good idea of possible choices.

Deadlines and Crisis Projects

Two other areas that often cause problems for communicators are meeting regular deadlines and responding to crisis projects in a timely fashion. Many times, it's the crisis project we blame for missing other deadlines.

Let's think about deadlines first. Why do we have them? Obviously, there are a couple of reasons. Without a deadline, many of us would never finish our projects on a timely basis. But that's not the primary reason for deadlines. The reason for deadlines is to ensure a regular and timely flow of information to your audience. That's an important part of effective communication. And it is recognized even as such by laymen.

Recently, the communicator at a major United States manufacturing company that has sophisticated communication capability surveyed employees on the effectiveness of his programs. Most employees said they thought the programs were weak. Some were unaware of the programs. Why? The bimonthly newsletter, besides carrying little in the way of real news, was published only twice last year. The quarterly video report from top management came out three times. The communicator and his staff had problems meeting their deadlines, what with clearances and crisis projects.

How do you avoid that pitfall? It all goes back to your policy and objectives. If you have management's firm commitment to effective communication, you don't have to miss deadlines to wait for clearances or get a late-breaking story out. Your communication plan must include ways to get fast-breaking news to employees without holding up regular media.

What do you do about the hole in your program created when a story is held up? You plan ahead. If you are on top of what's happening in the company, you know what issues are likely to cause problems; you've got a back-up story ready just in case. In fact, there is no excuse for not having a current file of back-up material always at hand. I'm not talking about filler. Your publication and your video news programs are not made up entirely of news. There are some stories that are timeless. Features on employees, historical information on some part of the organization, reprints of material from your archives with some new perspective—all of these are candidates for filling the hole that periodically appears in your publication or A/V show.

The other aspect of meeting deadlines has to do with educating management on the importance of meeting schedules and the cost, both in dollars and in communication effectiveness, of missing your deadlines. Also, be sure you have given those who need to review your materials sufficient time to do so. If you aren't taking this into account, you may be the cause of the problem. If you don't show respect for others' time, they'll feel no obligation to respect your apparently arbitrary deadlines.

Crisis projects by their very nature will upset your office routine. Frequently, they require inordinate amounts of your time. There are two important aspects of crisis projects to consider: how to organize to get the job done and how to avoid or minimize crisis in the future.

The most important aspect of crisis management is the manner in which you react. Obviously, crisis is upsetting, and the first reaction is to do something about it. Many skip the analysis and planning steps and forge ahead, often with the wrong tools and the wrong approach. If you can, slow the tempo down. Take the time to get a firm understanding of the problem and execute the problem-solving process. It is the only way you can be sure you have considered alternative solutions and the pros and cons of each. Take the time to write a plan so that everyone knows what has to happen, where it should happen, and who is responsible for which part of the plan. In the long run, this will save you time and ensure a better chance of success.

A written plan will do even more for you: it will put management on notice about the deadlines necessary for successful completion of the project. It will help management set some priorities and choose the parts of the plan they can accomplish successfully within the given time frames. It will show your ability to respond thoughtfully in crisis.

If you are really thoughtful, you will create a plan that anticipates crisis and minimizes it in your organization. (We spend far too much time reacting, and far too little anticipating and correcting to avoid crisis.) How does one anticipate and avoid crisis? By listening and planning. Listening can take many forms. Informally, get plugged into the grapevine and take the time to talk with people. That way, you can stay on top of employee concerns and bring them to management's attention before they reach crisis proportions.

Formal listening programs also can help. Most companies today have at least considered or even experimented with them. Regular, ongoing attitude studies help you identify concerns and spot trends before they become crises. It is important to review this kind of information regularly. Upward communication programs, ranging from "letters to the editor" to "telephone hotlines" and "speak-up" systems, should be charted and analyzed to the same ends.

As the organizational communicator, your role is to keep management informed of the trends and encourage action to alleviate concerns. Your job also entails using your media to tell employees that management hears them and is taking action based on what it's hearing. With dialogue taking place between employees and management, you create trust and credibility that alleviates the need for much crisis communication. The problem-solving process is useful here in deciding how to deal with employee concerns constructively and keep the dialogue flowing.

Working with a Highly Decentralized Staff

Managing creative people can be difficult, especially for communicators who have little or no management training or experience. The problem can reach critical proportions if you are relying on a staff that is highly decentralized. When you're not in daily touch with those who report to you, you have to rely on their ability to do the job and their motivation to do it well. Given the right environment, you can rely on most people to do a job to the best of their abilities. The manager's job, then, is to create the proper environment and help the staff develop as communicators.

Start by telling people what their responsibilities are. Most managers of decentralized operations find that their staffs need a written guide explaining what management's expectations are, what policies and procedures apply in that job, what general information people in that job ought to know, and whom to go to for more information. Call that your "communicator's guidebook" and supplement it with other regular communications that show ideas, approaches and changes in corporate direction.

Most managers of decentralized staffs find it important to conduct periodic workshops with their staffs. This ensures a common understanding of policies, objectives and plans; helps to keep the staff up to date on new and emerging communication theory and techniques; provides an opportunity for counseling on skills improvement, and creates an esprit de corps among the far-flung staff.

Finally, most managers of decentralized staffs find it necessary to deal with their staff's communication products on an "exception" basis—that is, the manager discusses products that are below expectations with the staff person involved, and they agree on recommendations for improvement. Similarly, the manager recognizes outstanding work by phone and letter.

Use the problem-solving process to identify problem areas and develop solutions. Start with a list of questions. Who are the members of the staff? What are their responsibilities? How well do they carry them out? For each staff person:

- Are skills up to par? Where is remedial work necessary?
- Is his or her knowledge of the organization and the job satisfactory? What are the apparent weak areas?
- Does the person have the tools and facilities to do the job well?
- Are resources (time and budget) available to support this staff person?
- Does local management support the effort, or are they uncooperative?
- Is the person enthusiastic and supportive of communication policies and objectives?

Based on the analysis, determine who needs what kind of help. Build that into your workshop agenda or deal with it on an individual basis. In some cases, you may be able to provide assistance directly by supplying information that has been missing or by interceding with local management for better support or more resources. In any case, you should communicate your concerns to your staff and let them know your plan of action. You should poll your staff periodically to discover their concerns and recommendations. Once they see that you're supportive in their effort, they'll support you in yours.

The Problem Is You

We cannot take all the blame for the problems that face us as communicators, but we often *are* a part of the problem. We should be aware of ourselves and the part we play in making communication happen in our organizations—or in keeping it from happening.

Many of us build boxes for ourselves and never venture outside the boundaries of our box. We limit ourselves, our capabilities and our potential for growth. Think about it. How many times have you stopped yourself from doing something that would help your organization either because you thought you couldn't get support for it or because it wasn't in your job description? If any of the following apply to you, you should consider the problem and understand its effect on you and your organization:

1. Do you limit your contacts in the organization to those you receive permission to see? An effective communicator must have access to all the sources of news. If you're limiting yourself, you're limiting the effectiveness of your program.
2. Do you believe you've seen it all or read it all so that you don't need to continue your education about how people and organizations work and what's happening in the communication field? If that's the case, time is probably passing you by while you are putting out the publication.
3. Is it your attitude that organizations generally take advantage of people, and so your role is to represent the downtrodden masses to the unfeeling captains of industry? You're probably not very happy in your job, aren't trusted by management, and know from experience that every organization is that way—at least it's been that way everywhere you've worked.
4. Are you frightened by the phenomenal technological advances that have taken place in the communication field and not confident you can master them or manage some smart aleck who can? You probably have managed, then, to convince your management that video is a fad and feedback programs will just cause people to become upset. How long will you be able to hold out?

Ideally, each of us knows areas where we can do better. It is our responsibility to develop a plan to improve in those areas. Our profession is not an easy one. We need to know so much about how people think, how they interact, what various media can do at what cost, how to build surveys and select representative samples, how to train supervisors in interpersonal communication, and on and on and on. So it is important for us to keep learning and keep talking with one another, both in our organizations and in our professional associations. The key is realizing what we know and don't know, and knowing how or where to find the information.

The communicator's role in an organization has to do with helping management achieve organizational goals through communication. If you have a communication policy and objectives and a plan to meet those objectives, you are far ahead of many of your peers. You'll avoid many of the problems they'll face. If you can find a problem-solving process that works for you and use that process in your work, you'll be still farther ahead. Finally, if you can identify some other successful communicators and share your experiences and problems with them periodically, you'll find help in solving even the "insurmountable" problem.

FREDERIC HALPERIN, ABC, is a communication consultant at Hewitt Associates in Houston, Texas. He is accredited by the International Association of Business Communicators.

◆ 18 ◆

Legal Considerations

Frank Walsh, JD, APR

Introduction

Mass communication law, admittedly, is complex, and the practitioner needs to be aware of legal applications and know when legal advice is needed. For ordinary public relations activities, the communicator should know enough of the law to keep from committing the more common legal mistakes. The general considerations of libel, privacy, freedom of information, and broadcast law are examples of areas in which the public relations writer should be able to apply a general understanding of the law. In other areas, the practitioner should recognize the questions so answers can be sought before a serious error is made. Financial reporting, in particular, raises some of these more serious questions.

This chapter offers an overview of mass communication law, but the practitioner should understand that the law changes rapidly. A general understanding of the law must be matched with continued reading in the area for updating.

The contents of this chapter are not intended to put the communicator in the position of becoming legal counsel to management. Rather the communicator must raise mass communication law questions and seek advice. The practitioner with a basic understanding of the law will be in a much better position to work with organizational attorneys.

Defamation

A *defamation* can be verbal (slander) or in fixed form (libel). Communicators work primarily with printed matter and audiovisual material, and are

291

therefore more concerned with libel. Generally speaking, a *person* is libeled when he or she is *identified* in a *publication* that *defames* (damages) him or her by exposing him or her to public hatred, contempt or ridicule.

Three elements are necessary to maintain a defamation suit:

1. *Identification.* The person or corporation does not have to be identified by name, but the information must point to an individual and give the reader reason to believe that an identifiable person has been defamed.
2. *Publication.* A broad term, publication is not limited to printed matter. Photographs, statues, cartoons, slide shows and hangings in effigy are all "publications" when they are communicated to one individual other than the person libeled. A person also may be libeled in a caption, headline, display, or classified advertisement, or anywhere on an opinion page.
3. *Defamation.* This is a statement impugning the honesty, virtue, or reputation and/or alleging mental or physical defects in the person libeled and causing some damage. Damages are often in the hundreds of thousands of dollars, and million dollar libel suits are not unusual.

Damages means the words or combination of words that cause loss of reputation and whose interpretation results in an amount or award of money. It is impossible to list all the words, actions or illustrations that may constitute a loss of reputation. However, some general categories may be helpful:

- Word(s) suggesting professional incompetency, such as "quack" in referring to a medical person; "idea-stealer" referring to a supervisor, or "should be pushing a broom rather than sitting behind a drafting board" in referring to an engineer.
- Word(s) suggesting dishonesty, such as "hustler," "on the take," "buys his way to the top," "writes his best fiction while filling out his tax return."
- Word(s) suggesting sexual impropriety, such as "affair," "loose," "keeps her job with off-duty favors," or "the office camp follower."
- Word(s) suggesting mental or physical condition, such as "mental breakdown," "alcoholism" or a veneral disease such as gonorrhea.

Defamatory words or phrases can result in damages that may translate into dollar awards. These are the three most common classifications of damages:

1. *General or compensatory* damages relate to loss of reputation, shame, hurt feelings, embarrassment and pain and suffering. General damage

awards are often high and it is not uncommon for them to reach hundreds of thousands of dollars.

2. *Special or actual* damages relate to tangible loss such as hospital bills, loss of salary or clients. These damages must be proven to the court and usually are out-of-pocket expenses only.
3. *Punitive* damages relate to any additional damages assessed by the court as punishment for the libel. Punitive damages also may be extremely high and assessed by the court for intentional libel or libeling with malice. While "mistake" is not a defense to libel, a full retraction, depending on individual state statutes, may limit punitive damages.

The law of libel is complex and is constantly being redefined. Within a broad framework constructed by the United States Supreme Court, many states have different interpretations of the law and also different standards for awarding damages. In the past, libel suits usually targeted the medium that disseminated the libelous information. A trend in recent years, however, has been to sue the source of the libelous information. A noteworthy case in this regard is *Hutchinson* v. *Proxmire* (1979). Dr. Hutchinson, a reputable scientist, had received a grant from the United States government to study stress in monkeys. Wisconsin Senator William Proxmire ridiculed this research in a press release and in a newsletter; he referred to the study as "monkey business." The press release was picked up by the wire services and the story ran in many newspapers. However, the press release and the newsletter were the culprit rather than the newspapers, and Dr. Hutchinson was successful in his suit. The practitioner must be very careful to avoid libelous statements in all of the tools he or she uses, including news releases and newsletters.

The law does not leave the communicator without the protection of some broad defenses for libel. The most far reaching of these defenses is *The New York Times* rule dealing with public officials/public figures, discussed below. Other defenses include truth and qualified privilege.

In libel law, an important distinction is made between public officials/ public figures and private individuals. The communicator has considerably more freedom to make critical (potentially defamatory) statements about public figures. This was established through case law to encourage public debate and the flow of ideas. However, the definition of "public figure" is still evolving. In the Proxmire case, the research scientist was not held to be a public figure, despite his employment by a state-owned university and his reputation within his field. In some cases, the courts have recognized the concept of a "limited purpose" public figure. This means that a person who has made a name for him- or herself through a specific act or narrow range of activity may have to suffer defamation in connection with that act or activity, but not in other aspects of his or her life.

The standard that allows increased criticism of public figures has evolved from the famous decision in *Times* v. *Sullivan* (1964). To be awarded damages in a libel suit, a public figure must prove, in addition to the standard elements of a libel case, that the defamatory material was made with a malicious intent or with reckless disregard for the truth. If a communicator finds it useful to make a point by attacking someone, he or she is on safer ground if that person is a public figure. Conversely, if the client is a public figure, the practitioner may have to counsel him or her to accept a certain amount of defamatory criticism with grace.

Yiamouyiannis v. *Consumer's Union* (1980) is another case in which an advocate criticized a scientific researcher. However, this had a different result from the Proxmire case because the researcher in this case was deemed to be a public figure. Dr. Yiamouyiannis had published studies that linked cancer with fluoridation of water. Consumer's Union, through its magazine, *Consumer Reports*, characterized the studies as "amateurish." The researcher charged defamation by innuendo. However, by his own admission, the researcher had thrust himself into the forefront of a controversial issue. The court, declaring Dr. Yiamouyiannis to be a public figure, granted summary judgment—that is, the judge threw the case out of court without trying the issues.

Truth provides a complete defense in most states against libel. Truth is a significant defense for communicators, but also contains some limitations. First, truth must be shown by the defendant—the practitioner. This is not always easy to do, especially if the libel is in the area of such loosely used words or phrases as "near bankruptcy," or "is close to a nervous breakdown." Second , "truth" is not the same as "accuracy." The communicator may accurately quote a source. If the statement is libelous, the accuracy of the quote does not relieve the communicator. Often the communicator and the source become joint defendants.

Public relations writers, like reporters, have the defense of "qualified privilege." This defense is based on accurately and without malice reporting statements and activities of officials who, because of their public positions, have "absolute privilege." Absolute privilege is the right, regardless of the nature, to be free from claim of libel. It is ordinarily limited to such persons or situations as judges and judicial proceedings, counsel, litigating parties and witnesses, legislative proceedings and legislators (state and federal), and members of the executive branch.

This defense becomes increasingly important to communicators as government involvement with business increases. The defense is "qualified" to the communicator to the extent that written reports on the "absolute privilege" situation are substantially accurate and without malice. The substantially accurate qualification sometimes creates a problem for communicators. Often, testimony, court orders or decrees, bills and resolutions are stated in legal jargon and not easily understood. If this is the case, the communicator has the responsibility to seek clarification of the material before writing the story.

Invasion of Privacy

Consistent with the tendency to litigate matters, people today are more aware when their privacy is violated or when they are exploited commercially without compensation.

The communicator should check the privacy law in his or her own state or province. Only a few states—New York, California, Oklahoma, Utah, Virginia and Wisconsin—have statutes recognizing privacy. Thirty-five other states and the District of Columbia have recognized some kind of privacy rights through court decisions. Federal courts also have recognized an action for the invasion of a person's privacy. While all of these recognize privacy in a somewhat different manner, the similarities are generally greater than the differences. Whereas a defamation suit can usually be defeated by proving that the alleged defamatory material is true, truth may not be a defense in an invasion of privacy suit.

There is, contrary to widespread belief, no constitutional right "to be left alone." If a person is involved, actively or passively, in a newsworthy event, he or she cannot successfully bring an action against a publication that truthfully portrays him or her in the context of reporting that event. Therefore, a person who is photographed at the scene of a fire or a political happening has little recourse if the photograph is published in connection with a news story. Proving that an item is newsworthy is a viable defense.

Privacy also becomes an issue when the likeness or name of a person is exploited in some way to promote an idea, another person, or a product, without permission or compensation to the person so exploited. This is known as appropriation.

The balancing factors to these invasions of privacy are generally accepted defenses. These are the most frequently stated defenses:

- *Newsworthiness* of the event or activity that makes it of public interest. The courts have defined "news" in a variety of ways; perhaps the best guide for communicators is the definition "news is whatever interests the public."
- *Consent* by the person to use the information. Because so much of what a practitioner writes falls close to or into the appropriation area, consent is an important defense. Because of its importance, practitioners should become knowledgeable about the various elements of consent—its limitations and the most convenient methods of obtaining it.

To have broad and lasting protection, certain elements of consent are required. Among the requirements are

1. *It must be written.* Several court cases and all of the states that have privacy statutes require that the consent to use a name or likeness be in writing. Only in limited circumstances has a court found an implied

consent when it has been obvious the employee knew that the photo was being taken and how it was to be used, and did not object.

2. *Proper parties.* This means the organization's representative and the person whose name, photo or other information is going to be used must be included in the consent form.

   If the person is a minor, the minor's parent or guardian would be considered one of the proper parties, along with the name of the minor. In some rare instances, agents are authorized to give consent for the subject involved. For a practitioner's protection, he or she should ask for a copy of the agreement showing that the agent has such authority.

3. *Consideration.* This legal term describes value given for something received. If a person gives the organization the use of his or her name, photo or other information, the organization has the legal obligation to give the person something of value in return. The courts are not concerned over whether the exchange is fair, but they do require an exchange to make the consent irrevocable. Without consideration, the party permitting the use of his or her name or photo may revoke his or her consent, even if the organization has spent considerable money in the use of the information.

   Consideration may be direct—payment of $1 at the time the consent release is signed—or indirect— included with other interests as part of the consent release. Payment of $1 is a typical amount and approach; inclusion with other interests is preferred when the consent is part of an employment form.

4. *Scope.* This describes the intended use of the information. For the communicator, the description of intended use should be broad in terms of actual use and who may use the information. It's not unusual for an organization to want to release a photo to the National Safety Council or an industrial association. In order to do this safely, the release should give the organization the right to release the material to assignees, transferees, subsidiaries or licensees.

5. *Duration.* This is the length of time during which consent is valid. Courts will not hold release to be "perpetual." Consent releases should include a specific term of years or a terminal date. Five years is not an unreasonable term, although courts have upheld much longer terms. In the case of an employee, the term is the length of employment, or less if stated in the release. It is generally accepted that consent given by an employee terminates with the conclusion of employment. (In the sample consent form, duration is stated in terms of an "unlimited period," which a court may not uphold.)

6. *Words binding on personal representatives.* These should be a part of the release. Such wording makes the release binding upon the heirs of the subject as well as on any other persons who may succeed to the rights of the person. This element has limited application for the

communicator. If an employee dies, employment is terminated and so is the consent to use the information. Such a phrase would be appropriate for a celebrity who is hired to help the company for a promotion and signs a consent release.

7. *Tie the release to parts of a broader agreement, if possible.* This is not unusual in contracts of employment where the employee agrees to several terms including consent; salary or wage acts as consideration. Some nonprofit organizations use this method for patients or clients. In these instances, tying the release to other parts of a broader agreement is the preferred method.

8. *Disclaimer.* Another consideration is that the practitioner should state that no other *inducements, statements or promises* were made to the person permitting the use of the information. Such a statement prevents the person from saying additional promises were made that were not included in the release.

The model consent form (Fig. 18.1) fulfills the requirements of the consent being in writing. It includes the proper parties, consideration, scope, duration and disclaimer, and makes it binding on representatives. The form applies to an employee but could be adjusted to others by omitting the reference to employee on the form. The form does not include consent as part of another agreement. However, with changes to meet specific circumstances, this form can become part of a broader agreement.

Right of Publicity

The "right of publicity" is a rather new but important aspect of privacy for the communicator. If an individual's name or appearance has commercial value, he or she is said to have a "right to publicity." This means that the communicator must bargain in advance before using a celebrity in a promotional activity. Using the celebrity's name or likeness doesn't necessarily invade his or her privacy, but it may deny him or her potential income. Even within the context of a newsworthy event, televising the essence of a celebrity's performance or printing the comic routine of a comedian may be an infringement of his or her right to publicity. The practitioner also must be alert to the possibility that clients have rights to publicity that must be protected.

Zucchini v. *Scripps Howard* (1979) resulted in a $25,000 award to a human cannonball whose entire 15-second act was telecast, without his consent, during a regular newscast. He successfully maintained that few people would pay to see his act in person after having seen it on television. This case has a limited application due to the brevity and uniqueness of the act. Nevertheless, the communicator should be mindful that he or she is

---

Model Consent Release

In consideration of the sum of (amount) dollar(s) and other valuable consideration, the receipt of which is hereby acknowledged, I certify to being over twenty-one years of age and hereby give (organization's name), its successors and assigns, and those acting under its permission or upon its authority, the unqualified right and permission to reproduce, copyright, publish, circulate or otherwise use photographic reproductions or likenesses of me and/or my name. This authorization and release covers the use of said material in any published form, and any medium of advertising, publicity or trade in any part of the world for ten years from date of this release or as long as I am an employee of said organization.

Furthermore, for the consideration above mentioned, I, for myself, my heirs, executors, administrators or assigns, sell, assign and transfer to the organization, its successors and assigns, all my rights, title and interests in and to all reproductions taken of me by representatives of the organization. This agreement fully represents all terms and considerations and no other inducements, statements or promises have been made to me.

_____   _____
Signature of Employee   Date

_____   _____
Signature of Organization Representative   Date

Figure 18.1.   While this model consent release is suggested as providing most of the requirements of a valid release form, each person and organization should consider circumstances special to the particular organization before designing a consent form. As written, this model consent release may or may not provide adequate protection.

open to charges of appropriation if critical elements of someone's material are used. For example, the court recognized bandleader Guy Lombardo's exclusive right to the use of the title "Mr. New Year's Eve."

Broadcast Law

The broadcast industry in the United States in regulated by the Federal Communications Commission (FCC) under the authority of the Federal Communications Act of 1934, as amended.* In contrast to the print media

---

* Both Congress and the FCC are in the process of deregulating the broadcast industry. These activities may significantly modify this area of law.

publisher, the broadcaster is heavily regulated in theory, if not in practice. Obligation to the public is the price the broadcaster pays for the franchise, which the government grants.

Two concepts that have emerged from the Act that are critical in FCC evaluations of broadcasters are (1) the fairness doctrine and (2) the equal time rule.

Communicators will have a better opportunity to place material on the airwaves if the constraints under which broadcasters operate are understood. They also should be aware that they have a "right of reply" under the *fairness doctrine* (discussed further below) when clients come under personal attack, and that they may gain access to valuable air time by taking advantage of the general obligation that broadcasters have to present both sides of controversial issues.

The *equal time* doctrine (formally the equal opportunity doctrine) applies to political candidates. The theory behind the doctrine is to provide all candidates running for office with equal time to share their views, and not permit stations to allow one candidate an advantage over another. Stated very practically, the doctrine allows all candidates for the same office the same approximate broadcast time during the same approximate time of day.

There are certain qualifications to the doctrine: (1) The candidates must be "legally qualified," which means they must have met all local criteria to be on the local ballot. (2) The "licensee shall have no power of censorship over the material broadcast under the provisions of the sections." (3) Perhaps the most powerful qualification, the broadcaster has no obligation to "allow the use of its station by any such candidates."

Many broadcasters simply do not allow candidates to use their stations in order to avoid application of the equal time doctrine.

While the equal time doctrine is stated in broad terms, there are equally broad exceptions that significantly narrow the use of stations by political candidates. The equal time doctrine doesn't apply to news. News is defined by the law as meaning a bona fide newscast, bona fide news interview, bona fide news documentary (if the appearance of the candidate is incidental to the presentation of the subject or subjects covered by the news documentary), or on-the-spot coverage of bona fide news events (including but not limited to political conventions and activities).

For communicators involved in political campaigns, knowing these rules is important, but it's also important to note that a station does not have any obligation to seek out other candidates. These candidates must ask for equal time.

While the *equal time doctrine* is limited to political candidates, the *fairness doctrine* is exceptionally broad and applies to controversial issues, so it may have importance for almost all communicators because so much of public relations deals with controversy.

The FCC grants broadcasters broad discretion in meeting the fairness obligation. In theory, stations have the affirmative obligation to present all sides of a controversial issue of public importance. The FCC will not interfere unless the stations act unreasonably or in bad faith. There are no "news" exceptions to the fairness doctrine; it applies to public service announcements as well as all other programming. An example will illustrate the extent of discretion the FCC allows stations. When the United States government reinstated draft registration, the Defense Department prepared public service announcements urging young men to register at their local post offices.

Antidraft and antiwar groups prepared public service announcements with a contrary message. The Defense Department, using opinions of the FCC, presented stations with a memo indicating that while the draft may be controversial, registration may be considered legislative action or bureaucratic regulation and need not be considered controversial. According to the Defense Department, the fairness doctrine would not be triggered if its public service announcements were used. Many stations ran the Defense Department's public service announcements and did not run the contrary messages.

While the section of the fairness doctrine dealing with controversial issues of public interest appears somewhat vague in its application, other sections are quite specific. The "personal attack and public editorializing" sections provide specific guidelines. These sections of the Communications Act provide

(a) When, during the presentation of views on a controversial issue of public importance, an attack is made upon the honesty, character, integrity, or like personal qualities of an identified person or group, the licensee shall, within a reasonable time and in no event later than one week after the attack, transmit to the person or group attacked (1) notification of the date, time and identification of the broadcast; (2) a script or tape (or an accurate summary if a script or tape is not available) of the attack; and (3) an offer of a reasonable opportunity to respond over the licensee's facilities.

(b) The provisions of paragraph (a) of this section shall not be applicable (1) to attacks on foreign groups or foreign public figures; (2) to authorized spokesmen or those associated with the candidates in the campaign; and (3) to bona fide newscasts, bona fide news interviews, and on-the-spot coverage of a bona fide news event (including commentary or analysis contained in the foregoing programs, but the provisions of paragraph (a) of this section shall be applicable to editorials of the licensee).

(c) Where a licensee, in an editorial (i) endorses or (ii) opposes a legally qualified candidate or candidates, the licensee shall, within 24 hours after the editorial, transmit to respectively (i) the other qualified candidate or candidates for the same office or (ii) the candidate opposed in the editorial (1) notification of the date and the time of the editorial; (2) a script or tape of the editorial; and (3) an offer of a reasonable opportunity for a candidate to respond over the licensee's facilities:

> Provided, however, that where such editorials are broadcast within 72 hours prior to the day of the election, the licensee shall comply with the provisions of this paragraph sufficiently far in advance of the broadcast to enable the candidate or candidates to have a reasonable opportunity to prepare a response and to present it in a timely fashion.*

Communicators should remember that the right of reply provided by the fairness doctrine applies only to broadcast stations and not to the print media. In *Miami Herald Publishing Co. v. Tornillio* (1974), the United States Supreme Court ruled that a Florida law requiring newspapers to publish replies from candidates whenever they had been attacked by those newspapers was unconstitutional. Communicators should also be aware of the possibility of changes in these areas because of current interest in the deregulation of broadcasting.

Newspaper Advertising

Under the First Amendment to the United States Constitution, the press has an almost unlimited right to publish whatever it wishes without prior restraint. To a significant degree, communicators use advertising as part of communication packages. However, there is the problem of regulation of advertising material by the United States Federal Trade Commission (FTC) or by various state agencies that impose limits on professionals whom they license. Can a state pharmacy board prohibit drugstores from advertising prices of prescription items? Can attorneys and physicians be denied the right to advertise their services? Can a state confine corporate speech to specific issues?

Answers to these questions began to surface when *The New York Times* case (1964) opened a new era in advocacy advertising. A civil rights group had placed a paid advertisement in the *The New York Times*. The advertisement, which contained major errors of fact, defamed a public officeholder. The officeholder sued and received damages in a state court. The United States Supreme Court reversed the damage award on the theory that a public official should be prepared to accept defamatory remarks unless he could prove that they were published with malicious intent or reckless disregard for the truth. This was done in the interest of furthering public debate. Note that the newspaper, not the originator of the advertisement, bore the brunt of this legal attack.

The communicator is not relieved of the burden of truth. It has long been a principle of law that a corporation, characterized as "an artificial

* 47 C.F.R. 73 123 (1971)

being, invisible, intangible, and existing only in contemplation of law," doesn't enjoy the same constitutional rights as a "natural person." However, recent decisions have given corporations the right to speak out on matters of importance to them. In *1st National Bank of Boston* v. *Bellotti* (1978), the United States Supreme Court supported the position of a bank that had used corporate funds to finance an advertising campaign directed against a referendum that would authorize the state legislature to impose a graduated income tax. This decision was very narrow, however, and it didn't address how far a corporation could go in taking a public position on issues of political importance. The decision did not allow corporations to support political elections or campaigns directly, nor did it permit violations of the Federal Corrupt Practices Act or other federal and state laws that limit corporate political activity.

Financial Public Relations

In order to make intelligent decisions about the sale and purchase of stocks and other intangibles, an investor requires current and accurate information about the health and prospects of the company represented by the stocks. Throughout most of history, the maxim "let the buyer beware" has applied. However, after the collapse of the New York Stock Exchange in 1929, the United States government took strong action. The Securities Act of 1933 and the Securities Exchange Act of 1934 resulted in a new doctrine, "let the seller also beware." The Securities and Exchange Commission (SEC) was given the responsibility of regulating the securities market and making disclosure available to those individuals who buy and sell securities. The registration and reporting procedure regulating disclosure is complex and a full review is not possible within the scope of this text. Briefly, new issues of securities offered to the public must be registered with the SEC and a prospectus (formal summary of the commercial prospects of the venture for which money is being sought) and other information must be furnished to potential purchasers. Annual reports (Form 10 K) must be filed, showing profit and loss statements and a wealth of other information necessary for the understanding of business.

Quarterly reports (Form 10 Q), which contain summarized profit and loss statements, also are required. In the event of an unanticipated or unusual occurrence, which could have a positive or negative impact on the value of the company, a Current Report (Form 8K) is required.

Rule 10 b-5 states that it is unlawful to make any untrue statement of a material fact or to omit a material fact in connection with the purchase or sale of any security.

This rule was not tested in court until the SEC sued Texas Gulf Sulphur (TGS) in 1965 over a press release issued in April 1964. The purpose of the press release was to suppress rumors about an important mineral find that TGS had made in Canada. The press release greatly understated the value of the find, while company officials were purchasing all the stock and call options they could. When the extent of the find was made public, the stock soared and many investors who had sold at low prices felt cheated. The SEC was upheld by the United States Court of Appeals in taking action against TGS and its officers.

Soon after this decision was handed down, the SEC took action against a large brokerage house. Through its underwriting of a stock issue for Douglas Aircraft, Merrill Lynch had learned that the company was not in good shape financially. Merrill Lynch adviced 14 of its largest clients to sell their stock in Douglas Aircraft before public release of the unfavorable financial news. The SEC, which had monitored the flow of large blocks of stock before the inevitable plunge, learned about the improper dissemination of information and brought charges against Merrill Lynch. The case was settled out of court and Merrill Lynch suspended two of its brokerage offices and censured several officers.

The SEC has developed complex rules regarding the holdings of officers in a corporation and the time periods in which they can trade in their stock. Theoretically, an officer who engages in "insider trading" to the detriment of outside investors can be liable for the full extent of "paper losses" incurred.

The decision in Texas Gulf Sulphur and its aftermath tended to inhibit communication among corporate officials, outside financial analysts and the public. Fortunately, later decisions have modified the rule in favor of officials who have acted in good faith with no intent to deceive or manipulate.

In *Dolgow* v. *Anderson* (1971), the issue was a misleading earnings forecast that had led investors astray. A district court held that the officers and directors responsible were protected against private suits for liability on the grounds that they had acted in good faith. *Ernst & Ernst* v. *Hochfleder* (1976) held that no damages could be recovered without proof of *scienter* (prior knowledge) on the part of the officials; to recover damages, it must be proven that the officials, charged acted with intent to deceive, manipulate or defraud.

A more complex case is *SEC* v. *Bausch & Lomb* (1977). This company, an early marketer of soft contact lenses, experienced turbulence in its earnings. When earnings were leaked prior to publication of the quarterly report, the company attempted to correct the leak with a hasty and poorly conceived press report. The release supplied the knowledgeable specialist with enough information to deduce probable earnings. The SEC sought an injunction against the company, but the court rejected this as an "extreme measure." Although the release contained several links in the chain of analytical information, the total "mix" of information was not affected.

There also was no evidence of *scienter* on the part of the preparer of the press release.

Financial analysts routinely seek and are granted interviews with corporate officials. In these interviews, an astute analyst may put together enough clues from seemingly innocent remarks to obtain what might be considered "inside information." In *Elkind* v. *Liggett & Myers* (1980), which dealt with nonpublic disclosure of financial information to an outside financial analyst, the court compared the corporate official dealing with such an analyst to a man engaged in "a fencing match on a tightrope."

The recent tendency of the courts seems to grant some relief to corporate officials who act in good faith in disseminating information, even when mistaken. Where blatant fraud or manipulation is suspected, the SEC is now seeking criminal prosecutions rather than civil injunctions.

How is the communicator expected to deal with these circumstances? It is important to have a broad plan for the routine distribution of corporate information. This allows the company to show that it has treated material information in a consistent manner. The communicator should maintain regular contact with corporate financial officers, legal counsel and, to the extent permissible, the research and development staff.

Sound judgment as to what is and is not "material" is required. Discussions of mergers and acquisitions are particularly sensitive. Plant closings and openings may or may not be material depending on the size of the operation involved relative to the company's overall strength. All publications for which the communicator is responsible should be carefully screened for "leakage" of potentially material information. For example, employees should not be informed of major developments within the company before a public announcement is made. The careful corporate communicator also will submit all copy of a controversial nature to legal counsel for approval.

The practitioner needs to understand the concept of "timely disclosure" required by the SEC. Basically this means that "material" information is released to the investing public at one time. The American Stock Exchange Disclosure Policies states

> As a minimum, any public disclosure of material information should be made by an announcement released simultaneously to (A) the national business and financial news-wire services (the Dow Jones news service and Reuters Economic Services), (B) the national news-wire services (Associated Press and United Press International), (C) *The New York Times* and *The Wall Street Journal*, Moody's Investors Service and Standard & Poor's Corporation.

Additional information on financial communication is covered in Chapter 16.

Labor Relations

The provisions of the 1935 National Labor Relations Act (Wagner Act) and the 1947 Labor Management Relations Act (Taft-Hartley Act), together with the decisions of the National Labor Relations Board (NLRB) and the court enforcement and interpretation of these statutes provide communicators with guidelines for employer-employee communication on labor issues.

The labor laws and court decisions restrict an employer's dialogue with employees and the public during a time of labor stress. The restrictions are aimed at preventing coercion of employees in the exercise of their rights. The basic law applying to employer communication is Section 8(c) of the Labor Management Relations Act:

> The expressing of any view, argument, or opinion or the dissemination thereof, whether in written, printed graphic or visual form, shall not constitute or be evidence of an unfair labor practice under any of the provisions of this Act, if such expression contains no threat of reprisal or force or promise of benefit.

While the section is written in the context of "free speech," the concerns of the NLRB and the courts have been to interpret and apply the exceptions "threat of reprisal or force and promise of benefit" phrases. Communications will not be judged in isolation, but are looked at in the "totality of conduct" of the employer toward employees. The "totality of conduct" concept simply means that the NLRB will look at the overall relationship of labor and management to see the context of communication rather than isolating the communication for interpretations. Specific cases, especially the 1980 General Electric case, provide some examples that help business communicators get a better idea of what is and what is not a communication that would be judged an unfair labor practice under the Act.

The unfair labor practice singled out in the General Electric case was management's communicating of offers directly to workers, independent of the union. The company also issued a statement indicating its best and final offer with a deadline for acceptance, suggesting that negotiation with the union was not needed. Other company statements held illegal under the Act are those that:

- Describe company wage policies, fringe benefits or other practices.
- Answer union arguments or charges against the company.
- Point out that union membership is not a requirement for continued employment.
- Justify company action against specific employees in the union.
- Explain the price structure of the employer and its inability to make a higher offer.
- Indicate company preference for one union rather than another.

Freedom of Information

If the communicator works for a public agency, the agency more than likely will be subject to freedom of information statutes relating to open records and meetings. The concept behind these acts, federal and state, is that the public has a right to know what its public servants are doing. The basic philosophy is that disclosure is the general rule, not the exception.

The Federal Freedom of Information Act (FOIA), which went into effect in 1967 and was amended in 1974, follows this general rule, but allows nine exceptions:

1. Matters (a) specifically authorized by executive order to be kept secret in the interest of national defense or foreign policy, and (b) properly classified pursuant to executive order.
2. Internal personnel rules and practices of an agency.
3. Matters specifically exempt from disclosure statute.
4. Trade secrets and commercial or financial information obtained from privileged or confidential sources.
5. Intra- or interagency memoranda or letters that would not be available by law to a party other than an agency in litigation with the agency.
6. Personnel and medical files and similar files, the disclosure of which would constitute a clearly unwarranted invasion of personal privacy.
7. Law enforcement investigatory records, but only to the extent that disclosure would
   (a) Interfere with enforcement proceedings.
   (b) Deprive a person of a right to a fair trial or impartial adjudication.
   (c) Constitute an unwarranted invasion of personal privacy.
   (d) Disclose the identity of a confidential source or confidential information obtained from that source.
   (e) Disclose investigative techniques and procedures.
   (f) Endanger the life or physical safety of law enforcement personnel.
8. Information related to agency regulation or supervision of financial institutions.
9. Geological and geophysical information, including maps concerning wells and so forth.

Almost all states provide similar open records statutes. The communicator needs to be aware of federal and state open records statutes and also needs to understand that how the act is administered within a particular agency will determine to a significant extent the agency's relationship with the news media. The agency that seeks minimal application will often find representatives of the news media working around the agency's practitioners. Often agency leadership needs to be aware of the value of more open general application of the statutes.

General application of the statutes fulfills the spirit of the acts and also creates credibility for the agency in the eyes of the media. Such general application still leaves the agency with the legitimate exceptions stated in the statutes.

Communicators can seek information from public agencies under these acts. You should be prepared to make an informal request for the information. A formal, yet simple, request may be necessary if the original request does not work.

A sample request for information is given in Figure 18.2.

Agency name   Return address
Address   Date

Dear _____:
I hereby request personal access to a copy of (describe the document, report or information sought as specifically as you can) under 5 U.S.C. 552 et seq., The Freedom of Information Act.

If you agree to this request in whole or in part, please inform me of the search fees and the reproduction fees in advance of fulfilling the request (or, Please supply me with the information if the search and copy fees do not exceed a total of $_____.).

If any part of this request is denied, please inform me of your appeal procedures. I will consider this request denied if I have no communication from you within ten working days of receipt of this letter.

Please be put on notice that I consider this information clearly releaseable under The Freedom of Information Act and that I consider any refusal to release the information to be arbitrary and capricious as defined in the Act.

Thank you for your kind attention.

            _____
             (Signature)

Figure 18.2. Sample letter requesting information. Such a request fulfills all the legal requirements of the act and puts the communicator in an advantageous position should the request have to be taken to district court.

Open Meetings

Open meeting statutes, often called Sunshine Acts, follow the same philosophy of disclosure as the FOIA. Like the open records statutes, the open meetings acts provide exceptions, generally describing when a "public" body can conduct closed or "executive" sessions. These exceptions are generally permitted for consideration of such matters as personnel, pending litigation, or those that would invade a person's privacy. Even with executive sessions, most of the statutes provide that final action must be taken in public.

Penalties for failing to apply these statutes vary but are most often stated in terms of misdemeanors. In some states, however, action taken in closed session will be declared void by the court. Communicators should check the specific federal and state statutes for detailed application to specific circumstances and locations.

Copyright Law

The United States copyright law of January 1, 1978, now parallels the Berne Copyright Union, an international agreement followed by major countries of the world. Under this agreement, authors receive substantially the same protection regardless of the country of publication.

Copyright Protection

The law provides statutory copyright protection as soon as a work is created in fixed form. For example, as soon as a story leaves the typewriter or word processor it has copyright protection. Nevertheless, formal steps have to be completed before the author has judicial remedies for infringement.

The duration of copyright protection is 50 years plus the life of the author. The life-plus-50-year term generally applies to unpublished works, to works published during the author's lifetime and to works published posthumously. For the communicator, there is an important exception to the life-plus-50-year rule. "Works made for hire" have copyright protection for 75 years from the first year of publication or 100 years from the year of creation, whichever is shorter. If a communicator writes an article for the organization's magazine as part of his or her job, the copyright is vested in the organization. If the article was written in 1980 but not published in the magazine until 1981, the copyright protection extends to 2,056, or 75 years from the year of publication.

When a person works full-time for an organization, the law is clear that the copyright on material created for the organization belongs to the organization, whether the employee is a writer, photographer, artist, or any other creative person.

Problems sometimes occur when a person works for an organization on a freelance basis. When a communicator hires a photographer or other creative person on a freelance basis, it should be made clear from the beginning to whom the copyright belongs. In the case of freelance work, ownership of the copyright is negotiable. A letter of agreement should state clearly the intent of the organization: to buy the first use of the material, or all uses.

Informal protection of works extends only to the time of publication. As defined in the statute, publication means

> the distribution of copies or phonorecords of a work to the public or sale or other transfer of ownership. Or by rental, lease or lending. The offering to distribute copies or phonorecords to a group of persons for purposes of further distribution, public performance, or public display constitutes publication.

Once publication has occurred, formal steps must be taken to maintain copyright protection. The initial formal step is copyright notice, though there is a five-year grace period after publication before the copyright notice is required. If the material doesn't display the usual elements of copyright by the end of the five-year grace period after publication, it becomes part of the public domain, available for use by anyone without recourse by the author. Notice of copyright simply means that three traditional elements of copyright must appear in an obvious position on the work:

> The letter "c" in a circle, or the word "Copyright" or the abbreviation "Copr."; the year of the first publication of the work, and the name of the owner of the copyright.

The other two formal steps are deposit of material and registration. In the United States, the owner of a copyrighted work that has been published and that displays notice must deposit two copies of the publication with the Copyright Office, Library of Congress, Washington, D.C. 20559, within three months of the date of publication. Registration is not a condition of copyright protection but it is a prerequisite to an infringement action. There is copyright protection from the time of a work's creation, but the work must be registered before infringement action can be pursued in the courts. Only one copy is needed to register an unpublished work. Application forms are free and available through the Copyright Office. The registration fee is $10.

Fair Use Versus Infringement

The copyright law gives guidelines to help determine whether a specific use of a work is a copyright infringement or "fair use." A general statement in the statute defines infringement as anything that "violates any of the exclusive rights of the copyright owner." The courts have the power to issue injunctions, impound and dispose of infringement articles, and award monetary damages as means of enforcement of the statute. A person who infringes a copyright willfully and for "purposes of commercial advantage or private financial gain" risks a fine of $10,000 or imprisonment for not more than a year, or both.

Fair use, including reproduction of records, may be made for "purposes such as criticism, comment, news reporting, teaching (including multiple copies for classroom use), scholarship or research." To determine whether the use of a work in any particular case is fair use, the statute offers four guidelines: (1) the purpose and character of the use, including whether such is of a commercial nature; (2) the nature of the copyright work; (3) the amount and substantiality of a portion used in relation to the copyrighted work as a whole, and (4) the effect of the use on potential market for, or value of, the copyrighted work. The United States House of Representatives, report on the copyright law indicates that more words may be used from a novel than from a poem and that the scope of the fair use doctrine should be "narrower in the case of newsletters than in that of either mass-circulation periodicals or scientific journals."

Permission to use copyrighted material is usually easy to obtain. Write the owner of the material and indicate exactly what you would like to use, how it will be used and what credit line will be included. The letter should indicate whether the organization is profit or not-for-profit. The holder of the copyright can then respond, indicating permission or requesting a fee for the use intended.

Organizational communicators should not confuse copyright with the protection of "patent" or with the concept of plagiarism. *Patent* is the legal protection provided to a process or method rather than something in a fixed form, a requirement of copyright. Plagiarism is an ethical rather than a legal concept. If a piece of material is within the "public domain," a communicator has the legal right to use it. If he or she does not attribute the source of the material, however, the ethical concept of plagiarism is violated. Most often, attribution of the source of material is sufficient to remove any consideration of plagiarism.

Canadian Copyright Act

The 1924 Canadian copyright act has strong parallels with the copyright code of the United States; both follow the international Berne Copyright Union provisions. As in the United States, there is only one federal Canadian copyright law. Officials indicate that the half-century-old law is outdated in several aspects and has been under study for statutory updating. The need for updating comes from new and advanced technology, which the current law does not take into consideration. Two such obvious advances not covered by the current law are the copying machine and cable television.

Government Regulations

The reach of government into organizations of every kind continues to grow. Statutes, executive orders, commissions and regulations have proliferated and the communicator's office has not been missed. These specific areas are of increasing concern for the organizational communicator: labor relations, discriminatory language and political information. Labor relations, having been discussed above, will not be treated here.

Discriminatory Language

Government has become increasingly involved in efforts to eliminate discrimination on the basis of sex, race, color and national origin, and in the areas of salaries, fringe benefits and promotion. Statutes, executive orders and commissions provide the basis for nondiscriminatory practices. Some that the communicator should become aware of are the U.S. Equal Pay Act of 1963, Title VII of the Civil Rights Act of 1964 (amended in 1972), the U.S. Equal Employment Opportunity Commission, the U.S. Fair Employment Practices Commission, and the U.S. Department of Labor. While these are not all the statutes or commissions that may affect the communicator, they are the trend-setters.

Typical of the language being enforced by the various commissions is that of Section 704(b) of Title VII:

> It shall be unlawful employment practice for an employer...to print or publish or cause to be printed or published any notice or advertisement relating to employment...indicating any preference, limitation, specification or discrimination, based on race, color, religion, sex, or national origin, except that such a notice or advertisement may indicate a preference, limitation, specification, or discrimination based on religion, sex, or national origin when religion, sex, or national origin is a bona fide occupational qualification for employment.

While a complaint may be based on discriminatory language contained in an organization's literature, more than likely an organization's literature will be only part of the commission's or court's review of a complaint. The organizational communicator should know that his or her publication may well be one part of the evidence considered in a hearing on discriminatory complaint.

An excellent source to help communicators write nondiscriminatory copy is IABC's *Without Bias: A Guidebook for Nondiscriminatory Communication*. It contains numerous examples of writing that show bias and ways to rewrite them without bias. A communicator following this guide should not have to worry about organizational publications being used as evidence of discrimination.

Canada provides both federal and provincial protection from discriminatory language. As with most Canadian law, the federal level handles only such organizations as banking, airlines and railroads. In these instances, the Federal Human Rights Commission hears complaints. The federal commission covers about 15% of the workforce; provincial Human Rights commissions cover the remainder of the workforce.

While provincial commissions vary in their statutory authority, they all seek to provide equal opportunity for Canadian citizens, according to Canadian authorities. They also say that while there has not been as much attention focused on discriminatory language as there has in the United States, it is important. As an example of importance, one official indicates that references to sexual or racial bias in organizational publications would become part of human rights violation investigations.

Political Information

Organizational communicators in the United States have established a rich tradition of providing employees and others with information about political candidates and issues. They must know and follow the Federal Election Commission (FEC) Regulations as well as guidelines provided by the Federal Election Campaign Act as amended in 1976. In general, the act and regulations apply only to federal elections and to profit-making organizations. Partisan communication, in both corporations and labor organizations, is permitted under certain conditions.

Corporations may permit presidential and congressional candidates, their representatives or representatives of political parties on corporate premises to address or meet employees as long as other candidates for the same office and representatives of all political parties are given the same opportunity. There can be no effort, either oral or written, to solicit or direct control of contributions by members of the audience in conjunction with the appearance, and there can be no endorsement or support of one candidate, group of candidates or particular party.

Posters, newsletters, or other communication can be published by a corporation to urge employees to register to vote or otherwise participate in the political process if

- The communication is restricted to urging such acts as contributing, voting and registering, and describing the hours and places of registration and voting.
- The communication gives the entire list of names and political affiliations of candidates on the official ballot, not just one particular candidate or party.
- Voter guides or other brochures describing the candidates and their positions do not favor one candidate or political party over another, and

the materials obtained from civic or other nonprofit organizations cannot endorse, support, or have affiliation with any candidate or political party.
- Nonpartisan distribution or reprints of any registration or voting information, such as instructional materials, are produced by the official election administrators for distribution to the general public.

Corporations may support nonpartisan registration and get-out-the-vote drives and even transport persons to the polls if the services are made available without regard to the voters' political preferences. A corporation may also donate funds for nonpartisan registration and get-out-the-vote drives to civic and other nonprofit organizations that do not endorse candidates or political parties. A civic or nonprofit organization conducting such political activities may utilize the employees and facilities of a corporation.

The laws involving business and organizational communication are complex and ever-changing. Communicators cannot afford to be complacent about them. They should know and confer with attorneys versed in the nuances of communication and law.

Ethics

Ethical considerations also are important to the communicator. The perception of unethical conduct can be as damaging as actual illegal activity. Sometimes practitioners find it difficult to separate legal from ethical considerations. One way to draw a somewhat arbitrary line between the two is to think of the law as the minimum standard that applies to everyone equally. The law is a floor. If a practitioner drops below the floor with a specific activity, he or she is open to legal liability.

Ethics, on the other hand, do not have standards that apply to all persons equally. Frequently, ethical considerations are personal and therefore vary from person to person. Professional organizations often bring to their memberships guidelines or standards that "should" be followed by the members. Business and organizational communicators should be aware of these ethical considerations. Out of necessity, they are general, but they can be applied to specific areas in order to provide guidance.

Public Interest. The public interest demands that the practitioner conduct his or her professional activities in such a way as to adhere to truth and accuracy and to generally accepted standards of good taste.

There are no circumstances in which lying to the public is acceptable professional activity. This should not only be a personal standard, but a practitioner's employer should be aware of this standard. The long-range interest of an organization is best served with truth and accuracy.

While good taste is open to broad definition, the temptations to use questionable techniques, illustrations, or stories to communicate should be avoided. In particular, sexual, religious and racial material lend themselves to possible questions of good taste.

Conflict of Interest. Practitioners should avoid situations that might result in conflict of interest. While it appears that this applies to practitioners in agencies, many communicators in not-for-profit or corporate settings can become involved in a variety of organization/community activities that may present a conflict of interest.

When a conflict of interest arises, the practitioner has an obligation to support one side's interest or to give full disclosure to both sides and continue the relationship only if both parties agree.

Source of Information. The practitioner shall be prepared to identify publicly the name of the client or employer on whose behalf any public communication is made. Along the same line, a practitioner shall not communicate on behalf of an announced cause or organization while actually serving an undisclosed interest, client or employer.

The public has the right to know on whose behalf communications are being made. The same communication made for one client or employer may have an entirely different perspective if made for a different client or employer. The receiver of information combines the information and the source to arrive at the meaning of the information.

Professional Courtesy. While it may seem obvious, practitioners should always deal fairly with fellow practitioners and not intentionally injure the professional reputation or practice of another practitioner.

Communication is a competitive business. Practitioners compete for business and for acceptance of their messages. While recognizing the reality of these statements, the best policy for the practitioner is to be as professional in dealings with fellow practitioners as in any other part of the business.

FRANK WALSH, JD, APR, is head of the public relations sequence at the University of Texas, Austin, Texas. He is accredited by the Public Relations Society of America and is a member of the Montana Bar Association.

· 19 ·

Feedback for Evaluation and Information

Roger Feather, ABC

In their formal communication systems, organizations often think of feedback in terms of a program to promote a flow of upward communication. But feedback is a crucial element in effective communication, not simply a program. It is a goal, not a tactic, that has to be rooted in an organization's operational and philosophical attitude—and primarily in the attitude of its senior management. When the concerns and feelings of each individual within the organization are seen to be important, and are important, effective feedback will result.

Feedback is at the very heart of humane, sophisticated management systems. It is also at the heart of the new demands of persons in the workplace, and of society in general. That demand is for individuals to be heard and to be recognized. It might well be the central issue in effective communication in the 1980s and beyond.

There are a number of ways to stimulate and improve the quality of feedback, but no method, however well launched and executed, can overcome a management or organizational attitude that relays the impression, "We don't care what they say or feel, we'll still do it our way."

Feedback requires an open atmosphere, and action resulting from that openness. When people within an organization participate, and have expectations that their participation will be meaningful, they want things to happen. When things don't happen as a result of their efforts and commitment, positive feedback quickly dries up. The efforts to promote involve-

315

ment when management has a "don't care" attitude can become counter-productive and damaging to the organization.

Candor in an organization depends largely on that organization having a strong sense of purpose and direction, and a strong sense of how the various parts fit together to make it work effectively. That purpose must be passed along and understood by all employees. When there is a firm knowledge of roles and the will to talk openly about those roles, organizations can come to grips with some of the real and important issues that involve people and business. They can talk about "why" things happen, rather than just "what" and "how."

The communicator's job should provide access to all levels and parts of the organization. That's an asset and privilege few others in the organization have; it should be used to advantage. The communicator should be attuned constantly to using in a constructive manner the information, or feedback, he or she gets.

To do an effective communication job and particularly to do a valid job on feedback, the communicator must study the organization carefully and methodically. He or she must become an expert in its style, culture,

Figure 19.1. Effective communication involves give and take. Management may use a variety of techniques to get a message to employees, who in turn may take advantage of other programs to send messages back.

audiences, and key personalities and their relationships with every segment of the organization. The communicator must then ask some hard questions —and find answers to them. What does top management really believe in? How do they back up, or act out, the beliefs? Do they really want to know what's happening? How will they use the information? How much, and what kind of change, is possible? Although the data are ever new and changing, when enough has been digested and evaluated, objectives and programs for feedback can be set or refined.

Feedback should be an integral part of any plan for communication within an organization. It is not something that can be tagged on afterward. Sophisticated, detailed planning is not an easy or fast task; it's built up slowly and constantly fine-tuned.

Feedback, by its very nature, can produce some surprises. It can bring to the surface issues and attitudes that were not known to exist. Some of the surprises can be frightening and difficult to deal with. In general, however, feedback will merely confirm what you already know. If you know, for instance, that there are negative attitudes on a specific issue or in a certain area, feedback data will not tell you what attitudes are positive. It can document and detail speculation, and that information can be a valuable lever for producing meaningful change.

Feedback is often threatening to management, particularly in the middle ranges. Some are concerned they'll be blamed for the attitudes of their subordinates; others know that in many areas they can't do anything about negative situations. To make feedback useful, it must be presented to management, like just about everything else, on the basis of, "Here are the positive things this information can do for you."

Feedback can uncover problems, and help solve them, but the results come slowly. It takes time to get an effective, upward flow of information in operation—and if it's starting in a neutral or negative climate, it takes more time.

Once the feedback element has been established as an essential component in the communication process, a wide variety of methods can be used to obtain information to provide a monitoring system for the organization. Methods fall into two general areas: formal ones such as climate or readership surveys, question-and-answer programs and focus groups, and a very long list of informal or casual ways, centered mostly around systematic listening and research by the communicator and other individuals. The methods described in this chapter begin with formal approaches.

The Climate Surveys

Climate surveys, also known as attitude or opinion surveys, are the key method for obtaining feedback in an organization. They come in a variety of

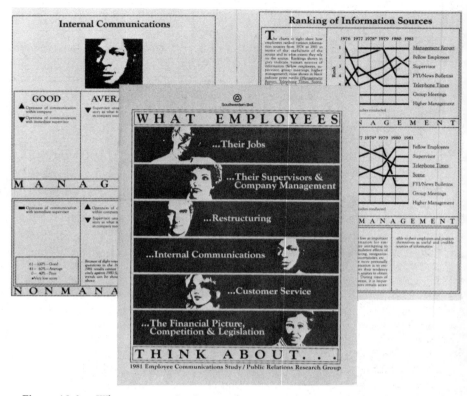

Figure 19.2. When an organization conducts an audit or survey, it tells employees that it cares what they think. To be fully effective, however, results of the survey must be communicated—good news and bad—as quickly as possible. This could represent an organization's most important effort of the year.

shapes and sizes but all are designed to find out what people think or feel—to find out their perceptions of the organization and their place in it. Other types of surveys measure behavior, or what a person does; climate surveys deal more with the emotional content of the job.

The structured survey is the key to get the best kind of information and, if collected, analyzed and used properly, the results can provide a solid basis for far-reaching decisions in an organization.

Most people in charge of managing the communication function believe that surveys deserve number one priority in effort and budget considerations in a communication plan. Before a well-managed organization acts, it seeks out the best possible information. Surveys can delve into the total workplace environment or be restricted to more specific areas or topics, but all, it seems, touch on communication in some way.

Who Does It and How

Although surveys are a major communication tool, rarely should they be conducted by in-house communicators. The communicator should be involved at all stages—and heavily involved in the latter stages of analyzing and communicating the results—but surveys should be administered by people outside the organization or at least by people not aligned with the department or function being surveyed. An outside consultant brings a level and range of expertise and experience to the job that most communicators don't possess. Conducting surveys requires a sound knowledge of scientific research methodology, workplace psychology and computer application.

Even more important, the outsider brings a degree of objectivity to the process that cannot be matched by any insider. Objectivity is an absolute necessity in conducting valid, useful surveys. Potential survey respondents must be assured that their feedback is going through independent and objective channels.

Because managements increasingly recognize the need to listen to employees, selling the idea of a survey is not as difficult as it was just a few years ago. In some organizations, however, there is still resistance. Some managements are afraid of surveys. Their objections are many: we have trouble dealing successfully with the information on hand; the cost is too high; it's just another toy; there's no beginning, middle or end to them; they raise expectations that can't be fulfilled; management already knows what's really going on "down there."

In an organization whose management doesn't care what employees think, there may be no point in even attempting to overcome the objections.

In most organizations, however, both communicators and managers know the information is vital. But on the first survey, it can still take a long period of educating and selling—up to a year or more—to get the final go-ahead.

When the green light does go on, there are usually still a number of decisions to be made or confirmed. One of the first is to choose the type of survey instrument or questionnaire.

Specially tailored survey instruments are becoming more popular, particularly in mid-size or small organizations. They usually include some questions that normally appear in packaged surveys so the results can be judged against some established norms.

Developing questions is a slow, painstaking process. Although the basic premise seems to be simply answers to "What do we want to know about?" and "How will that information be useful?", the questions must be checked by many people, many times to ensure they are free of bias, ambiguity and assumption. It's crucial that the questions be crystal clear.

One way many questions are developed is by holding meetings with employees or members and with managers. A group of employees might be asked, for instance, what they feel management should know about. Managers may be asked what they feel employees are concerned about, or what issues they need information on for future planning.

Packaged surveys sometimes allow space for questions of specific interest to the organization. On the IABC/TPF&C employee communication effectiveness survey, for example, participating organizations can add up to 10 questions directly related to their operation.

A survey targeted to a specific subject such as communication or benefits may have as few as 30 questions. For broader-based surveys, there may be 150 or more. Although the trend is away from long surveys, some packaged ones covering broad areas have as many as 300 questions. But, long surveys can produce fatigue and loss of concentration for respondents before they're completed.

An advantage of packaged surveys is that an organization can make judgments against a substantial normative data base. Norms can be misleading, however, so when responses are analyzed, a close study of the specific environment must be made.

Most survey questions are multiple-choice, usually offering four or five options. The choices range from "most" to "least," or some similar variation, plus an "I don't know" option. Although the order in which the questions are asked should have some rhythm, with easier questions usually at the beginning, the flow should not be obvious. Most questions are asked in a positive way but a few should be presented in a negative style to break the routine.

Brief demographic information is usually asked either at the beginning or the end of the survey. This information allows both for the profile of the respondent base to be checked and, where possible, matched with the demographic profile of the "real" population, and for answers to specific questions to be analyzed by such factors as age and sex. Care must be taken, however, to ensure that the information requested is general enough so there is not even a hint in a respondent's mind that he or she could be identified by the demographic information. Anything that's seen by respondents as an attempt to code survey forms for possible identification will lessen responses dramatically or make those that are received less than honest.

There should be at least one question on the survey, with adequate space following, requesting write-in comments. While the comments often tend to be negative, they can be of great value. Many surveys also include a question at the end asking whether respondents think the survey process is of value and whether they believe change will result from it.

In smaller organizations, the general practice is to survey everyone. In larger organizations, those with 1,000 or more employees or members, the survey usually goes only to a random selection. The selection must be made objectively, using the premise that everyone has an equal chance of being included, to be valid. The selection can be made by using the last digits of U.S. Social Security or Canadian Social Insurance numbers, by having a computer select every "nth" number on the list, or other similar means.

Surveys can be either mailed to homes or filled out at the workplace on company time or at meetings. The latter two, of course, will give close to 100% response but they're extremely difficult to handle if there are large numbers of people being sampled or if they're in a variety of locations. If surveys are completed at the workplace, they should be administered by someone outside the organization.

The response to surveys mailed to the home can vary widely. If proper explanations are given and advance promotion is good, responses can be as high as 70% or 80%. If the response is less than the number required for a proper scientific sample or if the demographics are significantly different from those of the "real" population, the quality of the results is usually suspect.

There should be advance promotion for any survey and some of it should spell out very clearly why the survey is being conducted, what the benefits might be, how the results will be used, and how they will be fed back to the respondents.

Making Results Useful

Even with relatively small numbers of respondents, information from survey forms should be processed by computer to save time and to easily and accurately obtain cross-references based on demographics and other factors.

Although questions may be "scrambled" on the survey form to obtain more spontaneous answers, at the analysis stage, they should be grouped under a few broad areas. The information should also be broken down by individual groups of respondents so that the groups can be compared with the overall response and with each other.

It takes time to get results back—inevitably, more than was estimated. Initial raw results can be misleading but they are sometimes helpful in deciding how to feed back final results. The time it takes to get final results, plus an outside analysis, varies greatly. It can take from one to three months or even longer for larger samples.

Because surveys produce vast amounts of information, long, intensive hours of analysis are needed to digest the material and put it in perspective. The results must be compiled and selected so that the information can be presented in an easily understandable form. The selection should be open and honest, with backup data available if requested.

Withholding information from participants, a common practice in many organizations until recently, runs counter to the concept of surveys as open feedback methods, and can damage the credibility of an organization. Results must be communicated as fully as possible. For a survey that delves into a broad topic or area, such as an overall climate survey, a story in the organization's publication is not enough; a special edition, or insert, is only slightly better. Results should be communicated with special booklets, A/V programs, group meetings and whatever other methods can be developed. Survey results can be the most important communication effort of the year for an organization.

Before approving a major survey, the senior management of an organization must commit itself to make changes if the results strongly suggest they are needed. When problems are indicated and changes aren't possible, management must explain why. Sometimes action can be taken quickly and sometimes it's a slow process. Before any action is taken, it's best to recheck the results with various levels of employees or members in small group sessions, which in themselves are feedback sessions, so that new interpretations of the results or lack of understanding about what they mean can be raised and discussed.

Although ideally, an outside individual or firm has prepared and analyzed the results, people inside the organization may find other or different items of significance. The outsiders' report is of great importance but still it should not be the end of the analysis done on the collected data, nor should their recommendations be the end of the result derived from the survey.

Obviously, both big and little changes may appear to be required from the results. Don't get caught up in the big ones and ignore the little ones, as often happens. By making the little changes quickly, an organization indicates it is responsive to the wishes and concerns of employees or members.

A climate survey is a big deal. It puts the credibility of a function, a department or a whole organization on the line. Both the survey, and the results obtained must be treated with great care and effort.

Readership Surveys

Readership surveys generally should attempt to measure primarily what people do or don't do when they approach a publication or other communication effort. Although they may contain questions relating to climate or attitude, basically they deal with behavior.

While readership surveys can be simple or sophisticated, they must be as objective as climate surveys to be really useful. Many readership surveys backfire or are invalid because they are not objective. Communicators who include survey forms as inserts or tear-out sheets in publications, or are involved closely in conducting their own survey, do a disservice to their organization and their readers. Attempting to do an objective survey on yourself offers great potential for conflict of interest, and self-administered surveys usually have such a low response rate that they cannot be matched to valid demographics and are invalid.

Brief readership surveys guaranteeing anonymity can be very valuable. A short, simple survey sent on a postcard with a return address, particularly if it has no direct connection to the communicator, can provide very useful information. Just the question, "Did you read the following article in the last issue of _____" and a list of the article titles can indicate what interests readers and what doesn't. The question asks what a reader did, not what he or she thinks.

Many communicators expect too much from casual readership surveys. Generally, they cannot provide in-depth information to prompt major changes. More than one organization has had readership results showing positive reactions to communication efforts and a climate survey that reveals communication as a major problem area.

A well-done readership survey, following the basic approaches and restrictions of a professional climate survey, is an extremely valuable feedback tool.

Formal Question-and-Answer Programs

Formal question-and-answer programs in organizations, often called "speak-up" programs because the best known and longest running one is IBM's "Speak Up," provide a direct, two-way communication flow from top to bottom.

The perception employees have of openness through all levels of the organization through these programs is often very important. Such programs say very clearly to all employees that senior management is listening and wants to know their opinions and concerns.

One danger in these programs, however, is that people at all levels can think of them as the beginning and the end of feedback. In fact, they should merely be a reflection of an attitude that welcomes openness and candor.

Most of these types of programs have common characteristics. They're based on confidentiality, have an independent coordinator, send questions and answers through the mails, and have access to and support from the top person in the organization.

Although all the programs strongly endorse and promote the idea that the prime way to get answers is to talk to your immediate supervisor, they recognize that supervisors don't always have all the answers—and they also recognize that some employees have trouble talking to their supervisors.

Even when the purposes of a specific program have been fully explained, some managers still see the program as a threat to their responsibility and authority. It must be thought of as a parallel channel for communication, not a substitute. For senior management, the program is a

HOTLINE REPORT

Caller: I just received the most recent issue of *Weyerhaeuser Today* from Tacoma. On the front page was an article boasting of Weyerhaeuser's 1979 record earnings. At the same time there are 1,400 people in the Eastern Oregon Region that have been curtailed due to market and economic conditions. What gives?

HOTLINE: It is easy—but incorrect—to think of Weyerhaeuser Company operations as just those that exist in the Klamath Basin. In fact, Weyerhaeuser Company consists of more than 50,000 employees involved in fourteen different operating regions throughout the United States, Canada and overseas, along with a variety of subsidiary company interests. Each of these regions or subsidiaries produces a different product mix, serves different markets and experiences different operating profits and losses. Recently, sales of pulp and paper products along with export trade have been strong areas for Weyerhaeuser Company while the housing industry has been softening at a serious rate. The Eastern Oregon Region, of course, is not involved in any of the pulp, paper or export markets which are currently strong. Also, our Region is not alone in reacting to the effects of a general slump in the housing market. Curtailments, layoffs and shutdowns have been in the news for the last several months wherever mills are closely linked to housing industry markets. It's not all gloom and doom for Eastern Oregon either. Of Weyerhaeuser's three Hardboard

facing. As early as last July our employee newsletter, *Growth Rings* began carrying notices, statements and feature stories indicating that curtailments were indeed possible if industry conditions continued to worsen. Similar warnings have appeared in almost every issue since July, as well as on Hotline. We didn't know how bad it would get, and we can't tell you what we don't know, but we have done our best to inform people about the possibilities. Some people were listening.

Caller: We've made it through poor markets before without drastic curtailments. What is so different now?

HOTLINE: For one thing, the current expected level of U.S. housing starts has dropped to the lowest point since July 1976, and is still declining. Some folks are speculating that it will turn out to be the worst period since 1946. Add to that our nation's current rate of inflation, declining levels of productivity and record high mortgage interest rates and you've got a number of factors that are different than they have ever been in the past.

Caller: We keep hearing how bad the lumber market is and yet turn around and work overtime to process lumber that the Merchandiser sends to the Sawmill. This could easily be run at the same time that the mill runs.

HOTLINE: Byron Dahlen told Hotline that when Mill #1 is cutting pine, the introduction of Douglas-fir flitches has created sorting prob-

Caller: Why can't Weyerhaeuser Company use profits made in other regions and businesses to keep the Eastern Oregon Region running?

HOTLINE: It's not a matter of funds, rather, markets and prices. Currently, demand and prices for local products are low. It is a fact of life that if you are running any kind of manufacturing business, at some point you simply must stop producing a product if there is no demand for it, or if the customers are not willing to pay what it costs to produce your products.

Caller: I'm concerned with the main crossing on Route "A." It's getting a lot of potholes and rough spots. I was wondering if it would be possible to get it repaired. Same thing goes for the road to the Truck Shop.

HOTLINE: Dave Wilson, Plant Engineer, said that the "A" Route crossing is an item that requires regular and frequent maintenance due to the heavy traffic of Sort Yark log movement, log trucks, and plant use vehicles. Wilson said that just prior to receiving the Hotline comment the area had just been graveled and graded again. Wilson said they'll try to increase the frequency of repair to eliminate the really serious problems of road roughness and potholes.

Caller: I've seen several Weyerhaeuser Company pickups on the highway that have been exceeding the speed limit. I have been passed by Company pickups while I was driving 55 m.p.h. I'm not perfect,

Figure 19.3. Publication of employee questions and the organization's responses strengthens the perception of openness and candor while protecting the anonymity of the employee.

system of checks on managerial behavior and performance. An appraisal of the concerns raised, even if only by one or two questions, can provide a special reading of the organization's climate and particularly the climate in one specific area.

Programs of this type are usually instigated by people at the top, unlike most communication programs that are planned and sold by the people handling the communication function. And while question-and-answer programs certainly are communication programs, they generally operate outside the formal communication systems.

Since they start at the top, there is no question about top-level support. One problem that can develop is that after the first flush of enthusiasm and success, senior level people can become bored with the program, which can diminish the programs' value and effectiveness quickly. They need continuous support.

While the main measure of these programs is in the quality and quantity of the questions, many organizations judge their success by being able to say, through them, "You're right, we're wrong; here's the action we've taken to fix the problem."

The key to any "speak-up" program is anonymity, and the key to that is an independent, credible coordinator. Both the safety factors of the program and the coordinator must have high visibility. People must see, and be constantly reminded, that there is no chance for participants to be identified. Because one of the advantages of the program is that it skirts the immediate supervisor, questions often concern the immediate supervisor. There can be a real fear of retaliation, so any indication that a name has been revealed will damage the program irreparably.

The coordinator must have the trust of employees. A good part of the job is spent talking to employees, individually and in groups, to build trust and promote confidentiality. Most coordinators widely advertise that only they open mail to the program and that after the question is answered, they destroy any and all records.

In many real ways, the coordinator becomes the organization's ombudsman, with the power to investigate at all levels. Normally, the coordinator does not have to accept answers to the questions regardless of who supplies the answer. Some coordinators estimate they send back 30% of the answers for a better response.

The coordinator is often seen as the emissary of the CEO, accountable only to that person. Some programs work out of personnel or administration areas, but that makes the job of promoting objectivity and freedom of action more difficult.

Normally, coordinators are not professional communicators; the job doesn't require that kind of background. In fact, many say that a generalist who has worked in a variety of jobs and levels, particularly in line areas of the organization, has the best training.

Before that first question arrives, senior management and the CEO must sit down and contemplate how to answer the most difficult, nastiest, most embarrassing question they can think of, because while most people are positive, the program will be tested with negative questions. The basic commitment is to answer all questions from whatever source, on whatever subject. A negative answer is completely acceptable if it's clear, candid and provides the answer to "why?." The asker may not like the answer, and it may not be in his or her best interests, but the point is that there was a way to ask it and to get an answer.

Most questions are rather ordinary. About 55% of all questions are generally complaints and 40% straight questions; the rest offer opinions. About two-thirds of all questions center on straightforward personnel administration or benefit issues, working environment, personnel policies, safety, and customer or community relations.

The programs are open to all employees, but since they tend to do end runs around managers, the assumption is often made that managers don't use them. In fact, most programs show that managers submit questions at a greater frequency than lower level employees.

All questions should be acknowledged when received and, if the answer is going to take longer than usual, the sender should be notified. Most programs commit to supply answers in 8 to 10 working days. The answers must come from the top. Although those people may delegate the investigation of the answers to someone else, the top person responsible for the subject area should review and sign the answer. If a question is directed to a specific person by the sender, that person also should sign the answer.

The number of answers prepared in a month varies in programs, from about two to six per 1,000 employees.

To submit questions, employees use a brightly designed question form that folds into a self-mailer. Although interoffice mail can be used, most forms are designed with a postage-paid business reply stamp. The forms should include a statement that the immediate supervisor is the best source of information and also that only the coordinator will see the question.

Some forms provide an option of sending the answer to a job location or a home address while others send them only to the home; some ask for permission to publish the letter without identification and others indicate that it may be published if it has sufficient interest.

Forms are made available in open racks in various locations of the organization. Because some employees fear being seen picking them up, programs often advertise that forms can be sent directly to the home on request.

All questions are retyped before they are sent on for answers, to eliminate anything that might reveal the sender's identity or specific job location.

Programs are heavily promoted through bulletin board notices, posters, stories in employee publications, and at general and special meetings. These programs need high visibility and consistent, lively promotion to be successful.

Question-and-answer programs operate mostly in nonindustrial, non-union organizations such as banks, insurance companies and utilities. There are some, however, in industrial, unionized organizations and they operate quite successfully in cooperation with the unions.

Direct costs for the programs are usually not high but when indirect costs, such as the time of senior managers, are included, the costs can be seen as high.

Question-and-answer programs are a valid feedback tool but they should be thought of as only one item in the organization's feedback tool chest. There are other formal methods for obtaining feedback, but like those already mentioned, they take considerable planning, are relatively expensive, and require a fair amount of time, care and skill.

Television, in various ways, is beginning to be used more and more to respond to the feedback element in a communication plan. Pratt and Whitney, for instance, has a regular "viewpoint" television show for employees, patterned on the Phil Donahue talk show.

Two or three senior executives start the show with a brief, well-prepared presentation on a specific issue, and then answer questions from the audience on that issue and any others that are raised. Each show is done from a different location and employees receive formal invitations. It's treated as a special evening out for employees.

Teleconferencing offers an excellent opportunity for discussions between employees at different locations. Although it can appear to be as freewheeling as a group meeting, teleconferenced meetings require more preparation and structure to be really effective. Videotape exchanges also are being used as a feedback technique, but they tend to be slow.

As the cost of communicating continues to drop, sophisticated methods of obtaining and evaluating feedback will increase, but the less formal feedback techniques will remain important.

Informal Methods

Informal (or casual and semiformal) feedback techniques require systematic data collection and documentation to be effective. It's not enough simply to hear something and react to it. In addition to developing a high awareness of what's useful, information must be sifted, categorized, assessed and reported in an understandable way to have a positive, direct impact in the organization.

Minisurveys on attitudes toward specific issues, or the behavior regarding a single event, can be very useful even though they may not hold up to scientific scrutiny. Although they should be treated with some caution, they can yield a great deal of information at little expense.

Communicators should be able to get an answer to one or two simple, direct questions from at least 100 people during a week in the normal course of the job. If that sample is not enough, or your days are crowded, two or three hours on the phone by yourself or a support person should produce a good reading.

Minisurveys can be done regularly or only on special occasions. Either way, the idea of them and the reasons for them should be publicized in advance. The results, of course, should be reported fully to everyone in the organization. The questions should follow the guidelines for any survey question and be free of bias, ambiguity and assumption. Treating the information collected as secret or not important can have a serious negative effect on the candor and participation level in subsequent minisurveys.

Communicators can expect too much from "Letters to the Editor" columns in publications. Unless the organization is quite large and, more important, has a hard-earned tradition of openness, letters columns can be an embarrassment. They are often promoted strongly, and when no letters appear or none expresses more than mundane sentiments, the credibility of the whole communication function can suffer. Certainly people should have the opportunity to write in comments, but never have high expectations that they will.

Question-and-answer columns fare a little better if they are set up with controls similar to formal question-and-answer programs. But again, expectations are often greater than results.

Listening posts are necessary for the communicator simply because he or she can't be in all places at the same time. The communicator must use other eyes and ears. Choosing a few people in strategic places in the organization and explaining to them in some detail what kind of information is needed and why can provide a steady stream of valuable feedback.

The people chosen should be informal leaders in the organization, the ones who are at the center of making things happen in an informal way—an organizer of recreational events, the person who always seems to plan the office get-togethers, or the one people go to to get the latest inside information. They generally do have a handle on what's happening.

The contacts have to be made, built up and used carefully. They are useful information sources, not spies. If possible, you should give them public recognition, and their supervisors should acknowledge their role. In the best sense, they should be one section of the communicator's regular "beat."

The grapevine is a broad, always active communication channel in all organizations. Many managements abhor the grapevine but it's a natural, normal information activity. It reflects the climate, good or bad.

The grapevine is tricky in that it moves irregularly, outside normal reporting relationships, and it moves fast. Studies show that about 80% of information on the grapevine is accurate at least 80% of the time. It usually has a high emotional content that reveals attitudes more than facts.

The communicator should treat the grapevine as a legitimate feedback source, get attuned to it, and collect the information in a purposeful way—and of course, correct the misinformation that sometimes flows through it. The worst thing you can do is ignore it or attempt to stamp it out with retaliation or censure.

Research from various sources in the organization that collect information for reasons not related to communication should not be overlooked as a feedback area. A regular check on the union grievance system, for instance, can tell you what issues are being raised, and whether they're single instances or larger, widespread problem areas. These systems are generally confidential and must be used with discretion. With the trend toward labor-management joint committees centered around "quality of worklife" issues, the channels should become more accessible. Employee records also can yield information that can be considered indirect feedback. Although individual records are confidential, such things as turnover rates and absenteeism levels can be very useful.

Suggestion systems are often closely aligned with the communication function even though most of them deal in manufacturing and safety issues. Getting involved in the plan as a communication advisor can yield considerable information. Some suggestion systems are broadly based and have, as one of their prime functions, general feedback. Most however, are award systems designed to bring in practical, workable ideas.

Feedback also can be collected regularly from sales figures, newspaper comments, community relations and public requests for information. All that material has a direct impact on an organization, and communicators should assess it, report on it and develop programs, where necessary, to respond to it.

Meetings of various types are another prime way of obtaining feedback. Communicators can arrange meetings specifically to gather feedback at little or no cost. For instance, getting together a randomly selected group of eight or 10 people for an hour or so, and using the last issue of the employee publication or some other communication effort as a talking point can bring in much valuable information. By structuring the meeting as a casual "focus group," you can start with some simple, direct questions such as "Did you read this article?" and let the attenders take the discussion into somewhat broader areas. Because of the time off the job, these types of meetings usually have to be cleared with the supervisory group. They also can be conducted in off-hours on a volunteer basis. Many employees will jump at the opportunity to express their opinions in a small-group setting.

Telephone information systems with a fast news output have been discussed in Chapter 11, but other systems designed to allow people to ask questions or offer opinions on tape are being used in a number of organizations to gather feedback. If a question is asked and a name given, the answer is sent directly back to the individual. Since these systems do not include the checks and balances of more formal systems, the questions are usually rather routine but they can still be a valuable outlet for employees. The anonymous comments that are sometimes offered on tape can be negative but often pinpoint a previously unknown problem area.

Since many would like the opportunity to talk to the top person in the organization, some organizations are arranging for their CEO or other senior people to be available at a phone to take direct calls for a few hours on a specific day. These programs are heavily promoted ("Phone-the-president-day"), and if the senior people can be convinced to handle some potentially hot questions—and some simple ones—on the spot, the programs can be very effective in promoting a sense of openness in the organization. The person answering the phone should be reasonable and candid; a few curt or less-than-honest answers can make the program counterproductive.

Getting Action from Reaction

Managing change in a busy, competitive, technological world is the prime task of organizations today. An effective management has to be based on good information. Managements want results and to get them, they need to know what's happening. If the planning is done properly, feedback programs and approaches can be sold in organizations because they do bring in the needed information. Ongoing education in attitudes will be necessary, but there is no question that most well-managed organizations want to listen and to respond to upward communication or feedback.

The key to good organizational communication is good information. Feedback approaches can get that information. Feedback is needed, wanted and demanded more than ever in organizations today.

ROGER FEATHER, ABC, is head of Feather Communication Services, an independent communication consulting firm in Toronto, Ontario. He is accredited by the International Association of Business Communicators and has served on the association's executive board.

· Part V ·

ORGANIZATIONAL COMMUNICATION TODAY AND TOMORROW

◆ 20 ◆

Trends and Issues: Challenges Ahead

Louis Williams, Jr., ABC, APR

An executive recruiter was asked what qualities he looked for when interviewing candidates for senior jobs in organizational communication. After detailing the expected points—experience, personality, skills—he said, "But those are really only superficial kinds of measurements. What I, and my clients, want to see is an individual who understands the world around him. Is that person able to relate to historical perspective and, more important, to make decisions that will show that the long view has been considered as an integral part of the problem-solving process? I want to know what kinds of books he or she reads, what he or she does in spare time, and how he or she places all that into the scheme of everyday living and working."

At first glance, that statement almost seems to be at odds with the fact that today's organizational communicator is being asked to initiate change rather than respond to it. Yet it's true. A person cannot initiate changes unless he or she understands where the problems came from. For example, the union movement in the United States has gone through several stages of development. In the beginning, there was the need for survival. The robber barons, and what passed at the turn of the century as big business, were exploiting labor. Security was nonexistent. Pay was abysmally low. Chances of being injured on the job were double or triple today's record. The union movement arose to combat all that. It did, most successfully.

Then things began to change. People began to look at work and the workplace as a place for individuals to develop as human beings. They began to talk about sharing goals. Union chiefs began to talk of participatory management—the worker should have a say in how an organization is run.

Although the worldwide recession of 1980–1982 has caused a pause in the movement toward shared decision making and reversion to concern about wages and benefits, the trend toward employee involvement will continue. As economics improve, the basic concern of unions will continue to be over basic management ingredients: Should workers be forced into overtime, against their will? How should we overcome the dulling drudgery of automation? How can we handle the displacement of workers caused by technology? What rights does an individual have to dignity on the job?

Unions continue to be strong and integral parts of the management process. They still can paralyze a city or region, even a country, in certain circumstances. But the "why" of their existence is so different from what it used to be that to attempt to communicate with today's workers in the terminology and issues of the past is to court failure. The communication expert of today and tomorrow should be looking introspectively at the organization, understanding the needs and frustrations of today's workers, and balancing them against the needs of the organization—walking a very fine line to obtain a meshing of those needs so that both can be satisfied.

The day when the editor of a publication could be concerned only with recording the life of an organization is gone. John Bailey, former president of the International Association of Business Communicators, puts it most succinctly:

> The specialist (the disseminator of news) still is in demand and will continue to be so, but those managing communication will be the generalists. This appears to be contrary to what is happening in society as a whole but it already is occurring. Even Little Sisters of the Poor Hospital uses a bulletin board, paycheck stuffers and an orientation slide show. The pure editorial positions are at the AT&Ts and Exxons.
>
> Specialization will be most obvious in the type of audience with which a communicator is involved: external, internal, investors, government, etc. They will use multiple media with specific audiences. . . . Communicators of 1990 will need a thorough knowledge of the organization and the industry of which it is a part because that knowledge will be the basis for their communication programs.

Harold Burson of Burson-Marsteller adds another perspective: "Today, we can no longer afford pat answers to difficult problems. The whole area of employee relations is studded with untapped possibilities for . . . practitioners who really understand the role of communication in an industrial society."

If you add to the informational need the explosion in access technology, you can be overwhelmed with choices. Educator Gerald M. Goldhaber calls it "information shock." He says, "A computer makes it possible for us to read immediately any book stored in the major libraries. A word-processing machine makes possible the revision of a book in less than a day. Within five minutes, we can talk by telephone to almost any part of the world. Satellite networks enable us to be eyewitnesses at the impeachment of a president, of the landing of a spaceship on the moon and even of a full-scale war— without ever leaving our living rooms."

The challenge is clear. The communicator of the future will have to manage information and assemble programs and media to meet objectives that solve the problems organizations face. Real power will fall to the communicator who not only can communicate superbly but also knows where the information can be found.

Looking Ahead

Historians and newspaper people are wont to assign to a period of history some sort of label that describes the era succinctly. For example, the decade recently ended has been called the "me" decade—with good reason. The 1970s produced 8 trillion, 160 thousand self-help books! We learned how to be more aggressive. How to be less aggressive. How to be thinner. How to live with our fat. We learned how to say no. We learned when to say yes. We bought self-help therapy books to "get it together." And then we went to therapy to pull ourselves apart—all to become the "new woman" or the "new man." All in all, it was a roller-coaster ride with lots of ups and downs and lots of buzz phrases: "I've got to get my act together," "I've got to discover the real me," "I'm OK, you're OK," "We've got an open marriage."

Throughout the 1970s, we kept getting hit over the head with facts. We found that people in our governments lied to us, that the glories of war weren't, that our gas tanks were empty.

Out of the glaring disappointment and disillusionment came a new decade, perhaps the most important in this century—not for what it promised, but for what it didn't promise. We seem to be on the threshold of a decade that will see the replacement of the "me" with the "we."

There are many examples, the first being the family. Psychologists and others have been bemoaning the demise of the family for years, and they have been right. The splintering of the family unit has been a dominating force in our society. To say the least, it is a phenomenon with far-reaching consequences. But, deep down, the need for family remains, and today it appears that need is on the verge of a comeback. The tremendous growth of worldwide religious cults is one outpouring of this movement. People want to be part of an identifiable group, especially one that will offer psychological reinforcement and love.

Of course, divorce rates are still high. In some places in the United States the odds of getting a divorce now are greater than the odds of a marriage lasting. Nevertheless, there is an increasing trend toward marriage. Yes, people still live together first. They may also enter into marriages with a contract and a view of the marriage's potential success that is different from their parents view, yet marriage still remains a stable and viable alternative.

Consider the television series "Roots." That story struck a vital nerve in much of the world. These weren't rich people checking out a genealogy because they had nothing better to do. "Roots" symbolized a deep-seated, widely shared feeling—namely, the need to know where we come from. A chance to discover *our* family. That's an emphasis on "we" not "me." It has almost become a justification of our person, our existence.

North America has been called a land of joiners. Studies indicate that the average American adult belongs to three associations, and it is estimated the same holds true for Canadians. It takes a book seven inches thick to list the hundreds of thousands of them. The reason for these   associations' existence goes beyond the need to promote an idea or belief. People want to "prove" they belong. We want to have reinforcement for convincing others about a point of view or a profession or, even, ourselves. Part of it, of course, has to do with trying to bring society down to a more manageable size. We find it difficult to identify with millions of brothers and sisters in a nation. An association or a club can make us very important within a specific group.

I mentioned earlier our proclivity for buying trillions of self-help books. What's the aim of those books? They are designed to make us more acceptable to our peers. *We* need to feel that *we* are able to make and keep friends. And the more governments create a numerical society, the more we will rebel against it with our own means of survival.

Governments of many countries are more socialistic than ever. Like it or not, we are headed toward an even more paternalistic point of view about our lives. In the United States, income taxes were nonexistent 100 years ago. Social Security didn't exist 50 years ago. Regardless of political beliefs, you have to admit that most countries have more social programs today than they did a few years back. The budget for the United States Department of Health and Human Services alone is larger than the gross national product of all but a handful of countries in the world. One could certainly make a case against the quality of programs we get from social agencies, but one certainly can't deny the "we" of them. Does anybody seriously believe that trend is going to change?

Consider what's happening to the subways and buses of the world's great cities. They're packed. Car pooling has become a national pastime. Freeways, motorways and autobahns around most major cities may be jammed, but imagine how much worse it would be without the impetus to find friends to share costs or an alternative means of transportation. We—that's "we"—are sharing our transportation. And the funny thing is that we have only begun.

Finally, look at the world of business. We discussed earlier the psyche of the labor movement and its modification in objectives. From gut-level problems of safety and money, big labor has moved to declare war on the "how" of business—how decisions are made, how people are motivated, and how profits are distributed. Unions want a piece of the decision-making pie. In Germany and other European countries this attitude has advanced to the point where management and labor literally share the decision-making process. Unions are often represented on the boards of directors and viewed as legitimate partners in the management of the company.

Governments, too, want to share in the management of business. They tell business the rules of safety and regulate the engineering of products; they tell us how we can compete with each other, the amount of money that can be made, what kinds of people must be hired; they protect pensions and profit-sharing plans from disaster and insinuate themselves into the management process in thousands of other ways. Yet many people are firmly convinced that governments need to do more. If that isn't a "we" attitude, what is?

Even today's shareholder wants to be part of the decision making. There was a time when a stockholders' annual meeting was a dull affair attended by people with time on their hands. They drank tea and munched cookies, congratulating the officers on how nice they looked. No more. The Evelyn Davises and Lewis Gilberts [corporate gadflies who attended numerous annual meetings to goad executives into "caring" about shareholder concerns] of the world have changed all that. To be sure, a couple of scandalous affairs like the Penn Central bankruptcy of a few years back helped mightily. Directors of large corporations have even found they are being sued by shareholders when things don't go right. What is the world coming to? It's coming to "we," that's what.

Those are some of the societal factors that are affecting the atmosphere inside the organization. Now, switch the scene to a single individual in an organization—the chief executive officer. He or she is the key element in the great "we" equation, because the CEO is the person who is converting all the philosophy into a reality-laden chain of events.

Look at a typical scenario. The chief executive officer, hero of hometown and leader of the masses, goes to Washington, fully expecting to be shown the respect he gets at home. Is he in for a surprise!

First, he hops on his private plane and heads for Washington to do battle with the politicians. But the *Washington Post* is waiting at his hotel and wants him to respond to the senator who has accused him of exploiting migrant labor. "No comment," he cries, and harrumphs his way across the lobby and up to his room. Standing at the door is a representative from

United States Immigration with a subpoena forcing him to testify on the matter of migrants who are illegal aliens, working in his plant.

That's only a beginning. Before the chief executive officer leaves Washington, he may be attacked by consumer activists who want to know why his products aren't safe, government regulators who say his plants aren't safe, and union representatives who berate him because his parking lots aren't safe.

Needless to say, he's glad when his business is completed in Washington so he can go back home to the safety of *his* plant and *his* people. What does he find there? The constituency he thought existed doesn't. He finds his plant is on strike, and National Labor Relations Board representatives are waiting at the door to his office. "Unfair labor practices," they scream at him.

Enough of that scenario: chief executive officers around the world are reacting to a variety of pressures and pains inflicted by sources both within and without the organization. They need help, just as the employees discussed earlier need help.

To obtain that help, the senior managers of our businesses are calling on communication experts. Communicators are working to build a bridge of trust that will carry ideas and joint objectives from the Land of Chaos to the Land of Accomplishment. That trust is based on a foundation of candor, credibility, and "we"—the sharing of the burden, the mutual solving of problems and the willingness to address the issues that most concern employees as human beings.

Issues of Concern

A look at one issue most experts believe will be paramount in the years ahead should give some feeling for the extent and depth of the problems facing communicators—productivity. In the first half of the twentieth century, the backbone of industrial success was the ongoing, seemingly forever rising levels of productivity. Wages and benefits skyrocketed and so did productivity, until the mid-1960s. Then things began to change. Technology slowed.

Add to that the impact of inflation, and one has the vicious "dynamic duo" that seems destined to plague the world of the 1980s. "How can I stay even with prices? If my company doesn't supply me with wage increases to match inflation, my family and I are the losers. Why should I work harder for less?"

How does this affect the communicator of tomorrow? The answer becomes clear when we begin to convert the need into the reality of problem-solving communication. A. Robert Abboud, former chairman of the First National Bank of Chicago, said it best when he pointed an accusatory finger at both workers and management, saying:

> There's a tendency to equate the terrible situation with productivity in this country with taking a smoke or going to the washroom too often. Well, that's not what it's about at all. I think everyone, including the unemployed, wants to put in a good day's work. We have highly educated, energetic, conscientious people. What we have to do is put the tools in their hands and give them enough leverage to get the job done. Licking inflation and helping productivity are the same thing. The average man is interested in stopping price increases. He understands that. At work, management must construct ways to improve productivity and convince him of their validity. He has to believe in their necessity. Then there won't be any problem.

If ever there was a call for the services of the broad-based communicator, this would seem to be it. The communicator is not going to design wide-scale systems for improving productivity, but he or she can assure that the message of why productivity must be improved is communicated in ways that will assure it will be improved. It means understanding, for example, that productivity improvements mean working smarter, not harder. It means understanding the issues that affect how the people feel about their jobs, and why. The communicator must appeal to emotions and minds to help bring about the necessary changes.

IABC conducted a survey of 50 chief executive officers, asking them to list the concerns and issues they thought would be most important over the next several years. Table 20.1 gives a pretty good overview of the kinds of issues ahead. CEOs were also asked if a communication program could have an impact in five specific areas. Table 20.2 shows their response.

Career Preparation

The task is gigantic. The process of filling an information vacuum with thoughts, words and deeds is mind-boggling. But it must be done, and there are any number of ways that a communicator—young or old, experienced or inexperienced—can help assure that the process will take place.

Formal education. There are basic attitudes of a communicator that can be learned best and most efficiently in a classroom. Study history and its role in the scheme of things; study writing and the technological aspects of communication; study the basic principles of business—economics, research techniques, psychology and so forth, and study the learning process.

Informal education. This is the kind of learning that people talk about but don't always factor into the total educative process. Everything will affect our learning patterns, from the way we decide to take a vacation to the books we read, the movies and plays we see, and the clubs we join.

Table 20.1
Major Public Issues and Concerns

Issues	Times Mentioned
Inflation and compensation	14
Government issues, including regulation	8
Equal opportunity employment and job opportunities	6
Technology	5
Economic education	5
Energy and environmental concerns	5
Retirement and pensions	4
Consumerism	4
Productivity	3
Quality of work life	3
Credibility	2
Health care	2

Table 20.2
Can Communication Have an Impact on these Problems?

Problems	Yes	No	Possibly	Unable to Answer
Labor relations	44	3	2	1
Productivity	47	1	1	1
Safety	46	—	2	2
Absenteeism	42	1	5	2
Quality control	44	2	3	1

Professional involvement.   Every profession has associations that can assist in the process of learning. The opportunity to lead in an organization can help to sharpen leadership skills for the job back home. Seminars and the opportunities to test ideas against peers and persons who may be further along the career track can be highly valuable.

Good reading habits.   Another basic, necessary ingredient to the learning process that needs to be expanded is our reading habits. Most of us tend to read materials for areas of narrow interest, especially those with which we agree. We need to broaden ourselves beyond what we already know, to look into areas of the unknown. We may not agree with the philosophy espoused, but if we do not study it, how can we understand why others *do* support a particular point of view? As any debator realizes, you must know your opponent's case as well or better than your own to argue a point successfully.

The mentor. Most people find role models valuable, whether they recognize it or not. It's common to hear about them in relation to sports, theater, television, or movies. Communicators also have a need to find some person or persons on whom to depend for guidance. That individual may be local—in your organization—or from afar. What is important is to search for the clues that helped him or her gain that success. What should you emulate? And what mistakes should you avoid?

Summary

The communication business is in flux. Technological and societal changes have an impact on us that is being felt with ever-increasing force and complexity. The demands being placed on organizations have never been more challenging or difficult—or potentially more rewarding.

We truly are at the dawn of a new communication age. More than ever before, pretty pictures, beautifully printed brochures and publications, and articulate narratives will need to be supplemented by substantive dialogue that considers the empirical needs of audiences of all sizes and kinds.

There is an additional, but just as important, thought to be considered: The "compleat" communicator of tomorrow will recognize and be able to factor in the universality of problems that face other organizations, and by so doing will further the cause of understanding among people in countries everywhere. That may sound grandiose, but in fact, our achievements will only match our objectives. If we plan small, we will achieve small.

LOUIS C. WILLIAMS JR., ABC, APR, is president of Savin/Williams & Associates in Evanston, Illinois. He served as chairman of the International Association of Business Communicators in 1979–1980 and is accredited by both IABC and the Public Relations Society of America.

Appendix A
Further Reading

Part I

D'Aprix, Roger. *The Believable Corporation.* New York: AMACOM, 1977.

D'Aprix, Roger. *Corporate Truth...and How To Tell It.* San Francisco: Harper & Row, 1981.

De Mare, George. *Communicating at the Top.* New York: Wiley, 1979.

Goldhaber, Gerald. *Organizational Communication,* 3rd ed. Dubuque, Iowa: Brown, 1983.

Levering, Robert, and Milton Moskowitz and Michael Katz. *The 100 Best Companies to Work for in America: An Insider's Guide to America's Favorite Employers.* Reading, Mass.: Addison-Wesley, 1984.

Peters, Thomas, J., and Robert H. Waterman, Jr. *In Search of Excellence.* New York: Harper & Row, 1982.

Part II

Albert, Kenneth J., ed. *Handbook of Business Problem-Solving.* New York: McGraw-Hill, 1980.

Berdie, Douglas R., and John F. Anderson. *Questionnaires: Design and Use.* Metuchen, N.J.: Scarecrow Press, 1974.

Burger, Chester, *The Chief Executive: Realities of Corporate Leadership.* Boston: CBI Publishing, 1978.

Cutlip, Scott M., and Allen H. Center. *Effective Public Relations*, 5th ed. Englewood Cliffs, N.J.: Prentice-Hall, 1978.

Dartnell Public Relations Handbook. Chicago: Dartnell, 1980.

Davidson, William L. *How to Develop and Conduct Successful Employee Attitude Surveys*. Chicago: Dartnell, 1979.

Drucker, Peter F. *Management: Tasks, Practices, Responsibilities*. New York: Harper & Row, 1974.

Dunham, Randall B., and Frank J. Smith. *Organizational Surveys: An Internal Assessment of Organizational Health*. Glenview, Il.: Scott, Foresman, 1979.

Lesly, Philip. *Public Relations Handbook*. Englewood Cliffs, N.J.: Prentice-hall, 1983.

Nager, Norman R., and T. Harrell Allen. *Public Relations Management by Objectives*. New York: Longman, 1983.

Newsom, Douglas Ann, and Alan Scott. *This is PR: Realities of Public Relations*. Belmont, Calif.: Wadsworth, 1981.

Oppenheim, A. N. *Questionnaire Design and Attitude Measurement*. New York: Basic Books, 1966.

Ross, Robert D. *Management of Public Relations*. New York: Wiley, 1978.

Steele, Fritz, and Stephen Jenks. *The Feel of the Work Place: Understanding and Improving Organizational Climate*. Reading, Mass.: Addison-Wesley, 1977.

Part III

Alexander, Louis. *Beyond the Facts: A Guide to the Art of Feature Writing*, 2nd ed. Houston: Gulf Publishing, 1982.

Arnold, William E., and Robert O. Hirsch. *Communicating Through Behavior*. Englewood Cliffs, N.J.: Prentice-Hall, 1977.

Ballinger, Raymond. *Art and Reproduction*. New York: Van Nostrand Reinhold, 1977.

Barker, Larry L., et al. *Groups in Process: An Introduction to Small Group Communication*, 2nd ed. Englewood Cliffs, N.J.: Prentice-Hall, 1983.

Baskette, Floyd K., and Jack Z. Scissors. *The Art of Editing*, 3rd ed. New York: Macmillan, 1982.

Booth, James L., and Kathy J. Wahlers. *Basic Public Speaking: Principles and Practices*. Winston-Salem: N.C.: Hunter Publishing, 1978.

Bradford, Leland P. *Making Meetings Work: A Guide for Leaders and Group Members*. LaJolla, Calif.: University Associates, 1976.

Brady, John. *The Craft of Interviewing*. New York: Random House, 1977.

Brennan, John. F., Jr. *The Conscious Communicator*. Reading, Mass.: Addison-Wesley, 1974.

Budd, John F., Jr. *Corporate Video in Focus: A Management Guide to Private TV*. Englewood Cliffs, N.J.: Prentice-Hall, 1983.

Callihan, E. L. *Grammar for Journalists*, 3rd ed. Radnor, Pa.: Chilton, 1979.

Charnley, Mitchell V., and Blair Charnley. *Reporting*, 4th ed. New York: Holt, Rinehart and Winston, 1979.

Click, J. W., and Russell Baird. *Magazine Editing and Production*, 3rd ed. Dubuque, Iowa: Brown, 1982.

Craig, James. *Designing with Type*. New York: Watson Guptill Publications, 1980.

Craig, James. *Production for the Graphic Designer*. New York: Watson Guptill Pulication, 1974.

Cronkhite, Gary. *Public Speaking and Critical Listening*. Menlo Park, Calif.: Cummings, 1978.

Egan, Gerald. *You and Me: The Skills of Communicating and Relating to Others*. Belmont, Calif.: Brooks-Cole, 1977.

Ferguson, Rowena. *Editing the Small Magazine*, 2nd ed. New York: Columbia University Press, 1976.

Frank, Ted, and David Ray. *Basic Business and Professional Speech Communication*. Englewood Cliffs, N.J.: Prentice-Hall, 1979.

Friant, Ray J., Jr. *Preparing Effective Presentations*. New York: Pilot Books, 1982.

Gifford, F. *Tape: A Radio News Handbook*. New York: Communication Arts Books, Hastings House, 1977.

Gray, Bill. *More Studio Tips*. New York: Van Nostrand Reinhold, 1978.

Gray, Bill. *Studio Tips*. New York: Van Nostrand Reinhold, 1976.

Gronbeck, Bruce E. *The Articulate Person: A Guide to Everyday Public Speaking*, 2nd ed. Glenview, Il.: Scott, Foresman, 1982.

Harriss, Julian, Kelly Leiter, and Stanley Johnson. *The Complete Reporter*, 4th ed. New York: Macmillan, 1981.

Herdeg, Walter, ed. *Graphis Annual*. Zurich, Switzerland: Graphis Press, (annually since 1952).

Herdeg, Walter, ed. *Graphis/Diagrams, The Graphic Visualization of Abstract Data*. Zurich, Switzerland: Graphis Press, 1981.

Hibbit, George W. *How to Speak Effectively on All Occasions*. Philadelphia: West, 1977.

Hilliard, Robert L. *Writing for Television and Radio*. New York: Communication Arts Books, Hastings House, 1976.

Hurlburt, Allen. *The Grid*. New York: Van Nostrand Reinhold, 1982.

Hurlburt, Allen. *Layout*. New York: Van Nostrand Reinhold, 1977.

Hurlburt, Allen. *Publication Design*. New York: Van Nostrand Reinhold, 1976.

Itten, Johannes. *Design and Form*. New York: Van Nostrand Reinhold, 1975.

Izard, Ralph S., Hugh M. Culbertson, Donald A. Lambert. *Fundamentals of News Reporting*, 4th ed. Dubuque, IA: Kendall/Hunt, 1982.

Kelly, Eugene W., Jr. *Effective Interpersonal Communication: A Manual for Skill Development.* Washington, D.C.: University Press of America, 1977.

Kemp, Jerrold E. *Planning and Producing Audiovisual Materials*, 4th ed. San Francisco: Chandler, 1980.

Kessler, Lauren, and Duncan McDonald. *When Words Collide: A Journalist's Guide to Grammar and Style.* Belmont, Calif.: Wadsworth, 1983.

Kirsch, Donald. *Financial and Economic Journalism.* New York: New York University Press, 1978.

Klein, Walter J. *The Sponsored Film.* New York: Hastings House, 1976.

Lem, Dean Phillip. *Graphics Master 2.* Los Angeles: Dean Lem Associates, 1977.

Mabry, Edward, and Richard Barnes. *The Dynamics of Small Group Communication.* Boston: Houghton Mifflin, 1980.

MacRae, Donald L., et al. *You and Others: An Introduction to Interpersonal Communcation.* New York: McGraw-Hill, 1976.

Metzler, Ken. *Creative Interviewing.* Englewood Cliffs, N.J.: Prentice-Hall, 1977.

Minor, Ed, and Harvey R. Frye. *Techniques for Producing Visual Instructional Media.* New York: McGraw-Hill, 1977.

Murray, Michael. *The Videotape Book.* New York: Bantam Books, 1975.

Nelson, Roy Paul. *Articles and Features.* Boston: Houghton Mifflin, 1978.

Nelson, Roy Paul. *The Design of Advertising*, 4th ed. Dubuque, Iowa: Brown, 1981.

Nelson, Roy Paul. *Publication Design*, 3rd ed. Dubuque, Iowa: Brown, 1983.

Olmsted, Michael S., and A. Paul Hare. *The Small Group.* New York: Random House, 1978.

Phillips, Gerald M., et al. *Group Discussions: A Practical Guide to Participation and Leadership.* Boston: Houghton Mifflin, 1979.

Pickens, Judy, ed. *Without Bias: A Guidebook for Nondiscriminatory Communication.* New York: Wiley, 1982.

Pocket Pal. New York: International Paper, annually since 1934.

Potter, David, and Martin P. Anderson. *Discussion in Small Groups.* Belmont, Calif.: Wadsworth, 1976.

Prochnow, Herbert V. *The Successful Speaker's Handbook.* Englewood Cliffs, N.J.: Prentice-Hall, 1977.

Publications Index. Rochester, N.Y.: Eastman Kodak, 1979.

Rivers, William L. and Shelley Smolkin. *Free-Lancer and Staff Writer*, 3rd ed. Belmont, Calif.: Wadsworth, 1980.

Rivers, William L. *Writing: Craft and Art.* Englewood Cliffs, N.J.: Prentice-Hall, 1975.

Roberts, Kenneth H. *Primer for Film-Making: A Complete Guide to 16 and 35mm Film Production.* Indianapolis: Pegasus, Bobbs-Merrill, 1971.

Robinson, Richard. *The Video Primer*, 3rd ed. New York: Links Books, 1983.

Rosen, Ben. *Type and Typography*. New York: Van Nostrand Reinhold, 1976.

Saltman, David. *Paper Basics*. New York: Van Nostrand Reinhold, 1978.

Shuter, Robert M. *Understanding Misunderstanding: Interpersonal Communication*. New York: Harper & Row, 1978.

Smith, Dennis R., and L. Keith Williamson. *Interpersonal Communication: Roles, Rules, Strategies and Games*. Dubuque, Iowa: Brown, 1977.

Sovto, H. Mario. *The Technique of the Motion Picture Camera* 4th ed. New York: Communication Arts, Hastings House, 1969.

Strunk, William, Jr., and E. B. White. *The Elements of Style*, 3rd ed. New York: Macmillan, 1979.

Swain, Dwight V. *Film Scriptwriting*. New York: Communication Arts, Hastings House, 1976.

Toothman, John M. *Conducting the Small Group Experience*. Washington, D.C.: University Press of America, 1978.

Turnbull, Arthur T., and Russell N. Baird. *The Graphics of Communication*. New York: Holt, Rinehart and Winston, 1980.

Van Uchelen, Rod. *Paste-Up*. New York: Van Nostrand Reinhold, 1976.

Verderber, Rudolph F., and Kathleen S. Verderber. *Inter-Act: Using Interpersonal Communication*, 3rd ed. Belmont, Calif.: Wadsworth, 1983.

Wells, Theodora. *Keeping Your Cool Under Fire: Communicating Non-Defensively*. New York: McGraw-Hill, 1979.

Westley, Bruce. *News Editing*, 3rd ed. Boston: Houghton, Mifflin, 1980.

White, Jan. *Designing for Magazines*. New York: Bowker, 1982.

White, Jan. *Editing by Design*, New York: Bowker, 1982.

White, Jan. *Mastering Graphics*. New York: Bowker, 1983.

Wilkie, Bernard. *Creating Special Effects for TV and Film*. New York: Communication Arts, Hastings House, 1977.

Williamson, Daniel R. *Feature Writing for Newspapers*. New York: Hastings House, 1975.

Zettl, Herbert. *Television Production Handbook*. Belmont, Calif.: Wadsworth, 1976.

Zinsser, William. *On Writing Well*, 2nd ed. New York: Harper & Row, 1980.

Part IV

Ackoff, R. L. *Concept of Corporate Planning*. New York, Wiley, 1969.

Blake, Robert R., and Jane S. Mouton. *Making Experience Work: The Grid Approach to Critique*. New York: McGraw-Hill, 1977.

Davis, Keith. *Human Behavior at Work: Organizational Behavior*, 6th ed. New York: McGraw-Hill, 1981.

Francois, William E. *Mass Media Law and Regulation*, 3rd ed. Columbus, Ohio: Grid, 1982.

Goldhaber, Gerald, and Don Rogers. *Auditing Organizational Communication Systems: The ICA Communication Audit*. Dubuque, Iowa: Kendall-Hunt, 1979.

Hasling, J. *Group Discussion and Decision Making*. New York: Harper & Row, 1975.

Kepner, Charles H., and B. B. Tregoe. *Rational Manager: A Systematic Approach to Problem Solving and Decision Making*. New York: McGraw-Hill, 1965. (reprint)

Managerial Decision Making. New York: AMACOM, 1975.

Nelson, Harold L., and Dwight L. Teeter, Jr. *Law of Mass Communications*, 4th ed. Mineola, N.Y.: Foundation Press, 1981.

Rogers, Everett M., and Rehka Agarwala-Rogers. *Communication in Organizations*. New York: Free Press (Macmillan), 1976.

Sayles, Leonard R., and George Strauss. *Managing Human Resources*, 2nd ed. Englewood Cliffs, N.J.: Prentice-Hall, 1981.

Steele, Fritz. *Consulting for Organizational Change*. Amherst: University of Massachusetts Press, 1981.

Vroom, Victor H., and Philip Yetton. *Leadership and Decision Making*. Pittsburgh: University of Pittsburgh Press, 1976.

Appendix B
Trade Magazines
and Journals

Communication Management and Public Relations

ABCA Bulletin
American Business Communication
 Assn.
University of Illinois
English Building
608 South Wright Street
Urbana, IL 61801

Businesswire Newsletter
44 Montgomery Street
Suite 2105
San Francisco, CA 94104

Channels
Dudley House
P.O. Box 600
Exeter, NH 03833

Communication Briefings
Encoders, Inc.
806 Westminster Blvd.

Blackwood, NJ 08012

Communication Management
National Communication Services
875 Sixth Avenue
Suite 1001
New York, NY 10001

Communication Notes
Council of Communication
 Societies
P.O. Box 1074
Silver Spring, MD 20910

Communication World
International Assn. of Business
 Communicators
870 Market Street
Suite 940
San Francisco, CA 94102

Communications & Management
Towers, Perrin, Forster & Crosby
600 Third Avenue
New York, NY 10016

Communicator's Journal
4115 Broadway
Kansas City, MO 64111

Corporate Communications Report,
  The
Corpcom Services, Inc.
112 East 31st Street
New York, NY 10016

Corporate Public Issues
105 Old Long Ridge Road
Stamford, CT 06903

Hollis Public Relations
Hollis Directories
Contact House,
Sunbury-on-Thames
Middlesex TW16 5HG
United Kingdom

ICC Newsletter
International Public Relations Assn.
P.O. Box 3970
New York, NY 10163

IPRA Review
International Public Relations Assn.
49 Wellington Street
Covent Garden, London WC 2E
  8BN
United Kingdom

Jack O'Dwyer's Newsletter
J. R. O'Dwyer Company, Inc.
271 Madison Avenue
New York, NY 10016

Journal of Business
  Communication, The
American Business Communication
Assn.
University of Illinois
English Building
608 South Wright Street
Urbana, IL 61801

PR Reporter
PR Publishing Company, Inc.
Dudley House
P.O. Box 600
Exeter, NH 03833

Public Relations Journal
Public Relations Society of America
845 Third Avenue
New York, NY 10022

Public Relations News
127 East 80th Street
New York, NY 10021

Public Relations Quarterly
44 West Market Street
Rhinebeck, NY 12572

Public Relations Review
Foundation for PR Research and
  Education
Communication Research
  Associates
7100 Baltimore Blvd.
Suite 500
College Park, MD 20740

Ragan, Report, The
Lawrence Ragan Communications
407 South Dearborn Street
Chicago, IL 60605

Graphic Design and Photography

American Photographer
111 Eighth Avenue
New York, NY 10011

Art Direction
19 West 44th Street
New York, NY 10036

Communication Arts Magazine
410 Sherman Avenue
P.O. Box 10300
Palo Alto, CA 94303

Design Commentary
Britt Steward Communication
    Designs
3166 Maple Drive, NE
Suite 222
Atlanta, GA 30305

The Editorial Eye
Editorial Experts, Inc.
4600 Duke St.
Alexandria, VA 22304

Graphics Today
25 West 45th Street
New York, NY 10036

Graphis
Graphis Press Corp.
107 Dufourstrasse
CH – 8008 Zurich
Switzerland

Impact
203 North Wabash Avenue
Chicago, IL 60601

Industrial Photography
United Business Publications, Inc.
475 Park Avenue South
New York, NY 10016

Popular Photography
Ziff-Davis Publishing Company
One Park Avenue
New York, NY 10016

Photomethods
Ziff-Davis Publishing Company
One Park Avenue
New York, NY 10016

Print
355 Lexington Avenue
New York, NY 10016

U&lc
216 East 45th Street
New York, NY 10017

Association Communication

Association & Society Manager
Barrington Publications, Inc.
825 South Barrington Avenue
Los Angeles, CA 90049

Association Trends
Martineau Corporation
7204 Clarendon Road
Washington, DC 20014

Association Management
American Society of Association
    Executives
1575 Eye Street, NW
Washington, DC 20005

Editors' News
American Society of Association
  Executives
1575 Eye Street, NW
Washington, DC 20005

Miscellaneous

Administrative Management
Geyer-McAllister Publications, Inc.
51 Madison Avenue
New York, NY 10010

Audio-Visual Communications
United Business Publications, Inc.
475 Park Avenue South
New York, NY 10016

Business Screen
Harcourt Brace Jovanovich
757 Third Avenue
New York, NY 10017

Effective Speech Writer's Newsletter
Box 444
University of Richmond
Richmond, vA 23173

Folio
125 Elm Street
P.O. Box 697
New Canaan, CT 06840

Harvard Business Review
Harvard University
Graduate School of
Business Administration
Boston, MA 02163

Labor Law Journal
Commerce Clearinghouse
4025 West Peterson Avenue
Chicago, IL 60646

Management Review
American Management Ass.
Trudeau Road
Saranac Lake, NY 12983

Personnel Administrator
American Society for Personnel
  Administration
606 North Washington Street
Alexandria, VA 22314

Personnel Journal
A. C. Croft, Inc.
P.O. Box 2440
Costa Mesa, CA 92626

Successful Meetings
Bill Communications, Inc.
1422 Chestnut Street
Philadelphia, PA 19102

Video News
Phillips Publishing
8401 Connecticut Avenue
Washington, DC 20015

Vital Speeches of the Day
City News Publishing Co.
P.O. Box 606
Southold, L.I., N.Y. 11971

Index